Items should be returned on or before the last date
shown below. Items not already requested by other
borrowers may be renewed in person, in writing or by
telephone. To renew, please quote the number on the
barcode label. To renew online a PIN is required.
This can be requested at your local library.
Renew online @ **www.dublincitypubliclibraries.ie**
Fines charged for overdue items will include postage
incurred in recovery. Damage to or loss of items will
be charged to the borrower.

**Leabharlanna Poiblí Chathair Bhaile Átha Cliath
Dublin City Public Libraries**

Baile Átha Cliath
Dublin City

Date Due	Date Due	Date Due
- 9 JAN 2017	0 9 MAY 2018	

D1333889

The
COLLEGE

The Irish Military College, 1930–2000

COLONEL TOM HODSON

First published 2016

The History Press Ireland
50 City Quay
Dublin 2
Ireland
www.thehistorypress.ie

The History Press Ireland is a member of Publishing Ireland,
the Irish book publishers' association.

British Library Cataloguing in Publication Data.
A catalogue record for this book is available from the British Library.

ISBN 978 1 84588 899 2

Typesetting and origination by The History Press

Contents

Acknowledgements

A work such as this could never have been attempted or brought to completion without an immense amount of help, and my first grateful acknowledgement goes to Dr Michael Kennedy. From the time Michael first became aware of what I was attempting, he has provided me with continuing advice, criticism, support and encouragement. Whatever merit this book may have is due to his generous contribution.

Next in the ranks comes, of course, the Defence Forces. When I approached the then chief of staff, Lt Gen. Seán McCann DSM, for his support and authority to access documentation, his response was immediate and favourable. His successors Lt Gen. Conor O'Boyle DSM and the present chief of staff, Vice Admiral Mark Mellett DSM, have been equally supportive. Military discipline being what it is this was of great help to me, but it does not explain the extraordinary openness and welcome that I received from every member of the Defence Forces with whom I renewed contact while working on the book; at the same time, they never attempted to influence what I was writing.

At the risk of unintentionally omitting some, I must thank the following: the assistant chief of staff, Brig. Gen. Colm Campbell, the general officer commanding 2nd Brigade, Brig. Gen. Michael Beary, the general officer commanding the Defence Forces Training Centre, Brig. Gen. Joe Mulligan, the director of Defence Forces training, Col Jim Byrne, the commandant of the Military College, Col Howard Berney, and his predecessor Col Eamon Caulfield, the commandant of the Command and Staff School, Col Brendan O'Shea, the commandant of the Infantry School, Col Dave Dignam, the commandant of the Cadet School and Cadet Master, Lt Col Tom O'Callaghan, and his predecessor Lt Col Paul Condon. Sgt Maj. Phil Hayden was most generous with his time and knowledge of the amalgamation of the Military College and the General Training Depot. All of the staff of the Military College who gave generously of their time could not have been more helpful. Lt Col Maureen O'Brien and Comdt Jayne Lawlor provided me with valuable insights. Lt Col Ted Shine and his colleagues of the Directorate of Ordnance delved into the Ordnance Corps ledgers to verify dates. I also owe a debt of gratitude to Comdt Noel Conway from the Defence Forces legal section, who generously researched and put me straight on Defence Forces regulations dealing with training and education. Comdt Seán Ó'Fáharta, the Defence Forces press officer, Capt. Declan Barrett and Sgt Wayne Fitzgerald of *An Cosantóir* kindly assisted in sourcing illustrations.

If I run the risk of omitting serving members of the Defence Forces, I run a greater risk of omitting former colleagues who supported me throughout my endeavours. Their invaluable help ran from allowing me to annoy them with my meanderings, literal and figurative, on various mountain walks. They allowed me to interview and converse with them. They read and commented on sections of the book, and two in particular, Paul Pakenham and Billy Campbell, very generously undertook the onerous task of reading the entire manuscript.

I take great pleasure in including Mr Liam Cosgrave among this list of former colleagues. I hope they will all forgive me for dropping ranks as I would not like to place any hierarchy, of which there was decidedly none, on their invaluable contributions. They are: Joe Ahern, Noel Bergin, Mick Boylan, Liam Cosgrave, Jimmy Farrell, Jimmy Flynn, Jim Goulding, Dick Heaslip, Graham Heaslip, Eddie Heskin, Anita Hogan, Dermot Igoe, Paul Kearney, Mick Lucey, Colm Mangan, Brian McKevitt, Gerry McMahon, Con McNamara, Terry McNulty, Jim Mortell, Len Mullins, Mick Mullolly, Seán Norton, Billy Nott, Barry O'Brien, Mark O'Brien, Malachai O'Callaghan, Donal O'Carroll, Brian O'Connor, Don O'Keeffe, Donal O'Laoire, Mick O'Malley, Charlie O'Rourke, John O'Shea, Jim Parker, Paddy Purcell, Jim Sreenan, Dave Stapleton, Des Travers and Wally Young. My sincere apologies if I have omitted anybody else who has helped me.

Of course not all of my benefactors were military, retired or serving. Ms Lavinia Greachen very kindly shared with me her research on the fascinating Brig. Dorman O'Gowan, and Prof. Anne Doyle and Dr Tony Walsh very kindly gave of their time and expertise in discussing Military College and NUIM post-millennium cooperation.

Individual contributions to a work such as this as are vital. On the other hand, the Irish Military College has had such an influence on the lives and careers of all Defence Forces officers that it is inevitable that memories and opinions should differ. Here facts should intrude on, and if necessary, correct memories and opinions. To achieve this, I have tried to rely on a wealth of archives and documentation to which I was so fortunate as to have access. First to be mentioned must be the director and the staff of the National Archives of Ireland. Ms Aideen Ireland, head of the Reader Services Division, the archivists with whom I had contact, and all of the reading room staff were outstanding in their professionalism and courtesy. Mr Declan Smyth introduced me to Ms Maureen Sweeney of DFA Archives, who helped me find DFA references to officers attending foreign courses. Military Archives must nevertheless take pride of place. Comdt Padraic Kennedy, officer in charge of the Military Archives, his second-in-command Captain Claire Mortimer, archivists Hugh Beckett, Lisa Dolan, Noelle Grothier, company quartermaster Sergeant Tom Mitchell, Sergeant David Kelly, Sergeant – then Corporal – Andrew Lawlor, Corporal Kevin Byrne and Private Adrian Short, all responded unfailingly to all my demands, and more importantly sourced documents for me which I had no idea existed. All this while dealing with increased demands for access to new collections and the preparations for the opening of a new Military Archives building. I am forever in their debt, as I am to Pat Brennan and Michael Keane, also of Military Archives. The National Archives in London provided me with access to an important file showing reluctance on the part of the 1920s British military hierarchy to allow Irish officers to attend the Staff College at Camberley. Ms Megan B. Dwyre of the National Archives, Maryland provided me with a copy of a US G2 (intelligence) report of the workings of the 1920s Defence Plans Division in Dublin. I have also received generous support from UCD Archives. The National Library and the Library of the Military College and their staffs were unfailing in their assistance and cooperation. I owe a great debt to all of these institutions for their help in allowing me to base my work on the facts. Needless to say, the conclusions and any mistakes that occur are entirely mine.

I also wish to acknowledge a largely anonymous and disparate group of people, the administrative staff of the Irish Military College. From the College's beginnings in the 1920s to the present day, these unsung heroes, both military of the 'College Company' and civilian secretaries, provided the background resource for its efficient and continuing operation. Without them, there would have been no Military College and no story to tell. Nor would the story have been told without Ronan Colgan, Beth Amphlett and all at The History Press Ireland. They decided that an earlier collaboration was mutually beneficial and agreed to publish this book. It was again a pleasure to work with them.

Without a doubt, however, my greatest acknowledgement is to my wife and best friend, Hilda, for forty-five years of love and support.

Abbreviations

ABC	Atomic Bacteriological and Chemical (Warfare)
ACS	Assistant Chief of Staff
AHQ	Army Headquarters
AMC	Army Medical Corps
APC	Armoured Personnel Carrier
ARW	Army Ranger Wing
ASC	Army Service Corps
ASI	Army School of Instruction
ATCP	Aid to the Civil Power
Brig. Gen.	Brigadier General
Capt.	Captain
CMC	Commandant of the Military College
CO	Current Operations
COS	Chief of Staff
Col	Colonel
Comdt	Commandant
CPTE	Command Post Terrain Exercise
CPTX	Command Post Training Exercise
CSCE	Conference on Security and Cooperation in Europe
DFATD	Defence Forces Annual Training Directive
DFR	Defence Forces Regulation
DFTC	Defence Forces Training Centre, Curragh, County Kildare
DINT	Director of Intelligence
DPD (T)	Defence Plans Division (Temporary)
DPO	Director of Plans and Operations
DPR	Director of Plans and Research
DS	Directing Staff
DSM	Distinguished Service Medal
DTRG	Director of Training
EEC	European Economic Community
EOD	Explosive Ordnance Disposal

FCA	*Fórsa Cosanta Áitúil* (Local Defence Force)
G2	Military Intelligence
Gen.	General
GHQ	General Headquarters
GOC	General Officer Commanding
GPMG	General-Purpose Machine Gun
GTD	General Training Depot
HETAC	Higher Education Training and Awards Council
HMG	Heavy Machine Gun
IRA	Irish Republican Army
JC&S	Junior Command and Staff Course
Lan	Local Area Network
LFTT	Live Firing Tactical Training
2/Lt	Second Lieutenant
Lt	Lieutenant
Lt Col	Lieutenant Colonel
Lt Gen.	Lieutenant General
MA	Military Archives, Cathal Brugha Barracks, Dublin
Maj.	Major
Maj. Gen.	Major General
MBT	Main Battle Tank
MCL	Military College Library, Pearse Barracks, DFTC, Curragh, County Kildare
MINURCAT	United Nations Mission in the Central African Republic and Chad
NAI	National Archives of Ireland, Dublin
NATO	North Atlantic Treaty Organisation
NBC	Nuclear Bacteriological and Chemical (Warfare)
NCO	Non-commissioned officer
NCEA	National Council for Education Awards
NGO	Non-Governmental Organisation
NLI	National Library of Ireland, Dublin
NS	Naval Service
NUI	National University of Ireland
NUIM	National University of Ireland Maynooth
OC	Officer Commanding
ONUC	*Organisation des Nations Unies au Congo*
OTC	Officer Training Corps
PCBC	Platoon Commanders Battle Course
PDFORRA	Permanent Defence Forces Representative Association
PDF	Permanent Defence Force
PME	Professional Military Education
PT	Physical Training
PSO	Personal Staff Officer
RACO	Representative Association of Commissioned Officers
RAF	Royal Air Force
TNA	The National Archives, Kew, London
UCC	University College Cork

UCDA	University College Dublin Archives
UCG	University College Galway
YO	Young Officer
UDI	Universal Declaration of Independence
UK	United Kingdom
UN	United Nations
UNEF	United Nations Emergency Force
UNFICYP	United Nations Force in Cyprus
UNHCR	United Nations High Commissioner for Refugees
UNIFIL	United Nations Force in Lebanon
UNISS	United Nations and International Studies School
UNMO	United Nations Military Observer
UNOGIL	United Nations Observer Group in Lebanon
UNTSI	United Nations Training School Ireland
USAC	University Student Administrative Complement
SHAPE	Supreme Headquarters Allied Powers Europe
WEU	Western European Union
WSC	Women's Service Corps
WRAC	Women's Royal Army Corps

Introduction

'An Coláiste'

The traveller on the M7 Cork to Dublin motorway crosses the Curragh plain about 45km from Dublin. Attention is immediately drawn north of the motorway to the nationally and internationally renowned headquarters of the Irish horse racing industry, the Curragh Racecourse. Directly facing it on the southern side of the motorway is another national – though infinitely less well-known – institution, the Irish Defence Forces Training Centre (DFTC), more colloquially known as the Curragh Camp. A line of dark-green conifers, broken only by a nineteenth-century British water tower and a twentieth-century Irish church tower, hides the DFTC from view. Further hidden behind the bank of conifers is a Defence Forces institution, the Irish Military College, which owes in large part its existence to the vision of the first commander-in-chief of Óglaigh na hÉireann, General Michael Collins. When people think of military colleges, they readily call to mind famous names such as West Point, St Cyr or Sandhurst. To the Irish Defence Forces officer the Irish Military College, An Coláiste, or simply the College, is all and none of these famous academies. The vast majority of Irish people have no knowledge of the existence of the Irish Military College. This unawareness is hardly surprising as the Defence Forces, during the period covered by this book, have infrequently entered into the national consciousness.

The Military College was conceived of by Gen. Collins during the Civil War; he dispatched a fact-finding mission to the Swiss Embassy in London in August 1922 and planned to discuss the formation of an Officer

Training Corps at a staff meeting on his return from his fatal inspection visit to Cork.[1] Eventually, it evolved pragmatically or compromisingly into an institution catering for the training and education of officers from cadet to general. None of the above-mentioned military academies attempts this multifaceted task: their mission is to train civilians to become commissioned officers and they maintain separate establishments such as their staff colleges at Fort Leavenworth, Shrivenham and the École de Guerre in Paris, for further training as their officers progress through their careers. It was not, however, as if the successors of Gen. Collins did not have ambitions for a similar model for the emerging Irish Army. Maj. Gen. Hugo MacNeill, who became an important figure in the creation and development of the Military College, had ambitious plans for the establishment of an Irish Staff College in the then Vice Regal Lodge, now Áras an Uachtaráin, the official residence of the Irish president and head of State. While his choice of location would now seem absurd, it was not so in 1932 when the future role of the building was by no means established. MacNeill, as will be shown later, was fully aware of foreign military education systems and he informed the chief of staff, Maj. Gen. Michael Brennan, that one of the advantages of the Vice Regal Lodge for a staff college was:

> Proximity to the Department of Defence so that ready access may be made to Defence Plans; that such plans may be worked out in a practical manner between the general [sic] Staff and the College (as in the case of the U.S. War College, French Ecole de Guerre and British Imperial War College), and that practical staff work can be demonstrated at first hand.[2]

Maj. Gen. MacNeill's Vice Regal Lodge efforts came to nought and when the Military College was finally established in Keane, later Pearse Barracks at the Curragh Camp, it was composed of the Cadet School, the Command and Staff School and the Infantry School in that chronological order. These were not the only schools established, as legislation and Defence Forces regulations provided for the establishment of schools for service corps other than Infantry, such as the Artillery, Cavalry and Engineer Corps. While the history of these schools remains necessarily outside the scope of this work, the implications of the Infantry School, almost by default a constituent part of the Military College, will, of course, be discussed.

The College and its predecessor, the Army School of Instruction, were fundamental to the professionalisation of the officer corps of the Irish Defence Forces. As the numerical strength of the army decreased, the College increased its knowledge, albeit often theoretical, of modern military thinking and developments. On the outbreak of the Second World War, the officers who held command and senior staff appointments in the greatly expanded Defence Forces had all been trained at the Military College. When drastic post-Emergency strength reductions saw the Defence Forces slip into almost terminal decline, the College kept alive its professional responsibility to the flame of educating the officer body, not only in its craft but also in its assigned responsibility for defending the State against external aggression. Disagreement with General Headquarters on the content of its courses would at times cause it difficulty. It may well have focused for too long and too rigidly on the task of defence against external aggression, as new or renewed Defence Forces roles, United Nations service and aid to the civil power became more dominant. It adapted, nevertheless, as evidenced by the introduction of university education for cadets and officers in 1969 and the establishment in 1994 of its fourth constituent school, the United Nations Training School Ireland (UNTSI).

Throughout this journey, the Military College has been both of and – if such a claim can be made of such a fiercely loyal institution – not of the Defence Forces. It has been and is integrally a part of the wider organisation in that it conducts its mission of education and training directly under the command of the chief of staff, albeit often being left to its own devices, and through the Cadet School it moulds the character and loyalty of all Defence Forces officers. On the other hand, it exists somewhat apart from the day-to-day existence of the organisation. It is to the College that officers go to be educated and trained. It has been the arbiter of the right way to do things, even going so far as to proclaim the sanctity of the now somewhat discredited 'College Solution' in tactical matters. Frequent and cyclical low unit strengths have often laid the burden of tactical training on the College, a task which it has embraced against often seemingly insurmountable obstacles. Officers are also aware that their performances will be judged by the College, a not inconsequential matter for today's merit-driven Defence Forces. These factors have contributed to an at times ambiguous view of the College among officers, particularly when they are no longer students.

This book attempts to chart and record the journey of the Military College from its origins in the Civil War to its place in the Defence Forces as it entered the new millennium. There are some things it cannot do; regrettably, the important work of telling the story of the Corps Schools remains outside of its scope, and my late colleague Sgt Billy Norton would be rightfully aghast and disappointed with my failure to record the sporting activities of the College. Not all courses conducted at the College are recorded; the aim is to situate the activities of its schools within the wider general history and prevailing conditions of the Defence Forces. Nor will the rich field of academic investigation into the military as a profession and its interface with civil society be ploughed. The pioneering work of Huntington and Janowitz had limited impact on instruction at the College during the period covered by this work. This lack has of course since changed out of all recognition and will be referred to in the Conclusion.

In his 1990 history of the 1870 Franco-Prussian War, François Roth recorded how, in an attempt not to repeat the disastrous mistakes of that war, the French Army established the École de Guerre. While it had a promising start, he considered that it had slipped back into a dogmatic system that educated 'mandarins and not leaders'. In his opinion in 1990, 'The history of that institution is still not well enough known from within to form a definitive judgement'.[3] This book is not written from within. It is, however, written by one who had the privilege of being for a while within, and while it may not form a definitive judgement it may, at least, record the story of an important national institution and bring it to the attention of a wider readership.

1

Beginnings

The National Army that emerged from the War of Independence and confronted the Anti-Treaty forces during the Civil War was not a well-trained army. The War of Independence was a guerrilla war, both urban and rural, and the military units of the Irish Republican Army rarely if ever exceeded 120 Volunteers. During the Civil War, the National Army had an authorised strength of 35,000, it conducted seaborne landings and had artillery and air support. In August 1922 almost 2,000 men were deployed in Cork under the command of Maj. Gen. Emmet Dalton, a former decorated First World War veteran of the British Army.[1] Dalton's command was just one of five deployed against the Anti-Treaty forces. This brief listing of the National Army's capabilities masks, however, an uncomfortable and potentially disastrous situation facing the Provisional Government. Its army was effectively untrained, and 'The huge majority of the new army possessed no military knowledge and experience and must have been motivated by consideration of the regular pay when enlisting, rather than out of any commitment to the pro-Treaty cause'.[2] This is not surprising as those who continued in the army after the truce with Britain had had little experience other than the sporadic if brave operations of the War of Independence.

Training was in progress at the Curragh for the influx of recruits at the start of the Civil War, but 'on the job' instruction of troops was often necessary. Gen. Seán McMahon, a future chief of staff, recollected that 'men were often taught the mechanism of a rifle on the way to a fight'.[3] Important as was the training of troops in the elementary requirement of weapon handling, more important still was that of the training of officers whose military knowledge, training and experience were doubtful. One senior member of the army, Acting Director of Training Diarmuid MacManus, 'described the military knowledge of average junior officers as "absurdly nil" and stressed the need to employ ex-British soldiers'.[4] MacManus was wounded at Gallipoli and 'came from a well-to-do family in County Mayo, was a Sandhurst-trained officer with the Royal Iniskilling Fusiliers in the Great War'.[5] This experience would qualify him to make such a damning judgement on the standard of the training of junior officers. It was in this perilous situation that the military authorities sought to establish and to develop a structure not alone for training officers for combat, but also to educate them as the leaders of the future army of the State.

The First Steps

Training and education occupied the early thoughts of the leaders of the National Army. A Volunteer Reserve Depot was established in Beresford Barracks in the Curragh Camp by July 1922 under the command of Comdt Gen. Peadar McMahon, a future chief of staff and long-serving secretary of the Department of Defence. The Volunteer Reserve was organised to cater for 'all men who have joined the Army or who have been engaged in active service since the outbreak of hostilities and who were not at that date attested in the Regular Army'.[6] The men of this reserve 'were draughted to the Curragh Camp for a short period of intensive training before being posted to the Commands as required'.[7] The sentence refers to the five commands organised in July 1922 to conduct the campaign against the Anti-Treaty forces. McMahon replied on 30 July 1922 to a request for information on the forming of an Officer Training Corps (OTC) from the director of organisation, Comdt Gen. Diarmuid O'Hegarty, who subsequently became director of intelligence and in 1923 cabinet secretary. He forwarded proposals from Col J.J. Hunt, the officer in charge of training the Volunteer Reserve for such a corps. Hunt recommended that it should be based in the Curragh, that it should cater initially for approximately 100 men, that the course should last for six weeks, and 'that the men selected must be of good education – the minimum being that of Seventh Standard, National School. They must be men of good character and intelligence with an inclination towards Military life'.[8] Hunt also attached a proposed syllabus of training for the course that had the aspiration of training up to infantry company level.

Lectures would be given in leadership, discipline, morale, power of command, organisation and the duties of a commander, system of supply, sanitation and military law. The main part of the course would consist of practical work in drill, musketry, physical and bayonet training, attack, management of the Lewis gun, cooperation, messages and reports, map reading and study of ground, and the company in attack and defence.

This comprehensive and daunting syllabus showed much ambition on the part of Col Hunt, considering that he proposed a course of just six weeks' duration. A suggested general order for the establishment of the OTC, which was also draughted by Hunt, outlined, at least, his understanding of the purpose of the corps. 'An Officers' Training Corps is being formed to enable existing Volunteer Officers and selected NCOs and men to qualify for Commissions in the Army'.[9] The commands would select personnel, according to quotas set by GHQ, to undergo an interview so as to consider their suitability, and those so selected would undergo the six-week course. Following tests at the end of the course they would be graded as either 'Officers, men suitable for NCO rank only or unsuitable men. Selected officers would be posted to Commands as vacancies arise. The remaining grades will be returned to their units'.[10] It is clear that Hunt's intention was to train existing serving soldiers to become officers in the army; what is not clear is how commanding officers were to deal with returned soldiers graded as unsuitable men. Differing views on the purpose of the OTC might also be discerned in McMahon's comment that he had received a visit from Gen. Emmet Dalton, who instructed him 'to select from among the Reserves suitable men to form an OTC, these men to receive special training and instruction'.[11] Emmet Dalton had been assistant director of training and then director of training of the IRA in 1921. The director of organisation forwarded and endorsed McMahon's and Hunt's proposals to the chief of the general staff, Gen. Richard Mulcahy, on 1 August 1922. Dalton's suggestion seems to have caused Mulcahy some disquiet, but he proposed 'to allow Maj. Gen. Dalton's instructions to Comdt-Gen. McMahon to stand. He may have a little trouble over it, but I think this can be overcome. Comdt-Gen. McMahon will, I have no doubt, be judicious in his selection.'[12] It is not clear what was in question here, or what significance was to be placed on Dalton's preference for members of the Volunteer Reserve.

However, the simmering background of the Civil War is apparent in suggestions in McMahon's letter as to where the OTC should be housed. Gen. McMahon felt that it could be accommodated in the Army Service Corps (ASC) Barracks in the Curragh, but for the fact that it was presently occupied by men of the Northern Division who had been transferred to the Curragh because of split loyalties in Frank Aiken's command in Dundalk. He suggested that since the director of organisation proposed increasing the numbers of the 'Northern Detachment' to 1,000, they should be moved to another barracks. Their transfer was delayed by O'Hegarty, who informed Mulcahy on 17 August 1922 that 'owing to the situation in Dundalk I had verbally postponed the transfer of the North Eastern men'.[13] On their eventual transfer they were removed from the ASC Barracks to the refurbished but rudimentary Hare Park Camp on the extreme western fringes of the Curragh Camp, indicating perhaps a concern that the 1,000 men transferred from Dundalk might have an unsettling effect on the running of the Curragh. O'Hegarty added a postscript to his letter, informing Mulcahy that 'I will be glad to learn whether you now consider issuing General Order regarding the Formation of Officers' Training Corps'.[14] The next letter on file is a copy of a poignant letter from the chief of the general staff of 19 August 1922 to O'Hegarty, 'A Chara, The formation of an Officers' Training Corps, is having the consideration of the Commander-in-Chief at present. We should arrange to discuss it at our next Staff Meeting.'[15] Gen. Collins departed on his inspection visit of Maj. Gen. Dalton's Cork Command the following day and was killed at Béal na mBláth two days later.

GHQ's interest in training extended further than the proposed OTC at the Curragh. Gen. J.J. (Ginger) O'Connell visited the Swiss legation in London on 4 August 1922 in connection with a mission to Switzerland to examine its training, organisation and equipment.[16] J.J. O'Connell received £50 in expenses for the visit from the Minister for Defence Richard Mulcahy at the end of July.[17] He was a prominent senior military officer who had also been director of training of the IRA during the War of Independence and was appointed general officer commanding (GOC) the Curragh Command in July 1922. While the Curragh was identified as an important training area, it also had responsibilities for conducting operations. O'Connell may well have been dispatched on the Swiss mission because of his earlier training activities, but it is also possible that he was sent because of dissatisfaction with his command's showing against the Anti-Treaty forces. Hopkinson recounts an inspection visit report from Collins in August, 'The entire organisation and command is defective and, in my opinion, has been defective from a long date. There is no real grasp either of the actual forces in the area or of what is required to be done by these forces'.[18] It may well have been harsh on O'Connell who had only been in command since July. He was nevertheless replaced as a commander, but went on to have a distinguished career as an instructor: the principal lecturer hall in the eventual Military College would be named in his honour.

In addition to the Swiss initiative, which got no further than London and which will be explored later, Gen. Richard Mulcahy, as minister for defence and Michael Collins' successor as commander-in-chief, received a minute concerning training on 13 September 1922 from O'Hegarty, the director of organisation. He forwarded 'rough notes of a proposed scheme for Military Training which were handed to me today by GEN. LOONE'.[19] Loone was most likely a British officer then still serving in Ireland or a retired British officer living in Ireland. His proposed scheme outlined the organisation of a possible training department. This department would organise and conduct 'Schools of Instruction for the training of Officers and NCOs to act as instructors in musketry, machine guns, bombing, signalling and gymnastics'.[20] The subject matters mentioned are similar to those listed by Col Hunt in his proposed syllabus. A clue to the nationality of the author can be found in his use of the British rank of warrant officer, a rank not used at the time in the Free State Army. Loone also recommended that a British manual be used and, in what will be seen later as a prophetic remark, he recommended that 'Instruction must be given in English for obvious reasons'.[21] Mulcahy's tenure as commander-in-chief proved difficult. He took firm control after Collins' death, continued and terminated the campaign against the Anti-Treaty forces, but then had to deal with disciplinary matters that eventually culminated in 1924 in what became known as the Army Mutiny. Therefore, his attention to training matters is commendable and his response to Loone's initiative was to request the director of organisation 'to send copy of syllabus of training at present operating in the Curragh and advise me of the position of the OTC opening on the 6th prox'.[22] It is clear that Mulcahy was determined to continue the interest in officer training shown by his predecessor Michael Collins.

The Officer Training Corps (OTC)

It is also clear that Mulcahy was under the impression that the OTC, which the director of organisation envisaged would ensure that 'the Officers as turned out will be used to officer the formal battalions that are to be made up',[23] would commence on 6 October 1922. The same memorandum also includes a postscript that 'The Director of Training reports that he has not been able to get anything going in this matter yet'.[24] This is hardly surprising as at the time Gen. Dalton was planning 'a major sweep in West Cork, overseen by Gen. Tom Ennis, to root out the remaining republican fighters in the region'.[25] The OTC for which Peader McMahon had submitted a draught syllabus and general order would be expected to conduct courses of instruction for the imparting or the improvement of military knowledge, depending on the level of seniority and future appointments of the officers concerned. Given the known low level of competency then prevailing in the army, the OTC could only aspire to small-arms training, i.e. pistol, rifle and light machine gun, and some tactical training, at most, in the tactical deployment of a company approximately 100-strong, although, at platoon level, thirty-strong would be more realistic.

The OTC was to be organised and run during a civil war that brought an increase in the strength of the army. In spite of this increase and the continuation of hostilities, the army authorities were farseeing in their requirement for the establishment of a professional, trained and educated corps of officers. The Curragh (Training) Command where the OTC was to be established was already organising courses such as battalion commanders, company commanders and adjutants courses for the large intake of officers. There is no indication of selection criteria for attendance on these more advanced and focused courses. They went way beyond the elementary training conducted at the OTC and officers selected as students would, on completing the course, expect to be appointed to the command of 100 men in a company or 600 in a battalion, or to oversee the administrative requirements of a battalion. These were significant responsibilities at a time of active operations. Were these students of a better calibre than those who were to be considered for the OTC? The necessary records are not available to differentiate between these students and those selected for the OTC, but it is unimaginable that officers known to be inadequate would be selected for such courses. Nevertheless, *An tÓglách* of 10 March 1923 reported that:

> It must be realised that these short courses are simply an outline, and cannot deal exhaustively with the work of any subject. When circumstances will allow, it is intended to put every Officer and Non-Commissioned Officer through a definite course of professional training with an examination following. The Curragh will become, as the Commander-in-Chief aptly describes it, 'The University of the Army'.[26]

While establishing an entity such as the OTC was imperative, its purpose had in the meantime undergone a crucial change from the role perceived by McMahon and Hunt. The name of the corps obscured another, contrary function: that of reducing the number of officers serving in the army. These, at that time, publicly unacknowledged dual roles were to prove problematic, resulting in a relatively short lifetime for the OTC. A series of memoranda makes it clear that 'weeding-out' was to be achieved at the OTC. A staff minute, unsigned and unaddressed, of 18 August presumed that 'in this organisation you have already absorbed any Brigade or Battalion officer, who was any good … A proposal is waited for the taking away from the various Commands of all supernumerary Officers, for training'.[27] The students for the battalion and company commanders and adjutants courses could have been selected from among the officers who were 'any good' while the others were destined for the OTC.

Continuing hostilities during the Civil War contributed to the delay in establishing the OTC. It became a difficult issue as correspondence, some three months after McMahon forwarded Hunt's syllabus, shows. Mulcahy wished to clarify some points.

> Is this camp going to be, as far as the first run goes, a kind of crèche for keeping innocuous officers until such time as they can be told that they are not fit to be officers, and passed back into civil life. In so far as it is going to be a testing ground for picking out the officers that we are going to retain, is it advisable that we would have it generally known that after the 1ˢᵗ April next provisions can be made in the Army for only a limited number of Commissioned [*sic*]. When are you sending out this instruction and how many men do you intend to start with?[28]

Mulcahy recognised the problems faced by the army in attempting to reduce the strength of officers. He indulged in some wishful thinking, if not indeed vacillation, in thinking that officers who failed the course might be offered some back-door approach to a permanent commission. For his part, the director of organisation accepted these views but did not underestimate the potential difficulties involved. Both Mulcahy and O'Hegarty must have been acutely aware that reducing the officer corps, by whatever criteria, was going to prove difficult and traumatic for some:

In reply to the definite points which you make, I think that the Corps should be looked upon as a sieve through which we could strain a large number of redundant Officers at present in existence so as to give them a chance of showing any merit or aptitude for military service which they may possess. It would be easier to deal with any discontent that might arise when things have become somewhat more normal and when openings other than military service will become available for men unfit for positions in the Army. The proposal at present is, that these men should be kept in training for 3 months. We intend to take about 250 men for the course.[29]

It cannot be said with certainty that the OTC was just a cynical exercise in cloaking the discharge of unwanted officers. As will be shown shortly many officers were awarded permanent commissions. What is certain is that the scope for subjective selection and reaction to such subjectivity was great. So great indeed that the Department of Defence became involved, and demanded copies of the syllabus, entrance tests and suggestions for the Board of Officers for the final examination. It is easy to see that students on the course could appreciate what was intended, which would then lead to possible disaffection and recourse by some to political influence. The syllabus, when it was produced for the department, was identical with that earlier submitted by Hunt, and the entrance tests seemed to be set at the seventh grade, national-school level of education also suggested by Hunt, with just two questions requiring candidates to calculate the rate of pay and allowances for soldiers. These questions were somewhat convoluted but could be solved easily arithmetically. On the other hand, the questions related to military subjects were set at a very low level. Candidates would be required to 'Define the positions of sections in a Company drawn up in close order' or to 'Define the meaning of a Column in route'.[30] The questions might seem somewhat esoteric but should have caused no difficulty to any prospective officer who had drilled troops. The weapon-handling prowess of the candidates was also set at a low level – they were asked to 'Describe the best method of cleaning a rifle after firing Ball ammunition, and state why it is so important to keep the bore of a rifle clean'.[31] Departmental officials should have been assuaged by the setting of such a low bar, while the final question, 'Write a description of any engagement in which you took part in the last two years'[32] should have gone some way towards assisting the difficult task of reducing officer numbers.

cooperation, sanitation, accountancy and business methods. It also stated that officers who achieved 75 per cent of marks for merit in this bewildering array of subjects on a general training course, and who were specially recommended by their commanding officers, would be trained in the school for 'the next higher rank to that which they hold on entering the School'.[45]

It also seems as if the intention of GHQ was to ensure that all officers should receive some formal military training, since the memo required that 'All Officers who have not passed through the Officers Course held at the Curragh Camp (OTC) will receive a month's intensive training in general military education at the above mentioned School'.[46] It is not clear if this was a separate category from the officers, who after having passed the general course could be considered for continuation training for the next higher rank. The memo's intention became even murkier when it stated that from those achieving 75 per cent of the marks a class would be formed of '30 Cadets, 30 Second Lieutenants, 30 Lieutenants, 20 Captains, 10 Commandants, 5 Majors',[47] who were then to be trained in the next higher rank. How any instructional staff could even attempt to implement such a directive is hard to imagine. To complete the confusion, General Staff Organisation Memo No. 8 informed the army, through its widely circulated magazine *An tÓg-lách*, that the officers trained for the next highest rank 'will be retained in the Course until they are appointed to fill vacancies throughout the Army in ranks next above their existing rank. All Commissioned appointments will be drawn from this Class. As the strength of the Class will be maintained in accordance with the above numbers it will also be regarded as a reserve of Officers.'[48] This administrative and potentially morale-destroying confusion was a very far cry from Col Hunt's proposed three-level grading for students of the OTC, and it must have been an extraordinarily difficult task for the officer in charge of the ASI to explain and sell the new programme to the students when they reported to Kildare Barracks. But it would be some months before he would have to face this task, as the then chief of staff, Gen. Seán McMahon, was confronted with serious administrative difficulties in preparing the barracks for the new school.

Gen. Seán McMahon, not to be confused with Gen. Peadar McMahon, the officer commanding the Curragh, was appointed chief of staff in August 1922 under Gen. Mulcahy as commander-in-chief and minister for defence. He intended that the ASI would open on 1 January 1924, but was forced to postpone the opening because of the unsatisfactory condition of the buildings and the lack of facilities at Kildare. Remedial work was carried out by the Army

Corps of Engineers but the authority for these works was questioned by the minister for finance. McMahon was asked by the secretary of the Department of Defence to provide for the minister of finance the history of the proposal to establish the school at Kildare. The Department of Finance was concerned that 'an entirely new service of this kind should not have been initiated without the prior concurrence of this department'.[49] They were insisting on their perceived prerogative to impose control over the army through financial means at a time when the minister for defence was also the commander-in-chief. Control would become ever more manifest and effective when the post of minister for defence rightly became the preserve of politicians. There was no reply to the secretary of the Department of Defence until 7 April. The chief of staff then stated that he was 'not fully conversant with the history of the proposal in as much as it was entirely in the hands of his predecessor'.[50] The unsigned reply coming from the acting secretary of the chief of staff masked the tumultuous happenings of the so-called Army Mutiny of 6 March 1924 when two senior officers, Maj. Gen. Liam Tobin and Col Charlie Dalton, had complained in writing about government demobilisation policy. In the resulting upheaval, Gen. Mulcahy resigned and the chief of staff, Gen. McMahon, was relieved and had his commission withdrawn for a short period. Gen. Eoin O'Duffy was appointed general officer command-ing the forces with Gen. Peadar McMahon, formerly officer commanding the Curragh, as chief of staff. It was, therefore, Peadar McMahon as chief of staff who professed no knowledge of the activities of his predecessor concerning the ASI. He did go on to point out that 'the barracks was reconditioned by the Army Corps of Engineers as an urgent military necessity in view of the reorganisation of the Army because no other suitable barracks was available for the training of Officers'.[51] Gen. Peadar McMahon was being a little disingenuous, as he must have been well aware, while he was general officer commanding the Curragh, of General Staff Organisation Memo No. 8.

The ASI in Kildare

Gen. O'Duffy, the general officer commanding the forces, quickly addressed the issue of the ASI and ordered Maj. Gen. Michael Hogan, stationed in Claremorris, to report to Kildare as officer commanding the ASI before Monday 7 April 1924. He arrived with the instructors course of twelve officers, which began on

3 April 1924 and which constituted the first course conducted in the ASI. A full-page cartoon in *An tÓglách* of 26 April 1924 entitled 'Arrivals in the town of Kildare' shows a red-faced and clearly discomfited officer carrying cases of books and notes, leading a less-than-impressed or impressive collection of staff and students past a group of equally unimpressed Kildare residents. The school's arrivals book shows the first non-instructor students reporting on 12 March 1924, followed by courses on 12 April, 5 May, 20 June and 27 August 1924 totalling 234 officers, an average of forty-seven students per course, ranking from colonel to cadet. All were armed with side arms and ammunition, ranging from Webleys long and short, Colts, Smith & Wessons and Peter the Painters. While the multiplicity of personal weapons is interesting, it is more interesting that students would be permitted to bring side arms on a course of instruction; personal security was clearly an issue at the time. What is not clear is which of the two course categories of Memo No. 8 were being catered for in the early courses; however, a submission from Maj. Gen. Hogan was soon to pass doubt not only on the implementation of the memo but also on the future of the ASI in Kildare.

Critical of the conditions in which he found himself, Hogan wrote to Maj. Gen. Joseph Sweeney, GOC the Curragh Command on 24 April, less than three weeks after taking up command of the ASI.[52] His judgements and opinions were uncompromising and unusual in their forthrightness and lack of bureaucratic circumlocution. He first made reference to the physical conditions of Kildare Barracks. The barracks was essentially a collection of huts that had fallen into disrepair since being evacuated by the British Army. It had been occupied by artillery troops and contained some gun sheds that were also in a dilapidated condition. The proximity to Kildare town and the lack of a perimeter fence or wall meant that the location was effectively open to pilferage and vandalism, not just to the physical environment but also to supplies, food and equipment. It was also quite an extensive site with only some barbed-wire protection, which made it very difficult to secure and demanded deployment of troops that could not be made available from the school staff. These defects would be difficult enough for any barracks, but were particularly so in a supposed educational establishment: 'There is no proper sleeping premises, no Library, no recreational Halls, and last of all comparatively no furniture. These are the absolute needs of any Army School'.[53]

Some fifty years later, the then commandant of the Military College (CMC), Brig. Gen. John O'Shea, made tentative moves to have the Military College moved back to Kildare Barracks, which since Hogan's time had been developed into a very fine barracks housing the Defence Forces Depot and Artillery School. In O'Shea's view, it would have provided a highly suitable location, self-contained and with multiple facilities both educational and recreational for the four schools within the Military College, which had outlived its inadequate facilities at Pearse Barracks in the Curragh Camp. His vision foundered against the opposition of what some consider the 'premier' corps in the army.[54] Kildare Barracks has since been evacuated; it is again prey to vandalism and is being offered for sale for the derisory sum of €2 million.[55]

While the OC of the ASI was clearly concerned about the physical conditions of the school, he was also preoccupied with the direction of the school and with the calibre and commitment of the students. Memo No. 8 had presented him with a very difficult task but he seemed to see in it a way to improve military standards in the army, probably through the requirement for a student to achieve a 75 per cent grading to advance to a higher rank. But after three weeks at the ASI, he had formed the opinion that 'There is no difference whatever between the old OTC on the Curragh and the Army School of Instruction at Kildare excepting a change of venue and this fact is apparent to every student'.[56] Adding to his difficulties were the administrative shortcomings, which saw officers arriving at the school in dribs and drabs leading to an indeterminate duration of courses. He was uncompromising in his opinion of the standard of officers sent to the school, considering them to be 'the refuse of different Commands, because they have been considered unsuitable for positions by their General Officers Commanding either because they have been sources of discontent or they are duds'.[57] Hogan was convinced that unless Memo No. 8 was fully implemented the ASI had no future, and that two categories must be established at the school, one for those who wished to advance and who were prepared to work hard and one for those presumably facing demobilisation. Failing this, 'it is evident that the School is condemned from the start, and the mere fact of changing its venue and the place will not make it an Army School of Instruction. The School at present is nothing more than a dumping ground for disgruntled Officers of the Army.'[58]

The OC of the ASI had been reduced in rank from major general to colonel in the less-than-three weeks between his reporting to the school and his memo to the GOC Curragh. This was not unusual, as many officers were reduced in rank at a time when 'an unsettling period of fluctuations and adjustments followed. It would be a mistake to imagine that things fell tidily and serenely into place'.[59] Notwithstanding his reduction in rank, it cannot be deduced, in spite of a modern lack of nuanced writing, that this caused him to write in a fit of pique. He seems to have been genuinely concerned that proper standards of training and conditions should be aspired to and enforced, and that despite its complexity Memo No. 8 should be put into practice. While Col Hogan's opinion on the officers attending the school was uncompromising and notably generalised, he does make the telling point that 'no Officer should enter the School unless it has been decided that he is a suitable Officer to hold a permanent position'.[60] If this had been implemented, albeit contrary in fact to Memo No. 8, it would have removed from the school its unenviable role of selection for permanent commissions, and allowed it to devote itself to instruction. Maj. Gen. Sweeney, himself a future chief of staff, passed on Col Hogan's memo to the chief of staff the following day. His attached comments were more restrained than Col Hogan's. He accepted that students were experiencing difficulties due to inadequate recreational facilities, inadequate numbers of officers' orderlies – an indication of how quickly a revolutionary army adopted the practices of the ousted army – and lack of furniture, and that the need to accommodate students in billets deprived them of personal privacy and privacy for study. He believed nevertheless that 'the main cause of discontent is the belief that they are going to remain there indefinitely'.[61] This is probably the most telling admission in his letter to the chief of staff, acknowledging the weakness of Memo No. 8, which instead of training officers was leaving them in a state of suspended career animation on the outskirts of the Curragh. Nor did Sweeney accept Hogan's damning definition of his students as the 'refuse of the Commands'. He considered some of them as being more worthy than others who had been placed in permanent positions in the army.

In spite of Col Hogan's jeremiad, his much-maligned students and no doubt his staff continued their work, with 246 students from cadet to colonel reporting to the school between March and September 1924. An attempt was made to introduce general education into the course through which English, arithmetic and basic mathematics would be taught under the guise of technical military subjects. Requests for furniture and for textbooks, which bizarrely had to be routed through the Department of Agriculture, continued up through the channels to the chairman of the Board of Works, Sir Philip Hanson. Bureaucratic delay, while often only frustrating, can in certain circumstances be also damaging, as in the case of the ASI where it increased unrest among the students. As seen above this discontent related directly to demobilisation. Unfortunately, figures relating to discharges from the ASI are not available as was the case for the OTC. But given the fact that after the mutiny 'the Army was reduced by 66%; 900 officers were demobilised'[62] some of those demobilised must inevitably have been found from among students at the ASI. Selecting those to be demobilised would always be contentious, and the stipulation of Memo No. 8 requiring a 75 per cent success rate in examinations before further advancement added to the difficulties. In one course in May, twenty-five of the fifty-two entrants gained over 60 per cent of the marks allotted. The GOC Curragh recommended that 'in view of the promises made to the officer Students at the opening of the Course and taking into consideration the feeling of unrest it would be well if those officers who received 60% and over were posted to such vacancies as now exist'.[63] Sweeney again emphasised unrest at the school when he recorded that 'there are some one hundred and thirty Officers now in Kildare simply marking time'.[64] He also recommended that an officer from GHQ should address the students at the beginning of each course so that they 'should get an idea of their position and that the rumours in circulation should be dispelled'.[65] The GOC Curragh had come to the same conclusion as Col Hogan on the impracticability of the school's dual mission and suggested that Hogan's proposal for an entrance examination be considered and adopted.

GHQ was listening to Sweeney, and it appears that Col Hogan's critical report had had some impact and that things were about to change at the ASI. Confirmation of the change appeared just two weeks after Hogan's letter, not in an admission of the inadequacies of Kildare Barracks but in a further episode of the bureaucratic quest for furniture. The acting military secretary to the chief of staff informed Thomas Gorman, the army finance officer, that it was no longer necessary to pursue the matter of furniture as 'some doubt existed as to whether Kildare will be the final location for the School'.[66] This was further confirmed in the minutes of an army finance meeting on 12 May 1932, which recorded that 'it is understood that the Kildare School of Instruction would cease to function at the place. It was desirable that all such Institutions should as far as possible, be at the Curragh'.[67] Sweeney was informed of this pending change in a letter on 10 May. Nevertheless, he found it necessary in a letter on 14 May to respectfully request that Gen. O'Duffy make sure that officers from the ASI to be posted to commands would be selected according to the results and placing they achieved at the school, 'otherwise the objects for which the School was set up will be defeated'.[68] In this letter, the GOC Curragh responded to the impending changes by asking for breathing space, in that GOCs be instructed not to send any more officers until a date for the next course was announced.

Following the indications that the school might not remain at Kildare, the institution was temporarily closed in early August with a proposed re-opening on 26 August. Sweeney planned a complete cleaning of the barracks during this closure, but the school was still at Kildare when he wrote a lengthy letter to Gen. Eoin O'Duffy, general officer commanding the forces and inspector general, on 2 September. By then he had completely accepted Col Hogan's arguments. He reiterated the unsuitable physical conditions and the unsuitable proximity to Kildare town, and had indeed become much more critical of the discipline of the students. Malingering had become endemic at the school with twenty out of 100 officers reporting sick on one Monday morning, a striking contrast with an average of only one officer per week sick in the Curragh. 'I find however, that it is almost impossible to deal with recalcitrant officers owing to their intimacy with the NCOs and men of the School who continually shield them.'[69] This was a very serious difficulty since collusion between officers and other ranks in the covering up of misde-meanours is utterly incompatible with military discipline, all the more so in a school that had discipline as one of its syllabus subjects. Sweeney proposed that the school should be moved to Keane Barracks at the Curragh, an early recommendation for the eventual home of the Irish Military College. Such a move would, in his opinion, greatly benefit the training and morale of the students and, if accepted, the students 'would lose the feeling of being as some complain of being the parasites of the Army'.[70]

While there is no specific documentary evidence available, it does seem that by this time a different approach to the school was being adopted at GHQ. It was most likely brought about by the slowing down of demobilisation and by what J.P. Duggan has described as the 'steadiness, professionalism and discipline dis-played by the bulk of Óglaigh na hÉireann during the crises'.[71] Gen. O'Duffy was taking a keen interest in not just the future location of the ASI, but also in its future in the training of officers. O'Duffy relinquished his dual posts in November 1924 and Gen. Peadar McMahon's appointment as chief of staff was confirmed in October 1924 by an established order of the government and by the Defence Act of 1924. McMahon held this office until 1927, when he went on to serve as secretary of the Department of Defence until 1958, an indication of the steadiness mentioned earlier. Before these changes, O'Duffy chaired a major conference at his headquarters at the Royal Hospital, Kilmainham on 5 September. In attendance were the chief of staff, the adjutant general, the general officer commanding (GOC) Curragh, the OC ASI and several senior staff officers from General Headquarters. A discussion of the perceived inadequacies of the syllabus gives an impression of how the training envisaged in Hogan's syllabus was proceeding. O'Duffy complained that not enough emphasis was given to musketry. Musketry, the study of the theory of small-arms firing, is not concerned with the actual personal firing of weapons but with the understanding of ballistics and how the individual can be taught to fire accurately and effectively their issued weapon. O'Duffy was concerned that officers were not learning how to impart instruction to troops. He was also concerned that the tactical instruction imparted at the school was too theoretical and at too low a level. He may well have been correct, but an existing example of an exercise shows admirable practical training including the live firing of weapons, a skill not often practised in later years. O'Duffy was also less than charitable to staff and students as they only had four weeks to complete the intensive syllabus, a workload that demanded cancellation of weekend leave.[72]

The conference was not limited to instructional lacunae; its greatest significance lay in the important decisions that were taken regarding the future of officer training and education. The recommendations of both GOC Curragh Command and OC ASI that potential students should undergo 'a suitable educational test which would enable them to hold commissioned rank'[73] were considered at length and eventually rejected. On the face of it, this seems strange and contradictory, but in effect, it can be considered as an important step forward in stabilising morale among the officer corps. It is also the beginning of a tradition that prevailed for long in the Defence Forces against establishing entrance criteria for certain courses at the Military College. Those attending the courses at the ASI should no longer see themselves as potential rejects as the meeting also decided that 'all Officers in the Army will receive a course of Instruction at the Army School'.[74] Two categories of courses would in future be established, a junior course for second lieutenants, lieutenants and captains, and a senior course for commandants, majors and colonels.

This was somewhat aspirational, as the chief of staff, for example, could not be expected to present himself as a student at the ASI. What is, however, anomalous is that senior officers and indeed captains were proceeding on courses to learn musketry and low-level tactics. But this was the general level of conventional training of officers in the army at the time, a situation that GHQ was determined to address. The division into two categories was implemented, with six junior courses and four senior courses conducted at the ASI during 1925.[75] By February 1925, the ASI had departed from Kildare Barracks and re-established itself at Keane Barracks in the Curragh, where the 6th officers course commenced on 20 February 1925.[76] The students on this course no longer carried side arms: this indicated a more settled political scene in 1925 than in 1924. The move to the Curragh established the Army School of Instruction as the forerunner of the Irish Military College in its future home. Keane Barracks would be renamed Pearse Barracks in 1928, honouring the memory of soldier/ educator Patrick Pearse – in fact, all the barracks in the Curragh would be renamed after the signatories of the 1916 proclamation.

The move to Keane Barracks, a physical and psychological signifier of a professional army, had been preceded two years earlier by an equally important legal development. The Defence Forces (Temporary Provisions) Act 1923, which established the legal basis for the Defence Forces, also established the legal basis for the Irish Military College. Section 23 of the act stated inter alia:

Out of the moneys specially appropriated by the Oireachtas for the purpose, the Minister may establish and maintain an Institution for training and instructing:-

Candidates for appointment to Commissioned ranks in the Forces.
Officers of the Forces, and
Such other citizens as the Regulations may declare to be eligible for admission to that Institution.

At the said institution there may be combined with the military training and instruction such other training and instruction of an educational nature as may be prescribed. The institution shall be designated the Irish Military College.

Conclusion

The provisions of the act displayed a detailed, farseeing view of how a military college might evolve, and a serious statement of intent. As we have seen, an army born in revolution and tested in a civil war was determined that its officers should become professionals, dedicated and trained to defend the State. They readily recognised the existing training deficiencies, understandable given the manner in which the army was created, and also understood how difficult the task would prove. Unfortunately, their first, faltering steps had to contend with the invidious task of selecting officers for demobilisation, as the State proceeded to decrease what, understandably, its politicians and bureaucrats considered to be a too-large and too-expensive standing army for the impoverished new Free State. We have also seen how Michael Collins, shortly before he died, looked beyond Ireland to Switzerland, a neutral country, as an example that the army could follow. His emissary, Col Ginger O'Connell, carried with him a document that outlined this inspirational vision. The document maintained that 'Ireland having reached the position of being permitted to have a standing army, and the conditions of maintaining such a force as understood in Europe not being familiar to us, it is hoped we may be able to investigate the Swiss Army Organisation'.[77] It is to these endeavours we will next turn as the army's leaders attempted to understand how the new professional army might be organised and trained to defend the State, and how the officers of that army might be trained in an Irish Military College.

2

The 1920s

Establishing the Military College

After having emerged from the Civil War and having overcome opposition to demobilisation from some senior officers, the army, imbued with solid constitutional allegiance to political authority, moved to address the pressing problem of training and educating its officers. A qualitative and quantitative progression was required. Other than those officers who had served in the British Army during the First World War, few officers had attended training courses and their combat experience was limited to guerrilla warfare and small-unit operations against the irregulars during the Civil War. What was now needed was the training in conventional warfare that would be required if the army was to defend the State against external attack. On 22 July 1925, the minister for defence and the military authorities acting as the Council of Defence sought direction from the Executive Council on its defence policy.[1] Following this request, the Executive Council approved and issued a secret document to the minister for defence on 14 November 1925.[2] This document contained some factors that, except for some modifications to the size of the army and political sensitivities to neutrality, have remained constant to this day. In 1925, the army should have a strength of between 10,000 and 12,000 men but with a capacity for rapid expansion if and when required. Expansion would be required because:

> The Army must be an independent national force capable of assuming responsibility for the defence of the territory of Saorstát Eireann against invasion or internal disruptive agencies; but it must also be so organised, trained and

equipped as to render it capable, should the necessity arise, of full and complete co-ordination with the forces of the British Government in the defence of Saorstát territory whether against actual hostilities or against violation of neutrality on the part of a common enemy.[3]

Such a clear, if secret, statement of geopolitical realities was accompanied by recognition by the Executive Council that 'the equipment and training should be directed towards the defence of Irish territory which involves specialised preparation of plans to resist invasion from any quarter'.[4] While GHQ could not have received a more definite policy statement, it left the general staff with considerable difficulties in implementing the policy with the limited means in personnel, equipment and funding available to them. There is no question but that training for conventional war was to be their focus, and one would have thought that, given the references to cooperation with British Forces, this would have led to training cooperation from a military point of view at least. But this was not to be the case, at least initially.

Where Shall we Learn?

The secret nature of the defence policy document shows that political and nationalist sensitivities were such as to make it impossible to embark on a programme of training cooperation with the British Army. A minute on foreign training by Comdt Liam Egan shows an awareness of these sensitivities and an understanding of the need for the army to look further afield than Britain. In the minute, the future chief of staff considered the requirement to provide the army with suitable training. He believed that this training could not be provided from within the army, but must be sought from outside, and discussed from where it might be provided. He outlined two possible alternatives, 'The first of these is to obtain the services of an expert training staff from the Army whose system is to be adopted. If no international difficulties arise as between England, Ireland, and the third country, the other problems will automatically disappear.'[5] Liam Egan obviously was not considering the British Army as the army to follow and he foresaw little language difficulty as, 'Officers who have not a working knowledge of English have no business posing as experts'.[6] The unsuitability of Britain as a location for training officers reflects the view of the Council of

Defence that this would be appropriate only if the State were to conduct its defence as an integral part of the defence scheme of the British Empire[7] – an option rejected in the government's statement of defence policy. Egan's second alternative 'would be to send a staff of Irish officers to make a prolonged study of military methods and undergo a six months course of training in a foreign military school'.[8] Comdt Egan was convinced of the need for one or other of these alternatives 'As we can never hope to have a really disciplined Army unless the private or NCO feels his Officers have other characteristics besides a Sam Brown and shoulder bars to distinguish them from the rank and file'.[9]

Cabinet files of August 1922 show that the government had accepted from an early date a need for foreign involvement. It had approved, subject to Department of Finance agreement, of a visit by a 'military delegation composed of four or five officers which it is proposed to send forthwith to Switzerland in charge of Lt Gen. O'Connell to examine into the Establishment, Training, Equipment, etc., of the Swiss Army'.[10] The initiative for this visit came from Gen. Michael Collins during the Treaty negotiations in London in 1921. According to Lt Gen. M.J. Costello, 'It was from there that Gen. Michael Collins sent an instruction back to Dublin for the compilation of all available information on the Swiss system of military establishment and education'.[11] The political attractions of a visit to the foremost neutral country in Europe must have been evident, but unfortunately, it seems that the visit did not proceed. A letter on the file from the Department of Finance indicated its lack of enthusiasm for the proposed expenditure and recommended that 'one officer of the delegation should be instructed to pay special attention to the financial system of the Army, and the means adopted to avoid waste in supplies and expenditure'.[12] Maj. Gen. O'Connell and a Mr Cronin did visit the Swiss legation in London in August 1922, most likely with the intention of seeking approval for the visit that Gen. Richard Mulcahy envisaged could last for three or four months. A London solicitor, J.H. McDonnell, forwarded a letter from the Swiss Chargé d'Affaires enclosing 'two copies of the Minute which Maj. O'Connell and Mr Cronin left with me on Friday last concerning the Military Mission which the Dublin Government desire to send to Switzerland'.[13] The unsigned and undated minute mentioned three areas of interest: general establishment, Quartermaster General's Branch and training of cadets, officers and NCOs. In the event, the visit did not proceed and an opportunity was missed for studying the political and military realities of neutrality, an opportunity which might have obviated the future formulation of the peculiar Irish position of military neutrality.

The Visit of the Chief of Staff to France 1923

The military authorities persisted in their desire to visit foreign military establishments, and the first such visit was conducted to France by the chief of
staff, Gen. Seán McMahon, in July 1923. Early evidence of the interest of the
Department of External Affairs in the benefits of military involvement outside
of Ireland is provided in a letter from President Cosgrave's private secretary to
the Minister for Finance:

> At a cabinet meeting held on 14 May, the minister for defence mentioned
> that he had been informed by the minister for external affairs that a French
> military review would be held in Paris on the following 14 July and suggested
> that the chief of staff and certain other officers should attend. The proposal
> was approved by the cabinet.[14]

Gen. Seán McMahon led a delegation of five officers, which included the then
GOC of the Curragh Command Maj. Gen. Peadar McMahon, with the intention
of attending the review of 14 July. Gen. McMahon reported that they experienced
some difficulty with permission to wear uniform, 'we learned that the invitations
to attend the French Army review were not direct, but that two admission cards
had been received through the British Embassy and that there was a difficulty
about wearing uniform at the Review'.[15] It required a meeting between Gen.
McMahon and the British ambassador, Lord Crewe, and a delay of a week before
the French Foreign Ministry granted permission. In the interval, the review was
cancelled because of a heat wave and the delegation requested permission to visit,
in uniform, some army establishments including the École Spéciale Militaire,
Saint-Cyr and the Centre d'Étude d'Infanterie at Versailles. That these schools
impressed Gen. McMahon is probably understandable, given his military training
with the Irish Volunteers on their foundation in 1913, and then his active service
with the Boland's Mills Garrison in 1916. The visit for him was most interesting,
'in so much as it showed that they realised the great necessity for training of officers
in order that they will not only know how to handle their men but also that they
may be able to use judgement and discretion when opposed by difficulties in the
field'.[16] The chief of staff's wider appreciation of officer education is apparent by
his comment that 'their scheme of training includes the training of officers for
civilian walks of life and it is a most excellent idea'.[17]

There is no indication of the response to the report from government, and it would be a further sixteen years before the Irish Army accepted a French invitation to attend their military educational establishments. There is, however, a detailed record of early Department of Finance antipathy to such military, foreign activity. Expense claims from the delegation were still being questioned in February 1924. The army finance officer, Thomas Gorman, himself an official of the Department of Finance, felt that the officers were being treated unfairly, 'Having regard to the quite exceptional circumstances of the occasion, when Officers of a new Army, scantily equipped, were called upon to go amongst Officers of one of the leading Armies of the world and to reflect credit on the National Army in doing so'.[18] Gorman also referred to his earlier experiences, 'I happen to have personal knowledge of the exceptional expenses that were allowed to Military Officers who went on the "Balfour" Mission to Washington in 1917; and I am bound to say that the exceptional expenses in the present case are relatively moderate in comparison'.[19] He then made a telling final comment, 'the officers who formed this delegation are, in common with most National Army Officers, poor men. They faced a severe ordeal with success; preliminary to doing so they incurred the present expenditure in what might be called a National Duty; and I venture to say that they should be re-imbursed such expenditure'.[20] The finance officer was only partially successful as the minister for finance approved payment of £30 to each of the officers of the delegation, less than half of their outlay.[21] If the government did not implement any proposals from Gen. McMahon's Paris report, most likely because of language issues, it continued to support the desire of the minister for defence and of the military authorities to advance officer education. It was decided to avail of a visit by Gen. Eoin O'Duffy to the United States and to ask him to discuss the matter with the government's plenipotentiary in Washington.

The Military Mission to the United States 1926

Gen. O'Duffy, then commissioner of the Garda Síochána, was attending an international police conference in Washington and made unofficial enquiries on the establishment and training of the US Army, and on the possibility of providing training for foreign officers. His enquiries led him to believe in the feasibility of Irish officers attending American army courses, and he submitted a report to the minister for defence on his return in May 1925. He recommended, 'that from 4 to 6 specially selected Officers be sent to Washington for three years to enable them to take the Basic, Advanced and Staff College Courses'.[22] O'Duffy was aware that his recommended period for attendance might seem too lengthy and that a shorter period might be preferable, but he cautioned that 'what we require most is Officers for staff work and for the proposed Military College, and I fear we have no Officers capable of taking the Staff College Course direct'.[23] He also recommended that the adjutant general, Gen. Hugo MacNeill, 'be sent for one year. It would not be necessary for him to attend any of the Courses, but I got a promise that if an officer of his rank and responsibility were sent, arrangements would be made whereby he would have facilities to study the Establishment and Training of the U.S. Army including the Academies and Colleges'.[24] Gen. O'Duffy was also aware of the alternative option of having American officers posted to Ireland as advisory and training staff for the army, but felt that, for international reasons, this might not be possible. He recounted the case of an American officer advising the Argentinean Army and the diplomatic difficulties this had caused. While not being specific, he was referring, and not without cause as shall be seen later, to possible difficulties with the Dominions Office.

O'Duffy's report provided the Department of Defence with the background information it required and it submitted a memorandum dated 1 August 1925, titled 'Staff for the Irish Military College' to the secretary of the Executive Council.[25] The minute, which closely followed the earlier arguments of Liam Egan, outlined the following position:

> The appointment in due course of a teaching staff for the College has been under consideration. It is not possible to supply from amongst the present Corps of Officers persons with technical qualifications such as would be required for the purpose. Two alternative methods for overcoming this deficiency suggest themselves:
>
> The acquisition for a period of the services of foreign military officers.
> The training of a number of our own officers in military academies abroad.[26]

In agreement with Egan and O'Duffy, the department stated that 'for political and linguistic reasons it appears that the only foreign country with which useful arrangements in either connection could be made would be the United States of

America'.[27] The department rejected the proposal that American officers should come to Ireland as being too costly and unlikely to provide sufficient trained Irish officers, but recommended the sending of four Irish officers to the basic course for one year only. 'At the end of that course lasting a year, it would be ascertained, whether two of them, depending on the progress they have made, could not be sent on direct to the Staff College. In any event, it is thought that we should not tie ourselves down to the completion of the three courses by all four officers.'[28] Gen. O'Duffy knew to whom he had been writing. Both memoranda, O'Duffy's and the department's, were attached to the agenda of a meeting of the Executive Council. The final paragraph of the department's memorandum requested approval in principle from the Executive Council to send 'a few specially selected officers to the United States to study military science and the establishment and training of the United States Army'.[29] It may be possible to discern the personal involvement of the then minister for external affairs, Desmond Fitzgerald, in the inclusion of military science, as he was to argue as minister for defence some years later in an article in *An tÓglách* that military science 'is of enormous importance'.[30]

The Executive Council considered the memoranda, and the recommendation from the Department of Defence on 17 August 1925, but felt constrained by political and diplomatic issues from making a decision. The minutes of that meeting record that, 'it was decided that the High Commissioner in London should inform the Dominion's Secretary, and if necessary the British Prime Minister of this proposal, and ascertain, whether if carried out, it would be likely have [*sic*] any undesirable political reactions in England'.[31] This concern may seem extreme, but an approach to the United States on military matters should also be seen in the context of the Treaty. The previous year the British secretary of state for the colonies had forwarded a copy of a report of a parliamentary committee on the education and training of officers to the governor-general, Tim Healy, requesting that it 'be forwarded for the information of his Ministers'.[32] It was decided that the high commissioner in London should seek a meeting with the dominion's secretary or, if necessary, the prime minister. The Executive Council's concerns regarding undesirable political reactions in England were eventually translated into a diplomatic request as to whether there 'is any diplomatic usage or understanding as to the way in which the U.S.A. Government should be communicated with if the proposal is approved of by the Executive Council'.[33] The Dominion's Office subsequently approved the suggestion from T.J. Kiernan 'that any further action which the

Government of the Irish Free State may wish to take in the matter should be taken by Mr Smiddy in Washington [the Irish Minister Plenipotentiary], steps being taken to ensure that His Majesty's Ambassador is kept informed'.[34] On 12 December 1925, with political and diplomatic difficulties resolved:

> The Executive Council approved of a proposal that a few specially selected officers of the Army should be sent to the United States to undergo a course of training at one of the Military Colleges there, with a view to their being utilised, when trained, as a nucleus of the staff of the Irish Military College provided for under section 23 of the Defence Forces (Defence Provisions) Act, 1923.[35]

From this decision came not only the military mission to the United States, whereby Irish officers would attend educational establishments in the USA, but also a continuing but not restrictive American influence on the future doctrine, education and training of the Irish Army.

However, even before dispatching the mission to the United States, the Defence Forces had formulated a comprehensive and clear understanding of how they would conduct tactical operations up to battalion level. A Defence Forces regulation on tactical drill was published in 1926, and in an almost modern, yet hardly military sense of transparency, this could be 'purchased through any Bookseller, or directly from Messers. Eason and Son Ltd., 40-41 Lower O'Connell Street, Dublin.[36] This regulation gave a very detailed account of the tactical training to be conducted by the army, from the private soldier up to the battalion. It explained procedures and included exercises as to how such training should be carried out. It was a significant publication as it outlined, at this very early stage of the army's development, the specificity of the State's defence position, a specificity that was to become a future leitmotif of instruction in the Irish Military College. In an exposition of the 'Guiding Principles for Instruction in Infantry Tactics', the regulation made clear that:

> The instruction of our Infantry for combat requires special consideration. Our forces are not equipped as liberally as those of large armies, but *a sound understanding of all modern means of combat* [italics in the original], including those which we do not possess (Aviation, numerous and heavy Artillery, Tanks, etc.) will enable us to find the ways and means to sustain a struggle against an enemy equipped with them.[37]

The regulation optimistically enjoined that such major difficulties 'must not make our Infantry Tactics weak or timid nor cause us to hesitate in attack'.[38] Disadvantages should be overcome by applying principles such as the discipline of all ranks, superior training, greater knowledge and use of Irish terrain, emphasis on night operations and concealment from the air. During exercises 'one side will frequently be composed of Infantry alone (unsupported by Artillery or Tanks), whilst for the purpose of the exercise the other side is supposed to have them'.[39] Even before it was established, the future ambiguous nature of instruction at the Military College had been evoked by a clear understanding of the lasting nature of Ireland's weak defensive posture. Neither was the individual infantry officer allowed to have any feelings of uncertainty. In a 'Note on the Company' the regulation recognised that:

> Whereas in the Battalion and Platoon there are four Sub-units, in the Company there are only two. This makes things much more difficult, but it is necessary to find a way out of this difficulty. It is no use for the Captain to say he would prefer three or four Platoons – he must do as best as he can with the existing conditions of organisation.[40]

It has to be assumed that the military mission to the United States was aware of this Defence Forces regulation on tactical training before its departure. The mission was composed of six officers: three senior officers, Maj. Gen. Hugo MacNeill then adjutant general, Col M.J. Costello and Maj. Joseph Dunne, and three junior officers, Capt. Patrick Berry, Lt Sean Collins-Powell, a nephew of Michael Collins and a future chief of staff, and 2nd Lt Charles Trodden. The three senior members of the mission were veterans of the War of Independence. MacNeill had been a member of Na Fianna, Irish Volunteers and the IRA. He carried out organisational and training activities as a company and battalion commander. He was director of training and also a member of the GHQ Active Service Unit. Costello served as intelligence officer of the 2nd and 5th Battalions of 1 Tipperary Brigade. Dunne joined the Irish Volunteers in 1917 and served with the IRA, notably manufacturing explosives and grenades.[41] Their US mission extended from July 1926 until October 1927. The objective was to study the defence and military education systems of the United States. It addressed its task by extensive visits and briefings given to MacNeill, and by actual attendance at courses by the remaining members of the mission. On its return and after submission of his report, Maj. Gen.

MacNeill's attention was directed to the development of the army's general staff and not, initially, to establishing the Irish Military College. The Defence Plans Division was set up with the aim of considering 'the Defence Policy of the Government with a view to an examination of the steps which require to be taken by the Department of Defence to implement that policy'.[42] The division's function was to examine defence policy and its possible implementation in the light of the experience gained by the military mission. It devoted considerable effort to disseminating the ideas absorbed by the mission's members during their year in the United States.

It is understandable from a political and a language point of view that the United States were chosen as a model. What is not so easily understood is an assumption that the American Army was the only suitable model for the Irish Army. One might have imagined that fellow-dominion Canada might have been chosen, but for whatever reason the Council of Defence had considered this option as unsuitable.[43] In his report on the military mission, MacNeill showed that he was well aware of this difficulty. He was careful not to make any comparison between United States and Irish defence requirements, 'because it appears to me to be obvious that the wide difference in the character of the problem which faces the two countries requires very different treatment in each case ... but some study at least of the systems of other countries which have more in common with us will also be essential'.[44] He was obviously referring here to the Council of Defence discussion – in which he participated – on cooperation with Britain and the subsequent statement of defence policy. MacNeill remained true to this aspiration and he embarked, with Col M.J. Costello, on an extensive visit of United Kingdom military training establishments; he also attended manoeuvres at Aldershot and Salisbury Plain in October 1928 with Col J.J. O'Connell and Maj. Dunne.

The Department of Finance was sceptical of such a visit, pointing out that in spite of the considerable expenditure of the American mission, 'so far as our official information goes we have so far seen no tangible results of that expedition' and 'the precise object of the present proposed examination of British Establishments is not stated'.[45] Nevertheless, the official felt that as, 'the invitation from the British is a direct outcome of a request made personally by our Minister for Defence, I am afraid that we could not successfully resist the proposal'.[46] In spite of such opposition, leadership elements within the Department of Defence, political, civilian and military showed themselves to be aware of the government's determination to address the problem of how, and for what purposes, the army should be educated.

Another element in the Department of Defence's desire to accept the British invitation is contained in the same Department of Finance minute. The department claimed that the secretary of the Department of Defence, Lt Gen. Peadar McMahon, had 'pleaded' that the visit should proceed because of its benefits both for the officers attending and for the Defence Forces. It also claimed that 'there was a certain pique that our Army had been in direct official association with the French, American and Canadian Armies but not with the British'.[47] There was no evidence of this 'pique' from the British authorities, either diplomatic or military, who went to considerable lengths to welcome and accommodate the visitors. They were welcomed by the secretary of State for dominion affairs and by the director of military operations. They facilitated requests from the delegation, including MacNeill's added request to visit the Senior Officers' School at Sheerness, 'as we are most anxious to make the visit of these two officers as pleasant to them as we can'.[48] There is evidence, however, that not all British officers welcomed these erstwhile enemies.

During their visit to the Staff College at Camberley, Col Bernard Law Montgomery 'promptly ordered a boycott against, as his notice put it, "shaking the bloodstained hands of Sinn Feiners"'. The Irish visitors 'found the building deserted except for the Commandant and one student'.[49] The one student was the future and controversial Brig. Gen. Eric Dorman-Smith, who as Brig. Gen. Dorman-O'Gowan was to deliver a lecture in 1968 at the Command and Staff School at the Irish Military College. His biographer's view of the genesis of MacNeill and Costello's visit is that 'the Irish Minister of Defence had been reproved, off the record, for the practice of using Fort Leavenworth in America instead of the Staff College, and had been invited to see British Army facilities'.[50] Among Costello's recollection of the visit was the fact that Dorman-Smith was anxious to discuss 'what should and should not be in the curriculum'.[51] Their reception at Camberley seems to have been mirrored by similar events during the manoeuvres. In a 1930 letter on a British cabinet file, which will be considered in depth later when discussing attendance by Irish officers at British staff colleges, the Cabinet Secretary Sir Maurice Hankey referred to, 'if not disagreeable incidents, at any rate unpleasant relations between British and Free State officers at Manoeuvres'.[52] These were likely to have been caused by a repeat of the Montgomery approach, as Sir Harry Batterbee of the Dominions Office replied to Hankey the following day that, 'I don't know what exactly happened at the manoeuvres last year, but I have no information to show that it was in any way the fault of the Irish Free State'.[53]

The Defence Plans Division

Unpleasant relations notwithstanding, following the visits to the United States and Britain, MacNeill, under the instructions and authority of the chief of staff, established the Defence Plans Division (DPD (T)). Its objectives were the formulation of a doctrine of war for Irish national defence, a theory of war to implement such a doctrine, a force structure to implement the theory, and then a Military College to teach the theory and its application. To this end the officers who had attended the missions to the United States and Britain and other selected officers set about disseminating the knowledge gained from the US Army by instructing staff officers of the Defence Forces at courses run in the Hibernian School in the Phoenix Park. These courses were inaugurated on 6 February 1928 with an address by Minister for Defence Desmond Fitzgerald and a lengthy detailed address on the intentions of the DPD by MacNeill. In matters of military knowledge, the minister deferred, as a civilian, to Maj. Gen. MacNeill and his officers, but declared that 'the particular application of the general military science to our own special circumstances has to be discovered, codified and applied. I believe that you are now laying the foundation of that Irish Military science.'[54] In his address, the director of the DPD emphasised the investigative nature of the process, and that the American experience was being used not as an example to be followed, but because of the instructors' greater knowledge of that system. MacNeill forcefully made the point that the establishment of a Military College before an understanding of the other objectives of the DPD would not be wise. 'For some years past we have all tended to look upon a Military College as a panacea for all ills in this Army. Suppose we decided to organise this College immediately and staff it with these foreign-trained officers?'[55] He was not convinced of the value of such an approach. 'Are we to adopt the Tactical Doctrines of America, or of England, from the mere academic point of view and utilise these as an artificial basis of instruction? Obviously that is not the solution.'[56]

One of the officers selected to assist the returned mission at the Hibernian schools was the future Adjutant General and Assistant Chief of Staff Col James Flynn. Capt. Flynn, as he then was, had been an intelligence officer in the Western Command working under the direction of M.J. Costello, who recognised his potential for higher rank. Flynn was tasked to understudy Capt. Paddy Berry, one of the members of the American mission, and Maj. Dan Bryan, the future wartime director of intelligence.[57] In Flynn's estimation, the course was conducted at a high level and, 'in effect it presented the salient relevant features of the Courses attended by the Mission; it covered leadership and command, and set tactical problems illustrating principles of war at Divisional, Brigade, Regimental and Battalion level.'[58]

An independent view of the progress of the DPD courses is contained in a G2 report from a visiting American military attaché based in London. The attaché noted the enthusiasm of the instructors, but remarked that:

> As all staff departments are busily engaged in re-organizing, the officers on duty in Dublin are finding it difficult to devote their mornings to this school, leaving only the afternoons for their office work. However, the course is designed to give these officers some conception of the scope of military art, enabling them to see beyond the limited field of their revolutionary experience.[59]

Some students queried the value of studying formations larger than those they were ever likely to work with; an enduring viewpoint that will become apparent in later chapters. Others 'were heard to comment rather unfavourably on a lecture on street-fighting stating that the revolution, and particularly their Civil War of 1922 had given them first-hand knowledge of the subject'.[60] Another senior officer seemed to take pleasure in sending a fake G2 message during a map exercise. Nevertheless, most students were taking the course seriously and 'in fact, the business-like way in which Gen. MacNeill and his assistants seem to be going about their work was particularly noteworthy'.[61]

It is understandable that some students would react in this way given their experiences to date. What was being attempted was the introduction of senior officers of Army Headquarters to the concepts and practices of modern military management both at command and at the senior-staff level, concepts and practices that were completely new to most of them. They were also being educated in politico-military relations, crucial to the period when the army was being rapidly reduced. Col Flynn recalls the course being opened by the minister for defence, Mr Desmond Fitzgerald, who 'was regarded as not being on easy or friendly terms with the Army Chiefs and had an exaggerated view as to the small number of Officers that would be sufficient to run the Army efficiently'.[62] The course organisers were aware of their responsibilities, however, and:

> The General Staff lectures were excellent: they brought out the nature of
> responsible relations between the General Staff and the nation's Statesmen,
> and the necessity for the Army Chiefs to understand and appreciate the
> responsibilities of the Statesmen in relation to International as well as National
> events and Situations.[63]

After the course, the DPD submitted some reports, one of which, on the organisation and strength of the Defence Forces, would in a short few years and the
breakout of the Second World War have a practical effect on the defence of the
State. Another report would, over a longer term, affect the conduct of courses at
the yet-to-be established Military College. With its main focus on defence planning and recognising economic and political realities, the division drew up an
establishment for a force tasked with defending the State based on the concept of
mobilisation. This establishment, with numbers, types and sizes of units, was termed
the War Organisation. A Peace Organisation reflecting the 'real' army that would be
mobilised in time of crisis was also drawn up. It was the War Organisation that was
to form the basis of instruction at the Military College. Col Flynn has written that
this organisation 'was accepted in principle by the Dept. of Defence and sanction
was given by the Department of Finance without very much delay as it seemed to
regard the War Organisation as simply a theoretical one'.[64] While this would have
serious implications some nine years later, it was also to provide a perhaps inevitable
conflict between GHQ and the staff of the future Military College, and a lasting
theoretical bias to certain levels of its tactical instruction.

   The fourth and final report of the Defence Plans Division discussed some
options for officer training. It outlined a system of officer education extending over
twenty years. Cadet training would be followed by attendance at arms schools, at a
senior officers school, a command and staff school and finally a school 'for the study
of the wider aspects of war by those who have a part in its supreme direction'.[65]
The report raised the question of the duration of the course of instruction at the
proposed cadet school. It queried if it was intended that it should last for four years
as at the Royal Canadian Military College, given that 'the references to a Military
College in our Defence Forces Act imply an intention to have such an institution
inasmuch as the provisions in question are copied from the Canadian Militia Act'.[66]

   The Defence Plans Division completed its work and submitted a report on
20 June 1928, which included 'proposals for the military education of the Defence
Forces'.[67] A striking element of the final report was the decision to adopt the

British Army rather the army of the United States as the foundation on which to establish the Defence Forces. The report stated, 'we are proposing to adopt the British Tactical Establishment and therefore Tactical Doctrines. We have already adopted their armaments and equipment. The application of American techniques is impossible'.[68] Here again was a realistic recognition that, in any future conflict, the State would be obliged to align its military doctrine and training with that of Britain. The report also outlined full and precise proposals for officer education. According to these proposals, military education of officers would be divided into definite phases as follows:

> Cadet Training
> Basic Training
> Advanced Training
> Combined or Higher Training

and would be provided in the following schools:

> Cadet College for Cadet training
> Service Schools for Basic, Advanced and Specialist training in each Branch
> Command and Staff School for Command or Higher training[69]

Important elements of these proposals were that the Cadet College would follow the Canadian example and last for four years. 'It was considered essential that the Cadet College be located at the University Centres of either Dublin or Galway, in order to avail of the services of extra lecturers and to facilitate attendance by Cadets at University lectures'.[70] Each branch of the army – infantry, artillery, cavalry, and so on, would have its distinct school for basic and advanced training. Farseeing as they were, these proposals were also recognised at the time as likely to be unfulfilled. Cadets were already in training in the ASI and, as the framers of the DPD proposals were aware, material and financial stringencies were likely to prevail:

> In practice, accommodation available demands that the Infantry School, the Command and Staff School (and probably the Cadet School initially) should be combined in one Establishment. For want of a better designation this com-bined Establishment could be known as the Irish Military College, although it is felt that this title should really be allotted to a separate Cadet College.[71]

In keeping with this somewhat grudging recognition of its likely structure, it was to take a further two years and a radical change of government before the establishment of the Irish Military College.

The College Emerges

John P. Duggan recounts that in 1929 Maj. Gen. Joseph A. Sweeney 'resigned after a row about the delay in setting up the Military College'.[72] No details of the row are given. It is possible nevertheless to trace separate strands of an argument involving the military authorities, the Department of Defence, and the Department of Finance before the Military College was finally established in 1930, and a Defence Forces regulation on the military education of officers and cadets was promulgated in 1937. These separate strands can be divided into military aspirations, which were themselves subject to internal organisational limitations, and reluctance on the part of the State to provide the necessary funding to concretise them.

The earliest recorded training for potential officers is that of a course organised for 130 students in Kilkenny Barracks in 1921 under the command of Comdt Barra O'Brian, but the Civil War made the continuation of this course impossible.[73] General Staff Memo No. 8 of 14 November 1923, which established the ASI, also provided for the selection of thirty cadets from among the officers attending courses at the school.[74] It appears, however, that these thirty cadets were never selected. Although the intention of establishing the Irish Military College was clearly enunciated in the 1923 Defence Forces (Temporary Provisions) Act, its tangible form was postponed until the return of the 1926 military mission and the subsequent proposals on military education outlined by the Temporary Plans Division in 1928. The first requirement of paragraph 23 of the act was the training and instructing of candidates for appointment to commissioned rank in the forces. The first step in implementing this requirement was the awarding of eight cadetships in the Air Corps in 1926 and one in the School of Music, and then in 1927 one in the Corps of Engineers.[75] Michael O'Malley recalls that 'Gen. O'Duffy, in his scheme of reorganisation of 1924, proposed a cadet scheme for the Air Corps. This scheme would evolve to become the cadetship intake system for the Army generally.'[76] The status of these Air Corps cadets caused some disquiet with the secretary of the Department of Defence insisting that cadets 'have no powers to give orders to anyone'.[77] After these early cadetships, the military authorities, through the Department of Defence, proposed in November 1926 a system for recruiting 'Officer Cadets for the Infantry Arm of the National Forces'.[78] The system was approved by the Department of Finance on 'the assurance given that an increased number of officers are to resign'.[79] An indication of the success of efforts to reduce officer strength can be found in a Department of Defence memorandum to the Department of Finance, which quoted the officer establishment as being 625 with the actual strength at 496.[80] Equally critical for ongoing officer intake was the fact that there were only twenty-nine 2nd Lieutenants from an establishment of sixty-one.

The first cadet class was formed in 1928 – not in the Cadet School, which was to await the establishment of the Military College – but in the Army School of Instruction in Pearse Barracks at the Curragh. The course was not long in operation before the chief of staff had cause to request the segregation of the cadets from other students in the ASI. He was concerned 'that there are a certain amount of dissatisfied remarks in the air which tend to create a bad impression of the Army generally on those young fellows who look to make it their career, also that it is not in their best interests to be in the same ante-room where drink is consumed'.[81] The chief of staff need not have been so concerned as a member of this first class remembered that the officers undergoing instruction in the ASI, who, as we have seen, were facing retirement from the army, 'showed no resentment – quite the contrary in fact. They seem to accept us with open arms and were as friendly and helpful to us as big brothers'.[82] Warranted or not the segregation must have proven effective as all thirteen cadets were commissioned as 2nd Lieutenants on 2 September 1929. The cadets' satisfaction at being so commissioned was no doubt eventually tempered by the fact that 'we were to remain "Young Officers" with one "Bar" for eleven years, and that when we would eventually get our second "Bars" as First Lts we would have to thank a certain Adolf Hitler'.[83]

These first steps towards implementation of paragraph 23 of the Defence Forces (Temporary Provisions) Act instituted a continuous system of education for Defence Forces cadets and a break from the existing methods of appointing officers to the Defence Forces. However, the second cadet class presented the authorities with the problem of cadets who failed to complete the training laid down in the early regulations. Maj. Gen. Hugo MacNeill, who was GOC Curragh District, had responsibility for recommending cadets for commissioning. Among the 1929 intake, five cadets had not reached the conditions required for commissioning as laid down in Defence Forces Regulation 26/1928, but the GOC, surprisingly given his commitment to maintaining high standards, recommended that they be awarded commissions. His recommendation was less than fulsome however, and in the same letter, he suggested that if this should be impractical 'the proper course would be to give them a further year as Senior Cadets, at the end of which they could be examined and gazetted or finally disposed of'.[84] While Maj. Gen. MacNeill again attempted to have them commissioned 'quietly', the five cadets who did not qualify were given an opportunity to complete a further twelve-month training. Altering the 1928 regulation on cadets proved difficult, with discussions on 'rustication' and non-existing final examinations making the matter almost intractable. In the event, a separate regulation providing for re-enlistment for a period not extending twelve months, DFR 15/1931, was signed into effect by the minister, Mr Desmond Fitzgerald TD, on 27 February 1931.

The correspondence surrounding this matter serves one useful purpose insofar as it is possible to narrow down the actual establishment of the Irish Military College to a matter of weeks, if not days. On 11 September 1930 Maj. Gen. MacNeill signed his correspondence as GOC Curragh Military District and then on 2 October Col S. MacLoughlin signed his as officer commanding Curragh Military District. Next, on 4 November, MacNeill was signing his as commandant, Irish Military College. DFR 64/1930, signed by Desmond Fitzgerald as both minister for finance and defence on 7 October, provided 'That personnel on the strength of or attached to the Irish Military College shall, however, be under the command of the General or other Officer for the time being commanding the College for all purposes'. It is reasonable to suggest that the Irish Military College was established by 4 November and probably around 2 October 1930. The attention and the efforts of the Department of Defence and the military authorities now turned to the provision of suitable accommodation for the College.

Pearse Barracks, originally Keane Barracks, had been the home of the ASI since 1924, but providing the barracks with an infrastructure capable of fulfilling the tasks of the Military College was to prove illusory if not indeed impossible. The secretary of the Department of Defence, Lt Gen. Peadar McMahon, a former chief of staff, had in fact begun his campaign for the adaptation of Pearse Barracks some time before the Military College was established.

The Department of Defence, at this time, aided perhaps by Lt Gen. MacMahon's military service, tended to present a unified front to the Department of Finance, in contrast with later developments that show the military authorities contending with opposition from the Department of Defence. Lt Gen. MacMahon informed the secretary of the Department of Finance on 15 November 1929 that:

> Following the representations made by the responsible military authorities as to the imperative necessity of establishing the College forthwith, the Acting Minister for Defence has given very careful consideration to the question from the points of view of providing the Defence Forces with efficient officers both for the Regular Forces and the Reserve, and for the training and education of such officers in command, administration and military tactics. After mature deliberations he has reached the conclusion that the College should be instituted with all convenient speed and that it should be performing the functions for which it was created early in the new financial year.[85]

A schedule of works to adapt Pearse Barracks to the needs of the Military College at an 'expenditure, estimated at an approximate basis, of £8,295'[86] was submitted with a request that the alteration works be allowed to commence during the current financial year. Imperative necessity, careful ministerial consideration or mature deliberations were to carry little weight, however, in the ensuing bureaucratic master class.

The Department of Defence left itself open to immediate and justifiable opposition when it stated in its request that accommodation was required for 192 officers. The Department of Finance promptly replied that this represented 40 per cent of the actual strength of officers, an unlikely figure to be involved in courses at any one time. An internal Department of Finance memorandum reveals a delicious *Yes Minister* passage when the official dealing with the Department of Defence request suggests that it may be 'advisable to consult with the Minister [of Finance], on whose authority as Acting Minister [of Defence] the proposal for making an early start with the preparation of plans has been put forward'.[87] These miscalculations led to lengthy bureaucratic wrangling, which depressingly lasted for some years. Eventually the Department of Defence capitulated on numbers of students and responded with a much-reduced accommodation requirement for twenty-four cadets, twenty-four students at the Infantry School and twenty-four students at the Command and Staff School, while continuing to demand that they all be billeted at the College. Internal Department of Finance minutes acknowledged that 'Defence have not given way on the subject of providing quarters, but I think we may agree given the considerable watering-down of the original plan'.[88] The memorandum also includes a somewhat self-congratulatory note that this result was 'one more good reason in reply to the query why should there be a Dept of Finance!'[89]

While a Department of Defence and military sense of urgency to finally start work after a more-than-two-year paper war is understandable, it was not sufficient to deal with continuing Department of Finance recalcitrance. In a short memo to the secretary of the Office of Public Works late the following year, on 30 November 1931, the Department of Finance informed him:

> With reference to your minute of the 17th ultimo (No.16628/1931) and subsequent correspondence relative to the provision of a Military College at the Curragh Camp, I am directed by the Minister for Finance to state that, in the present circumstances he has decided that the expenditure contemplated on the adaptation of Pearse Barracks should be deferred.[90]

The somewhat overwhelmed response from the Department of Defence to the decision by the Department of Finance to defer the approved works, while outlining the severe infrastructural deficiencies at the College, could only finally plead that:

> The Minister is seriously concerned at the position, inasmuch as the cumulative effect of the disadvantages under which the College is operating may seriously react on the training and education of those attending the various courses with consequent loss of efficiency. The revised scheme which was approved by your Minister was adopted after considerable discussion as the absolute minimum necessary to provide the essential facilities to enable the College to occupy the place it should fulfil in relation to the Army.[91]

Ministerial pleading was of no avail until wider political developments, and the installation of the Fianna Fáil Government in March 1932 intervened. The change of government prompted Department of Finance officials to query whether further representations by the Department of Defence should be reconsidered, and the new minister for defence, Mr Frank Aiken, was asked if he approved of the earlier proposals of his predecessor concerning the Military College. Aiken's personal secretary replied that:

> The Minister for Defence delayed consideration of this matter until he would have had an opportunity of a personal inspection of the Barracks in question. As a result of an inspection made by Mr Aiken a few days ago, he is satisfied that the work should be proceeded with and accordingly recommends that the proposals already submitted by this Department be approved by your Minister.[92]

In an uncharacteristically quick reply, the Department of Finance stated on 29 April that authority was granted for the scheme. Bureaucratic and financial rectitude was retained right to the end of a three-year inter-departmental battle for the expenditure of £7,000 on the refurbishment of Pearse Barracks as the home of the Irish Military College. The battle, which saved £2,000, provided facilities comprising accommodation for students of single, double and at times eight-bedded rooms, shared and cramped office space for instructors, basic administration accommodation, and training facilities of a drill shed, section rooms and three bare lecture rooms. It was indeed 'the absolute minimum' and was to remain thus for another fifty years.

While the Department of Defence, advised by the military authorities, was attempting to provide the infrastructural requirements for the Military College, an equally intense conflict was being played out within the military hierarchy; that for the establishment of the educational and instructional principles of the College. The origins of this conflict are to be found in the vision and ambition of Maj. Gen. Hugo MacNeill, then head of the Defence Plans Division, and the practical realities of directing the army being faced by the chief of staff, Maj. Gen. Joseph Sweeney. While MacNeill asserted early in the work of the Defence Plans Division that a Military College was not the answer to all the army's problems, he nevertheless was unequivocal in his 1928 view that:

> The greatest handicap to the progress and efficiency of the Forces to date, and one of the main contributory factors to the decline in morale which has been apparent during the past two years, has been the lack of any systematic Scheme of Military Education for Officers.[93]

A reason for this lack was the scarcity of instructors to progress such a scheme. Notwithstanding the military mission to the United States and courses attended by officers in England, MacNeill considered that there were only ten trained officers in the army and for specific reasons these were of limited use for the education of officers. Since the decision had been taken to adopt British tactical organisation and doctrine along with British armaments, the American-trained officers could at best contribute by using their knowledge of instructional methods learned from the US Army, which were applicable to any system of military education. Their knowledge, on the other hand, of American organisation and operational principles, would not transfer to the British model. The British-trained officers were specialists in chemical warfare, survey duties and military engineering, and so of little value in the general military education of officers. An immediate requirement, therefore, was the sending of Irish officers to complete courses at British infantry and artillery schools. This requirement should, perhaps, have been recognised before the dispatch of the military mission to the United States.

It was hoped that these officers could return and organise initial courses at the Military College beginning in 1930 or earlier. The courses proposed for the College were the 1929 and 1930 cadet intakes, an infantry company officers course and an infantry field officers course at the Infantry School, and a command and staff course at the Command and Staff School. These courses were not to be 'classified as Regular Military College graduate Courses, they would be really condensed versions of the future Regular courses'.[94] It was a pragmatic scheme that recognised the impossibility of stripping headquarters and units of officers for long periods so that they could attend courses at the Military College. The plan would give 'at least a nucleus of semi-trained officers to carry on with'.[95] Part of the plan was that these semi-trained officers would return to the College at some later date to complete regular courses. Pragmatic though the plan was, it is difficult to imagine that the initially trained officers would ever return for 'further training'. In fact, the seeds of the difficulties that would soon bedevil the future commandant of the Military College were sown in his desire to instruct relatively large numbers of 'experienced' officers for their professional roles in the 'modern' army.

In 1929, Maj. Gen. MacNeill was GOC of the Curragh Military District and set about attempting to implement the views of the Defence Plans Division, although these had not yet been approved by the chief of staff or by the minister for defence. In a somewhat modified version of the 1928 proposals, he submitted proposals in June 1929 for an instructors course at the ASI. The objective of the course was the provision of instructors for both the Command and Staff and Infantry Schools. If this instructors course commenced in the autumn of 1929, it would facilitate the establishment of the Irish Military College in 1930. He envisaged that all those officers detailed for the course would complete the infantry sub-course. Those intended as instructors for the Infantry School would then be posted to that school while the remaining students would continue to the command and staff sub-course and subsequently, if successful, transfer as instructors to the Command and Staff School. Again, this would be a pragmatic if difficult process, given the difficulties of selection and the fact that many of the students would also have to act as instructors on the courses. An indication of the selection difficulties can be seen in MacNeill's suggestion that the adjutant general, the quartermaster general, the chief staff officer, the director of training and the director of intelligence should also attend the course. Although he stated that 'It would give these five senior Officers an opportunity of getting some really systematic training before our future plans have really to be put into actual effect',[96] one gets the impression that he might have relished having such officers under his command during the course. He might also have included, if he could, the chief of staff on the list of students. It may be a harsh opinion, but there is little doubt, in spite of the civility of some of his future correspondence with the chief of staff, that an element of professional rivalry existed between these two equally ranked officers.

Thirty-two officers, not including the senior GHQ officers, were nominated for the course. But on 18 September the chief of staff informed GOC Curragh that the minister for defence had approved an instructors course for the Infantry School only and 'will not give any decision on the proposals advanced in favour of the Command Staff School until the Infantry School is in operation'.[97] Not welcome news for MacNeill, but, undaunted, he requested that the minister reconsider his decision and the arguments that he, MacNeill, had previously put forward. He seemed to have swayed, if at least temporarily, the minister in his favour – the course was now named as the Special Instructors Course ASI. The matter of nominations continued to irk, with headquarters refusing to nominate senior staff officers such as the future wartime Director of Intelligence Maj. Dan Bryan for the course as a student/instructor. The chief of staff went on record that Maj. Bryan was working on the upcoming Imperial Conference at which he would be part of the Irish representation and could not be spared. The matter went as far as a Council of Defence meeting with the Acting Minister for Defence Ernest Blythe, who was also minister for finance, agreeing to meet with Maj. Gen. MacNeill to discuss the matter of the course and nominations. In an extraordinary letter, seen from today's circumstances, MacNeill informed the chief of staff that, 'I interviewed the A/Minister on this matter on the 11th instant, when the following plans were discussed and tentatively agreed upon'.[98] One can glimpse the former Taoiseach Lt Liam Cosgrave's opinion that MacNeill had certain aristocratic tendencies, which became apparent during his future divisional command at Carton House.[99] What MacNeill understood to be agreed upon was effectively his concept of a combined Infantry School and Command and Staff School instructors course, but not, however, nominations for the course. Not having achieved agreement on the specific officers he required as students/instructors and on other administrative matters, he informed the chief of staff that it would not be possible to complete preparations for the instructors course before the end of January 1930. Shortly after, a minute from the Defence Council meeting of 4 January 1930 recorded that the acting minister directed that the instructors course at the Curragh commence at the earliest possible date – Maj. Gen. MacNeill may well have over-stepped the mark.

Col James Flynn, who was then personal staff officer (PSO) to the chief of staff, has recorded his understanding of relevant events at this time. Col, then Capt., Flynn became aware on 7 April 1930 that Maj. Gen. MacNeill 'had requested to be relieved of responsibility for the Military College'.[100] MacNeill attended a meeting with the minister and the chief of staff on 16 April to discuss his letter and the proposed instructors course. At the conclusion of this meeting, Col Flynn recorded, 'I learn confidentially that as a result of yesterday's conference, at which the Inspector General was also present, the Military College has been virtually abandoned. The Minister, Inspector General and Chief of Staff all of one mind – they don't want the ambitious College Course.'[101] The underlying impression is that MacNeill was forcing the pace, both on a personal basis regarding his status and in an attempt to possibly select and influence the future leadership of the army. In the event, he backed down and, on 24 April, 'there came a letter from General MacNeill referring to the conference (of 16th) stating that "not wishing to become indisciplined" he had arranged for a five-month's Infantry Course to commence on 02 June'.[102] The minister's and probably the chief of staff's earlier decision not to proceed with the Command and Staff School until the Infantry School was established had prevailed. No further reference appears to a combined Command and Staff School and Infantry School instructors course, and the twenty-four students of the 1st infantry officers (instructors) course, one of whom was Capt. James Flynn, reported to the Curragh on 10 June 1930.[103] The fact that the students on the first infantry officers (instructors) course were to report to the ASI indicates that the Military College was still not established. GOC Curragh Command was still complaining to the chief of staff that 'as I have already tried on repeated occasions to make myself clear on this matter (combined tactics) I suppose that nothing is to be gained by discussing it further'.[104] This gives the impression that the long delay in establishing the Irish Military College continued to frustrate both headquarters and the Curragh Command.

Legal matters were in hand, however, and the secretary of the Department of Defence informed the secretary of the Department of Finance on 30 September 1930 'that it has been decided to establish at the earliest possible moment the Irish Military College'.[105] Certain amendments to regulations were required as the Military College would absorb existing schools of instruction and 'in order that the Commandant may be in a position to devote his entire time to the College the reorganisation necessary to relieve him from other duties is contained in the draft amendment'.[106] Regulation 65/1930 of 6 October 1930 stipulated that in the schedule to paragraph 4 of Defence Forces (Definitions) order No. 5, reference to the officers' School of Instruction, Curragh Training Camp should be deleted and that the Irish Military College should be inserted. Also, Defence Forces Regulation 78/1930 of 15 November 1930 stipulated that paragraph 37 of Defence Forces (Organisation) Order No. 3 should be deleted and the following substituted:

37. The Irish Military College shall be organised by the following units:

The Administrative Staff,
The Military College Detachment,
The Command and Staff School,
The Infantry School,
The Cadet School.[107]

Insofar as can be ascertained from existing documentation, these two Defence Forces regulations, signed by Desmond Fitzgerald and by Mr Ernest Blythe, established the legal existence of the Irish Military College with Maj. Gen. Hugo MacNeill transferring from GOC Curragh District to be the first commandant of the Military College (CMC). There remains a poignant personal footnote to this appointment. Maj. Gen. Joseph Sweeney was replaced as chief of staff by Maj. Gen. Michael Brennan in October 1931 and in an unusual move he was appointed as GOC Curragh Command. A 1932 document shows him urging the AG that a new peace establishment proposed by the CMC 'be provided in its entirety'.[108] Maj. Gen. Sweeney's professionalism enabled him to rise above the often-hectoring treatment he endured from the pen of his predecessor as GOC Curragh Command. His forbearance was not, however, rewarded as the CMC did not hesitate to complain later to the chief of staff about pettiness on the part of the Curragh Command towards the Military College.[109]

Conclusion

With the establishment by regulation of the Military College on 6 October and 15 November 1930, the Defence Forces had reached the end of a long journey. A journey that could be said to have started with Ginger O'Connell's peripatetic training camps for the Irish Volunteers. It continued with his eventually abortive mission on the orders of Michael Collins to Switzerland, his role as a senior instructor at the Army School of Instruction and his input to the deliberations and recommendations of the Defence Plans Division. Maj. Gen. Hugo MacNeill took over the baton with the military mission to the United States and visits to the British Army, his direction of the Defence Plans Division and its proposals for the establishment of the Military College. Not all of these recommendations were implemented, notably that of a separate cadet college, and the de facto if compromised incorporation of the Infantry School into the College. Much bureaucratic resistance had inevitably to be overcome. But the Military College was now in existence, albeit a fledgeling College that would need nurturing and stability before it would face major upheaval during the looming Emergency.

3

The 1930s
'Bedding-in'

'Bedding-in' is the term for the first two rounds fired from a mortar tube when it has been relocated to a new position. These rounds drive the base-plate of the mortar into the ground and allow for subsequent accurate delivery of fire. It is an appropriate term to describe the Irish Military College during the 1930s, a period that saw the legal underpinning of not just the College but also of officer education. This chapter will recount this legal underpinning and the manner in which the Military College contributed to the development of what the Defence Plans Division hoped would be a modern army. An army tasked, organised, and equipped to defend the State against invasion, but also one which would cooperate fully with the United Kingdom in such a defence.[1] These two aspects formed part of a government defence policy provided to the minister for defence in 1925 that also envisaged that mobilisation of a small standing army would be required to conduct successfully such a defence. The emphasis therefore for the Military College would be on educating and training officers who would then, in times of emergency, form the nucleus of, and command and control a mobilised and expanded army. This emphasis remained following the change of government in 1932 and the future policy of neutrality.

The strength of the PDF when the new government took office in 1932 stood at 507 officers and 5,286 other ranks.[2] The officer corps, which had been greatly reduced from their 1923 numbers of 3,600, had also undergone some difficulties with the previous Minister for Defence Desmond Fitzgerald over the formation of an officers association. They nevertheless accepted the democratic change of government and the introduction of a new Volunteer Force, which provided an opportunity for former Civil War opponents to serve constitutionally in the army. The task of educating officers during this period suffered not only from low strengths and increased duties, but also by the difficulties faced by the general staff in convincing the Department of Finance and government that a statement of neutrality was of itself no guarantee that the State would be defended. Various schemes of organisation, based on various forms of reserves, were proposed for the Defence Forces, all of which remained purely theoretical without allocation of adequate defence funding. Theoretical organisations inevitably produce theoretical education, but these difficulties were not to the forefront in the early years of the 1930s.

A new location and focus had been established for the military education of officers and cadets, which during this period would establish the educational tradition that would grow and flourish and make such an impact on the Defence Forces. It should not be forgotten that other, separate schools had also been established for the other army corps, such as artillery, cavalry, engineers, supply and transport schools. But these schools, also established at the Curragh, did not form a part of the Military College and require their own distinct study. What remained outstanding was the Defence Forces regulation, which would codify military education and which was requested in the report of the Defence Plans Division. The report laid down a template for the education of officers that would influence the future structure and roles of the schools within the Military College.[3] The Cadet School was to provide training for young men to prepare them for commissioning as 2nd Lieutenants in the various corps of the Defence Forces. The next stage would be provided by the service schools, which would conduct basic and advanced courses. For the Infantry School, which eventually became a part of the Military College, the intention was that officers would be qualified up to the level of battalion commander. The final stage of education was to be provided by the Command and Staff School. It would educate and train senior officers as commanders and staff officers of combined and higher formations, i.e. a formation that included elements of all the various corps, such as infantry, artillery, cavalry, engineers, signals, required to conduct conventional warfare. In the organisation proposed by the Defence Plans Division, these formations were the brigade, the division, field forces (which combined more than one division) and also Army Headquarters. The Defence Forces regulation giving legal existence to this template would not come into existence until 1937, but in the meantime, the newly established Irish Military College set about implementing the vision of the Defence Plans Division.

During the 1930s, the Cadet School prepared and graduated for commissioning twelve cadet classes, the second to the thirteenth comprising 222 graduates. Unsurprisingly, given the worsening international situation, 106 of these graduated during the period 1938–1940.[4] The Infantry School comprised 1,152 students in forty-seven courses such as standard infantry, field officers, reserve officers, gas officers, and NCOs courses. The Command and Staff School completed nine command and staff courses graduating 125 students. A closer reading of such a solid body of work inevitably reveals lacunae, inconsistencies and deficiencies. A continuing theme will be the difficult task of conducting, particularly in the Cadet and Infantry schools, training for cadets and officers in the leadership and technical skills required in leading sub-units of platoon and company strength. Battalion and higher units and formations could only be addressed on a theoretical level.

The Schools

The Cadet School

The Cadet School was the more solidly implanted with its publication of vacancies, educational requirements and application procedures established under the auspices of the civil service commissioners, not that this was a seamless military procedure. In his half-yearly report of April 1932, the CMC Maj. Gen. MacNeill complained that 'training is seriously handicapped by the present haphazard system of sending cadets here at varying intervals, in some cases many months after the classes have been formed'.[5] Another difficulty quoted was the low military standard of training and discipline of cadets selected from OTC. The OTC were established in the universities and are not to be confused with the earlier OTC which was replaced by the Army School of Instruction. MacNeill advanced the view that while cadets from the OTCs were academically ahead and more self-reliant, 'it is all too evident that they compare very un-favourably from the point of view of discipline with their younger Colleagues from the secondary schools'.[6] However, he gave little convincing evidence to back up this view and this prompted a handwritten notation from the chief of staff that the Director of Training Col M.J. Costello should be asked for his views on the matter of cadets who joined the Cadet School from the OTCs.

Costello's views as director of training are not available, but he later expressed his opinion on the standard of cadets in his capacity as CMC in 1932. Costello's report highlights this difficult matter of the assessment of cadets for commissions at this early period of the Cadet School's existence. He adopted an opposed position to that of MacNeill. Costello's opinion was that 'with three exceptions, none of the class of cadets dealt with in this report is likely to make as good an Officer as any one of those recommended for Reserve commissions following the recent course for O.T.C. and Volunteer reserve Cadets here'.[7] A further indication of this difficulty is that several of the cadets criticised by Col Costello subsequently reached very senior rank in the Defence Forces. Three of the cadets whom Costello wished not to commission reached the ranks of adjutant general and quartermaster general.

The standard of Irish language of cadets selected from among serving NCOs, of whom there were four in 1932, militated against achieving a common standard of Irish in the school. The Cadet School included on its staff a language instructor, thanks to whose hard work, according to MacNeill, it became possible 'to teach many subjects entirely through the medium of Irish, to make Irish the sole medium of conversation in the Cadet Mess, and to have a weekly debate in Gaelic'.[8] While his enthusiasm for Irish was commendable, it is reasonable to speculate whether, Gaelic debates apart, Irish was the language of the cadet mess. Experience some thirty years later would tend to contradict the CMC's claim. An indication of the importance of Irish in the Cadet School at this time is to be found in an interim report by the chief instructor on the third cadet class, where three of the ten cadets were reported as having 'a good knowledge of the Irish language and a good national outlook'.[9] Irish was not the only language taught in the Cadet School. French and German were also on the syllabus but much less successfully so, as the entrance standard of cadets in these languages was very poor. Either the entrance standards would have to be raised or 'it would be better in the existing state of affairs to make French and German obligatory in the entrance examination and dispense with further instruction here'.[10] Sadly neither option was chosen, and foreign languages were dropped from the Cadet School syllabus, only to return again in the 1950s.

In 1932, the training syllabus, which underwent almost yearly modifications, comprised 1,657 hours of instruction and included 745 hours of military training, 82 hours of administrative training, 382 hours of drill, 69 hours of scientific training and 683 hours of educational training. It is significant that almost as much time was allocated to educational as to military training, which was composed of weapons and tactical training. It showed uncertainty concerning not only the function of the Cadet School but also the future duties and responsibilities of the junior officer when he reached his unit after commissioning. The impression is given that the school had a 'civilising' role, not of course in the civilian sense, but in the sense of emphasising the gentlemanly and patriotic role of the aspiring cadet to the detriment of his future warfighting roles. The tactical training provided was in no way significant as the allocated time of thirty-five hours was limited to minor tactics and 'on the occasion of Terrain Exercises carried out by other schools cadets were employed as runners with a view to familiarise them with Field operations of larger units'.[11] One omission from the 1932 syllabus and a glaring one from today's perspective is that of leadership training. Again, it seems that the general intention was to train the young civilian as a private soldier, to advance his general education, particularly in Irish, and not to be too concerned with his future employment as a commissioned officer in a military environment except insofar as he should be patriotic and loyal.

That this was the case emerges in a difference of opinion between the CMC and the Chief of Staff Maj. Gen. Joseph Sweeney on the posting of newly commissioned officers in 1930. As chief of staff, Sweeney stated that he favoured a suggestion that newly commissioned officers before posting to a corps 'should serve for at least six months with an Infantry battalion in order to allow of their acquiring some experience of the handling of men'.[12] The chief of staff visualised that the newly commissioned officers would be temporarily posted to the 3rd Infantry Battalion, which was based in the Curragh Camp and which had been foreseen as being a demonstration battalion for the college. MacNeill, at this time GOC Curragh, did not agree with the suggestion of his chief of staff, nor did he fulfil the request and instead arranged that they should act as understudies to other officers in their respective corps. No cadet gets to command men before commissioning, but the early lack of leadership training could not have helped the early cadets on appointment to their first command. This difference of opinion among senior officers again highlights a lack of clarity concerning the duties and responsibilities of junior officers. The 2nd Lieutenants posted to non-technical units would, because of the parlous strength of those units, have little opportunity to engage in tactical training. Perhaps concentrating on non-warlike education was a pragmatic if not essentially military compromise.

A change in the selection procedures for cadetship occurred in 1934 when it was decided that the Civil Service Commission would not hold open qualifying examinations in that year, in 1935, or in 1936. The reason for not holding an open civil service examination was the decision by the minister for defence that 'the only examination which it is proposed to hold this year for Cadetships in the Forces is one which will be confined to members of the Volunteer Force'.[13] This Volunteer Force, established by the Fianna Fáil Government with the intention of incorporating anti-Treaty participants into the Defence Forces, is not to be confused with the Irish Volunteers founded in 1913. Recruitment for the new Volunteer Force commenced in March 1934. This was a force that 'gave a shot in the arm to Óglaigh na hÉireann'.[14] A shot in the arm notwithstanding, educational requirements for entrance into the Cadet School and the limiting of the examination to members of the Volunteer Forces became an issue of major disagreement between the Departments of Defence and Finance in 1936. On this rare occasion, the minister for finance proved to be a sterner champion for the Defence Forces than either the minister for defence or the chief of staff.

The civil service commissioners published regulations for an examination that would take place in June 1936, from which fifteen cadet places would be offered. The educational standard set for this test was Leaving Certificate (pass), and applicants must have been members of the Volunteer Force. Before this class entered the Cadet School, the chief of staff, Maj. Gen. M. Brennan, requested a supplementary intake of thirty cadets for 1936. His reasons for this request were the effect on an under-strength officer corps of the training requirements for the Volunteer Force, the formation of Western Command Headquarters and a possible expansion of the peacetime establishment. At a Council of Defence meeting on 31 August 1936, the chief of staff stated that the Leaving Certificate standard for cadets was too high and was depriving the Defence Forces of suitable candidates. At the same meeting, the minister for defence, Frank Aiken, decided that 'in future the standard of the examination for such cadets will correspond to Matriculation (N.U.I.)'.[15] The minister later lowered the educational standard to Intermediate Certificate on the suggestion of an unnamed official of the Department of Defence. The same official discussed the matter with the secretary of Civil Service Commissions who expressed reservations at the lowering of the educational standards. He would have 'considerable doubt whether this would produce candidates of an educational standard sufficient to enable them to undergo the two years' Course at the Military College and to produce good Officers on the conclusion of that Course'.[16] There were also practical difficulties of timing between the average age of students sitting the Intermediate Certificate and the minimum entry age of 18 for the Cadet School. These difficulties also raised the possibility of having to extend the cadet course by a further two years. Notwithstanding these potential difficulties, the minister for defence re-affirmed his earlier decision and instructed that sanction should be sought from the Department of Finance for thirty cadets 'even though it may involve an extension of the Cadet course'.[17] It is astonishing that it could be considered appropriate that the minister for defence, secretary of the Department of Defence and the chief of staff could contemplate enlisting 16-year-olds into the Cadet School. They would then, as pointed out by the civil service commissioners, have to be educated to the standard of the Leaving Certificate before they could undertake the cadet course. The only defence that can be put forward for the chief of staff is that he was acutely aware of the impending war, 'an intelligence submission in February 1936 stated that war was likely to break out in two or three years',[18] and that there would be, as indeed transpired, a dire need for officers.

The case for a further thirty cadets, based on the low strength of officers and the training requirements of the Volunteer Force, also instanced the low number of candidates at recent examinations caused, according to the minister, by the Leaving Certificate (pass) educational standard. In his opinion, this was 'depriving the Army of the services of very suitable material, e.g. sons of small farmers'.[19] The minister may well have been speaking tongue-in-cheek as he, a noted veteran of the War of Independence, was the son of a builder and not a small farmer. Any impression that might have existed that the lowered educational standard would apply only to the supplementary intake of thirty cadets was dispelled when the chief of staff confirmed to the Department of Finance that the educational standard for the 'normal' 1937 cadet intake would also be at Intermediate Certificate level.[20] The Department of Finance's reply to the Department of Defence's case on 29 December stated that the minister for finance, Mr Seán MacEntee, approved of the proposal, provided that the lowering of the educational standard and the limiting of applicants to the Volunteer Force should be removed. 'From the financial point of view the Minister is concerned to ensure that the State will obtain the best possible return from expenditure and that the efficiency of the Army will not suffer as a result of appointing Officer personnel of poorer quality.'[21] Surely this should also have been the concern of a minister for defence or of a chief of staff? Mr MacEntee also considered that limiting entry to Volunteer Force members was artificial, doubtful in its application, not in the best interests of the army, and probably responsible for the limited numbers applying for cadetships since it was introduced in 1934. If this restriction were removed, the numbers and standards of applicants would rise and 'in his opinion it would not be advisable to subordinate the needs of the regular Army in the matter of the quality of Officer personnel to the necessity for increasing the numbers of the Volunteer Force'.[22] The request for a supplementary intake of cadets revealed internal disagreements within the Fianna Fáil Government over a central policy, the establishment and development of the Volunteer Force as a part of the Defence Forces.

In response, Frank Aiken agreed – somewhat surprisingly given that one would have expected the Taoiseach to support him – that the examination should not be confined to members of the Volunteer Force, but that the educational requirement should remain at Intermediate Certificate (pass) level. He did indicate privately that for this examination it 'might be tried experimentally'.[23] The minister for finance was not for turning or even for replying speedily to Aiken's proposed compromise. A letter from Aiken to MacEntee on 3 March 1937 stated that if he did not receive a reply to his January proposal it would be too late to hold the supplementary examination. There was also the danger of not being able to conduct the 1937 examination, which would cater for the additional thirty cadets. MacEntee replied two days later even more determined not to accept the proposed lower educational standards, which he was convinced 'would be a profound mistake'.[24] Finally, an internal Department of Defence memorandum of 13 March records that 'The Minister has decided to retain the Leaving Certificate for the next Exam.'[25] The minister for finance's bureaucratic but also principled victory was final and long-lasting. It was not a very edifying position taken by Aiken, Brennan and indeed the Secretary of the Department Peadar McMahon, all of whom one would have expected to be committed to maintaining cadet intake at the highest educational standards possible. Twenty-seven cadets were commissioned from the 1937 intake, the largest number since the Cadet School was founded. Of that twenty-seven, Cadets P.J. Delaney and T.L. O'Carroll became chiefs of staff. Cadets R.H.W. Bunworth and M.J. Buckley became GOCs. Cadets P.J. Crowe, D. Fitzgerald, M.K. Hanley, J.P. Kane, J. Larkin, I.P. Noone, T. O'Brien, J.J. Reilly, P. Stapleton and J.E. Walsh reached the rank of colonel. Seán MacEntee, while he could be parsimonious towards the army when he considered it warranted, as in his reluctance to pay for guests at an earlier cadet commissioning ceremony reception,[26] was fully vindicated in not allowing the lowering of the educational entry standards for cadets and future officers.

The Infantry School

As with the Cadet School, the Infantry School also had its beginnings in the ASI. The ASI, with Col J.J. (Ginger) O'Connell as chief instructor, conducted many infantry-based courses before the establishment of the Infantry School and Military College in 1930. But the purpose of the Infantry School was different. Although pragmatically or perhaps compromisingly so a part of the Military College, it was seen, particularly by Maj. Gen. MacNeill, as just one, albeit the premier, of several corps schools. These corps schools were to conduct young-officer and standard courses for officers commissioned into corps other than the infantry, i.e. artillery, air corps, cavalry, military engineering, signals, army ordnance, supply and transport, and army medical corps. They would have to wait until the promulgation in 1937 of the Defence Forces regulation cover-ing the education of cadets and officers. The thinking was that while all cadets received the same training at the Cadet School, the requirements of the different corps meant that officers posted to these corps required training particular to each of them, which could not be imparted at the Infantry School. Not all of these schools, when they were eventually instituted, conducted all the courses intended, leaving the slack to be taken up by the Infantry School.

The students on the 1st infantry officers course reported to the Infantry School on 10 June 1930, and subsequent yearly courses continued up until the end of the decade. A feature of these courses is the effort undertaken to ensure that a level of instruction would be imparted to as many as possible, including very senior officers. Between June 1930 and June 1933, from a total of 101 stu-dents all of whom attended a six-month-long course, nine were of colonel rank, eight were majors and thirty-one were commandants; almost 50 per cent of the students on the courses were senior officers.[27] From then on, the dominant rank was captain. A footnote on the fifth infantry officers course of June 1933 gives a glimpse of the developmental nature of the school and its courses. 'The Case of Capt. D.A. Kelly has to be considered separately. This officer was acting as an instructor for a considerable part of the time and did not do all the tests. Taking into account the results which he did, if he had done the full Course, he would have passed with distinction'.[28] The natural progression of student, qualification, and then perhaps later instructor on the same type, of course, could not be strictly applied in an educational system that was only then under construction.

Nor were difficulties confined only to available instructional staff. The scope of the infantry course was also causing concern for the CMC. The DPD report on military education envisaged that corps courses would be of two kinds, basic or company, followed by advanced or field officers courses. This model, based on the American system, saw students study first at the company level and then moving on to the advanced course, which studied the battalion, regiment, infantry brigade and reinforced brigade. It had been decided at Army Headquarters that the brigade should be studied at the Command and Staff School. So, attempting to devise an advanced course for an army that did not have regiments would, according to Maj. Gen. MacNeill, have resulted in an advanced course that 'would be a very short affair, probably a matter of a couple of months'.[29] All the more so as MacNeill considered the Irish army brigade 'a much more simple and smaller Unit than an American or Continental Brigade, it is in effect merely a big Battalion'.[30] Here MacNeill was reflecting the experiences and instruction received by the military mission to the US Army in 1926. At that time, the US Army was organised, on paper, in divisions of almost 20,000 men. A division is, in essence, a standalone formation that comprises all elements of an army from infantry through artillery, armour and all the necessary support elements such as transport and signals. The infantry in these divisions was further divided into two brigades, with each brigade containing two regiments, each of which contained two battalions. An American Army brigade would, therefore, contain four battalions.

The original intention of following the American course system would have seen the College attempting to devise a course for an organisation that did not include an infantry regiment; the Irish Army organisation went downwards from division through three brigades each containing three battalions, the triangular formation eventually adopted by the US Army in 1937.[31] The adoption of such an organisation, albeit on paper, as the force that would be tasked with defending the State implied that such a defence would be along conventional lines whereby these formations would oppose any attempted invasion of the State. It followed naturally that instruction at the College would also be along conventional lines. This adoption of a conventional organisation would be criticised by the Department of Finance in 1938 as lacking in original defence analysis when the Department of Defence put forward proposals for the equipping of two full conventional brigades.[32] Meanwhile, MacNeill's recommendation that the present course be continued for some years was adopted. This issue of whether or not the brigade should be taught at the Infantry School continued, and as will later be seen, was to be a controversial feature of course development in the Military College for many years.

Col, then Capt., James Flynn attended the first infantry officers course. He had earlier participated as an instructor on the DPD course for Army Headquarters officers. As he was also aware as personal staff officer (PSO) to the chief of staff of the controversy surrounding the course, his impression of the course would necessarily be an informed one. It was favourable, 'The Instructional Staff, pre-sided over by Maj. Joe Dunne (late United States Mission), were thorough and business-like; the Course Schedule, the system, scope and content of instruction were a vast improvement on anything I had experienced on previous courses'.[33] Flynn had previously been a student on the tenth general course at the ASI in April 1926, the most advanced course available at the time. The present course had a distinctly practical, and essentially non-academic content with 'subcourse in Weapon Training, Combat Orders, Field Fortifications, Military Intelligence, Topography, Machine Guns, Communications, Tactics – Battalion in Attack, Defence, etc., Leadership, Methods of Instruction and others'.[34] The students on the course were of mixed rank, majors (the modern equivalent of lieutenant colonel) commandants, captains and lieutenants. Several prominent names apart from Col Flynn's appear on the list of attendees: Comdt Liam Egan, a future chief of staff, and Comdts Tom Feely and Tom Fox, future senior staff officers. The second course also included two future chiefs of staff, Maj. Dan McKenna and Comdt Liam Archer. The students were 'the serious-minded, the studious, the over-serious and the less-interested … among whom there was no sense of personal rivalry or competition'.[35] The earlier limited military experience of the students is emphasised by Col Flynn when he refers to a sub-course on methods of instruction. All of the students had come 'directly into The Army during or before the Civil War (1922–23), and not having had the benefit of Cadet School training, for the good reason that such a School had only recently been set up'.[36] They were keen to absorb the instruction and the opportunity for public speaking it demanded. The CMC's view of the objective of the course was that over time infantry officers of the army would be trained in the 'nuts and bolts' of their trade at platoon and company level,[37] an objective that had not been achieved by their earlier military experience. Col Flynn responded exceptionally well to this objective: he achieved first place on the course and was immediately posted, along with Comdts Egan and Fox, as instructor in the Infantry School.

An essential element of the infantry officers course, which is highlighted in the 1932 half-yearly report, is that the school attempted to provide the practical hands-on experience of infantry tactics to the students. This experience was to be facilitated by cooperation with the 3rd Infantry Battalion based in the Curragh and organised as a demonstration battalion. In a highly polemical and thinly disguised attack on the then GOC Curragh Maj. Gen. Joseph Sweeney, the CMC complained that the battalion he, as GOC Curragh, had organised and trained at full battalion war establishment was unable to provide troops as required by the Infantry School. The result, according to MacNeill, was that 'No Regular Army Infantry Officer, who has passed through this school, has ever seen a unit as large as a war-strength rifle-company'.[38] Sweeney not unexpectedly replied with a long list of occasions in which the 3rd Infantry Battalion, under his command, did, in fact, supply troops for the Infantry School. He concluded that the complaint from the College 'is obviously intended to be an impeachment of District Headquarters, but has developed into an attempt at self-advertisement'.[39] The rivalry between general officers aside, the issue of the demonstration battalion clearly illustrated the fact that practically all infantry officers had little if any experience of command of troops in the field, and that the army relied on the Infantry School to provide even a minimum experience in this vital aspect of officer training. This difficulty continued throughout the school's existence whenever low strengths in the infantry battalions curtailed realistic tactical training.

The school did not confine its activities to the infantry officers course alone. Throughout the 1930s, it became something of an all-purpose school conducting a diverse range of courses such as gas officers, potential NCOs, rifle company instructors, special terrain exercise, Volunteer Force officers, Volunteer reserve cadet, reserve of officers, OTC cadets and intelligence officers courses.[40] The increased demands placed on the school and its instructors by the establishment of the Volunteer Force were considerable. During the decade, courses were run for 555 members of the Volunteer Force, 356 of whom attended four-month-long potential officers courses at the school.[41] The commitment to the training of these potential officers proved worthwhile as 'without them, the 1940 expansion would scarcely have been workable'.[42] In its first decade, the Infantry School established itself as a practical school with instructors committed to providing the infantry officers of the army with training in the techniques of a conventional infantry force.

This was no minor matter, as such expertise was worked up from an inadequate military base in much the same way as the Irish Diplomatic Service, and in contrast to the pre-existing British structures that applied in the Department of Finance and the legal system.[43] The Infantry School can be justifiably proud of this early practical commitment and the establishment of a tradition of professional adaptability.

The Command and Staff School

While both the Cadet and Infantry Schools can trace their roots to the ASI, the Command and Staff School can trace its roots to the experiences of the military mission to the United States of America of 1926–7, albeit with some instructional reach back to the ASI. Both Maj. Gen. MacNeill and Col M.J. Costello spent nine months at the US Command and General Staff College at Fort Leavenworth. They were careful not to recommend adoption of American defence systems. Nevertheless, the problem-solving procedures, staff structures and instructional methods made a deep impact on their hitherto limited, albeit distinguished revolutionary and Civil War military experience. The First World War had shown the absolute necessity of a trained corps of staff officers who could translate the tactical decisions of commanders into actual operations on the ground, exemplified by the Prussian and then German general staffs. All modern armies had recognised this necessity and trained officers and commanders in similar level schools. The establishment of a Command and Staff School at the Irish Military College was therefore considered one of the most important elements in the construction of a modern army capable of defending the State. In a covering note to a 'Tentative Syllabus of Instruction' for the 1st command and staff (instructors) course to be held in 1931, Maj. Gen. MacNeill expanded on the DPD vision and outlined the proposed scope and ambition of the Command and Staff School:

> The mission of the Military College in connection with Command and Staff Instruction is the training of eligible officers for: (I) higher command in the field (with particular reference to the Reinforced Brigade and the Division), and (II) for staff duty at the Department, District Headquarters, GHQ Field Forces, Division and Brigade Headquarters and [unclear] Headquarters. In attaining this mission the teachings of the College will obviously ensure that the Training and Tactical employment of Troops of all Arms is based throughout the Army on uniform principles and doctrines as laid down from time to time by the DEPARTMENT OF DEFENCE.[44]

The intended pre-eminence of the school within the Irish military education system could not have been made clearer. The ambition was clear but so too were the challenges and difficulties. This tentative syllabus, which in familiar fashion MacNeill circulated to all officers commanding corps without it having received 'official approval of any sort',[45] was for a course to train instructors who might then go on to establish the Command and Staff School. Given the limited experience in command and staff of most officers in the army, this was to prove a difficult task. The full syllabus is not now available, but correspondence between the CMC and the chief of staff concerning the release of the Director of Training Col M.J. Costello to lecture on the course gives an indication of its scope. Costello would be required to lecture on four subjects: combined tactics, command staff and logistics, training methods and military organisation. He would also be required to prepare and conduct map and terrain exercises. According to the chief of staff, this would, 'in effect, comprise the principal features of the Course'.[46] MacNeill's reliance on Costello also shows his reliance on the experience they gained at Fort Leavenworth. It is hoped that he was also aware of some criticism of that school 'for stifling creative thinking by rewarding only those who could produce the "school solution" to problems'.[47] Later students at the Irish Command and Staff School might echo the same criticism. MacNeill's request for the services of Costello was the subject of lengthy correspondence involving not only the chief of staff but also the minister for defence, Desmond Fitzgerald. As a fellow graduate of Fort Leavenworth, his value to the CMC was unquestionable, but an initial request that he lecture on the course for 209 hours was obviously going to cause difficulties. The request was eventually reduced to thirty-three hours but not before the chief of staff had to inform MacNeill that 'time and again your responsibilities with regard to the establishment and administration of the Irish Military College have been defined, and representations such as are contained in the first paragraph of your letter are decidedly objectionable'.[48] That this and other instances of the strained relations between both men seems not to have militated against the conduct of the course says as much for the forbearance of the chief of staff as it does for the ambition, vision and drive of the first commandant of the Irish Military College.

Sixteen officers, the most senior of whom was Col J.J. O'Connell, then director of intelligence, were detailed to attend the course that commenced on 23 February 1931. Col O'Connell, after whom one of the three Military

College lecture halls was named in August 1954, requested that the chief of staff excuse him from the course because he had been summarily removed from instructional work and posted as director of intelligence. The reason for this removal was he felt, 'that my ideas on technical matters did not agree with those being brought into operation'.[49] Furthermore, 'the new methods constituted a complete scrapping of all that I had been teaching for several years'.[50] In spite of this request, Col O'Connell not only attended the course as a student but played a very significant role as an instructor by delivering lectures and organising conferences on subjects relating to what was then termed 'mobile forces'.[51] Col O'Connell's detailed and well-prepared précis discussed modern developments in the use of armoured cars and tanks in operations that had formerly been conducted by horse-mounted cavalry, in particular reconnaissance. He did not, however, neglect specific Irish conditions and prepared a map exercise for cyclist troops. Following accepted military doctrine of the time, O'Connell informed the students that while, 'Infantry is the basic Arm, a doctrine which is in keeping with our country's circumstances and resources – on its Infantry this State must place its main reliance – but we must recognise also a need for Mobile Troops'.[52] The cyclist exercise was based on a map of the environs of Gettysburg, which indicated, again, reliance on US material for the conduct of this first Irish command and staff course. O'Connell's derived his lectures and preparation ability from his earlier training experiences. He established a link between the Military College and the ASI where he served as chief lecturer from February 1924 until March 1929.

The course commenced on the allotted date against the objections of the CMC. MacNeill attempted to absolve himself of any future recriminations by informing the chief of staff that it would be recognised that 'should any breakdown occur, that as the General Officer responsible for the College, I have advised the Department that the time allowed for preparation was entirely inadequate'.[53] As with the 1st infantry officers course, the students on the command and staff course, such as Col O'Connell, would also act as instructors. This expedient would eventually have consequences for grading students, and for course results. The CMC informed the chief of staff that the course would have to 'be conducted on the Syndicate Basis as in force in the British Staff College rather than on the Individual progress basis as approved by the United States Staff College'.[54] In the British syndicate system, students were grouped into almost permanent groupings and were assessed mainly on their performances during the collective work of these syndicates, as compared with the American system in which students were mostly graded according to their individual efforts. The CMC subsequently prepared a detailed efficiency report on each of the students based on the overall work of each student. Not an ideal situation, but understandable given that 'most of the instruction and many of the papers, problems, etc. are set by the students themselves'.[55]

The 1st command and staff course was followed by the 2nd, commencing on 2 November 1931, and was reported on by the CMC in his half-yearly report of March 1932. It is clear from this report that a step-by-step approach was being operated with an emphasis being placed on preliminary staff training for corps directors and senior staff officers of the respective corps. The next step would be to train senior staff officers serving at higher headquarters. A later consideration would be the training of infantry officers provided they had completed courses at the Infantry School. Later still would be the development of stage II of the command and staff course covering advanced training for war. The CMC had not yet attempted developing stage II. He considered that 'the administrative and instructional difficulties connected with this are so numerous and compli-cated that I think we had better defer it for another year'.[56] This admission shows that the syllabus was confined to staff procedures at a relatively restricted forma-tion level, not surprising given that the school instructors were also learning their trade and writing exercise texts and manuals relevant to Irish conditions.

Persistent themes in the report are: one, that students should be carefully chosen based on their future appointments; two, that instructors should also be carefully chosen and three, that resident instructors from all corps should be posted to the College. Maj. Gen. MacNeill also hinted at the beginning of a problem that was to persist: that of disconnect, or perceived disconnect, between what can be termed 'college life' and the life of the army. He was concerned that the Command and Staff School should have the same status as comparable schools in other armies, such as the British and American schools where qualification on the equivalent Command and Staff Course was a requisite for promotion to higher rank. He was concerned that 'a feeling was creeping into the Army that graduation from the Staff School has no bearing on the filling of higher Staff Appointments'.[57] It was a feeling that continued for some years, as can be seen in a letter from 'Felix' (perhaps Col Felix McCorley) to Col J.J. O'Connell in 1936. He recounted in the letter how he had spent some time with the command and staff students on Lough Sheelin where they were undergoing the final and most important tactical map-based tests at the end of their course. He was present when the adjutant general read a message from the chief of staff to the students informing them that he had them continually in his thoughts, and their work was much appreciated. 'Felix' understood this to mean 'that the old policy of putting Command and Staff graduates into the key positions is to continue and I was wrong to tell the students that the week's privilege leave at the end of the Course was the only thing they would ever gain as a result of their labours'.[58] Perhaps 'Felix' was being somewhat jocular as he did sign himself *Mishay lay Mass*.[59] This situation would in time be remedied somewhat with graduation from the command and staff course becoming one of a number of criteria to be considered for promotion. Even at this early stage, the risk of the Command and Staff School becoming 'other' was discernible. Nevertheless, while course objectives might lay down that successful completion of the course would qualify a student for a particular rank, this did not mean a promotion to that rank. The chief of staff continued to retain the authority for recommending to the minister for defence whether or not an officer should be promoted. This matter will come to the fore in later chapters when the question of whether all or only selected officers should attend the command and staff course will be discussed.

The course continued annually throughout the 1930s, with the 9th course commencing in December 1938 and bringing to 125 the number of officers who attended this, the most senior course then available to officers in the Defence Forces.[60] In spite of certain misgivings by some less-than-satisfied officers, the command and staff course was a serious undertaking as can clearly be seen from Col Dan Bryan's papers lodged in the UCD Archives. Dan Bryan, the much-respected head of military intelligence during the Emergency, completed the infantry course in 1932/33 and then proceeded to the 5th command and staff course in October 1934. The course syllabus provided for 108 days, comprised of almost 400 hours' instruction with a predominance of lectures, conferences and map problems over terrain exercises and demonstrations.[61] The emphasis of the course was on the theoretical instruction of the deployment of military formations from battalion to division in the various phases of conventional combat, attack, defence and withdrawal and the part played by the various arms in these deployments. All of this would have been new ground for most, if not all, of the students, given their previous limited active military experience. This limited experience, gained in the War of Independence and the Civil War, was reflected in only twelve hours of instruction devoted to street fighting, guerrilla warfare, and riot duty out of a total of 101 hours of instruction on combined tactics. The intention was clearly to educate senior officers in the professional knowledge and expertise required of commanders and staff officers of a standing national army. Both the command and staff aspects of this intention were catered for, with ninety-two hours of staff duties instruction matching the 101 hours of tactical instruction.

The school instructors played an important role in the process of establishing what could be called a baseline of tactical and staff doctrine, albeit the result was some way away from being the considered, debated and accepted doctrine for the Defence Forces requested by the DPD. The Irish Military College adopted the British nomenclature for its instructing staff by designating it as the directing staff (DS), with each instructor called a DS. The DS wrote and delivered lectures and conferences, constructed and conducted map and terrain exercises. They devised, submitted and provided solutions and conducted, marked and commented on tests and examinations. That this work was considerable can be glimpsed from just one commented tactical test solution in the Bryan papers. Tests were held following each block of instruction, and there was a total of twenty-five DS comments on a test submitted by Bryan on the tactical application of air power. One of the comments to a paper – just one paper, from one student – shows the professional commitment and attention to detail of the DS when he wrote 'It is too late to move the aircraft on the 15th. Comdt 'B' could not possibly order his Sqn to move before 1900hrs leaving 30 minutes to complete the move in daylight. NO facilities exist at this time for night flying.'[62] It was a level of commitment that early established the reputation of the DS of the Irish Military College. The general structure of the 1930s command and staff course remained constant, with relatively little change during the decade. As an example, the syllabus of the 7th course, conducted between 1936 and 1937, shows a duration of 107 days with a total of 316 hours of instruction. The remaining courses of the decade were similar in duration and content. The students on the 7th course were instructed to 'Avail of every opportunity to obtain practice in Equitation'[63] before joining the course. In spite of O'Connell's lectures on armoured reconnaissance, the Irish Army, like many others, still saw a role for horse-mounted reconnaissance. In the case of the Command and Staff School students, this took the form of what was known as staff rides during terrain exercises. These staff rides had an aura of the mounted staff of the First World War, an aura that would not survive the next decade of the Irish Military College.

Defence Forces Regulation (DRF)
Military Education Officers and Cadets

The regulatory position of military education within the legal framework of the Defence Forces was an important issue to be resolved, as while the CMC could propose courses and syllabuses, he did not have the legal authority required to do so. Regulation only, through the issuance of Defence Forces regulations as provided for in the Defence Act, could achieve this aim. DFR 54/1928 and DFR 52/1924, which considered military examinations, provided a framework. Further revision to these early regulations had been under consideration, and a comprehensive DFR on the military education of officers and cadets had been draughted and approved by both the minister for defence and minister for finance in 1934, but had not been promulgated. The probable reason for its non-promulgation was a proposed comprehensive network of general service and service schools. The general service schools proposed was the Military College comprising three schools: Cadet School, Command and Staff School and School of Educational Training. Further general service schools were the School of Music, Army Equitation School, School of Physical Culture, School of Military Intelligence and School of Technical Training. The listed service schools were the Infantry, Artillery, Air Corps, Cavalry, Military Engineering, Signals, Army Ordnance, Supply and Transport, and Army Medical schools.[64] This extensive listing of schools was designed to fulfil the DPD recommendation that basic and advanced education would be provided by each separate service or corps school. The continuing concept that the Infantry School should be considered as a distinct service school is emphasised by the parenthetical inclusion that '(The Infantry School shall be located in the Military College)'.[65] Several of the listed schools were not yet established and two in particular, the School of Educational Training and the School of Technical Training, would require much further consideration. In approving, the Department of Finance proposed the wording 'the schools may be established' instead of 'will be established' and informed the Department of Defence that the minister's approval was 'subject to the consideration that no additional expense will be incurred in respect of personnel or equipment without his prior sanction'.[66] This consideration, which would hamper the Military College well into the future, whenever expenditure over and above day-to-day activities was concerned, gave the military authorities food for thought, and a revised DFR was submitted for Department of Finance approval in 1936.

'DFR C.S.3 1937 – Military Education Officers and Cadets' provided the structure upon which the Irish Military College would build its future direction for decades to come. The regulation was promulgated in 1937 and is still in force. The concept of general service schools and services schools was retained, but the School of Military Education, the School of Technical Training and the School of Military Intelligence were not included in the 1936 draft. Paragraph 1 outlined the mediums of military education:

1. The military education of officers and cadets will normally be imparted through the following mediums:

Cadet Courses.
Young Officers Courses.
Standard Courses for each Corps and Service.
Refresher Courses.
Command and Staff Courses.
Technical and Specialists' Courses including Courses abroad.
Service with Troops including attached service with foreign armies.[67]

Subparagraph g was a remarkably prescient innovation. It may well have been intended solely to allow for attendance at courses conducted by foreign armies, but it also left open the possibility of actual service with foreign armies. This possibility has come to fruition with the deployment of Irish troops on United Nations peacekeeping missions. The purpose of each of the courses listed was laid down and the schools that were to provide the courses were detailed. Insofar as the Military College was considered, it would be responsible for the cadet course, the young officers and standard course for the Infantry Corps since the Infantry School was now part of the Military College, and the command and staff course. The standard courses for officers other than those of the Infantry, Medical, Air Corps and Naval Service were to be of two parts, with the first part conducted at the Infantry School and the second part in the respective corps school. While flexibility may well have been intended with this provision, the eventual result would be the future conduct by the Military College of standard courses, which were attended by officers of other corps and services.

Another important aspect of the DFR was that it laid down certain qualification objectives of the various courses:

> The Standard Course is designed to fit officers to hold a commandant's command and to acquire a knowledge of handling commands normally allotted to a Lt-Col. It covers the tactics and technique of the Service Corps concerned and the functions of all components of the Defence Forces.[68]

The command and staff course had a broader function:

> The course is designed to fit officers of all Corps and Services to hold the rank of Lt-Col and higher rank, to command formations of all components of the Defence Forces Arms and to perform the higher staff work involved in the handling of such formations. The course will include the study of war in its wider aspects, the handling of formations of all components of the Defence Forces, and staff duties.[69]

The regulation, while stating what rank qualification could be gained by successful completion of the course, did not state that successful students would be promoted to these ranks. Allied to the promotional aspect of the courses, the regulation set out the necessary rules for the setting, conduct and marking of examinations at all schools. The Department of Finance recommended to the minister for finance that the DFR should be approved on their standard contingency that it should incur no expenditure 'in respect of personnel, equipment or additional pay without the prior sanction of this Department'.[70]

The Military College implemented the DFR on its coming into effect in 1937 by conducting cadet, standard infantry and command and staff courses up until 1939 when 'War in its Wider Aspects' conspired to change how it conducted its business. The CMC Maj. Gen. Hugo MacNeill, who had the luxury in 1932 of engaging in an important debate on whether or not the GOC Curragh Command should also hold the dual appointment of CMC,[71] would soon be appointed GOC 2nd Division. He would then have an opportunity of learning if his efforts at the Military College were vindicated by the standard of training and military education of his unit commanders and staff officers. An intriguing aspect to MacNeill's change of appointment is that a student on the 9th command and staff course, which commenced on 31 January 1938, was the acting director of cavalry – Col Daniel McKenna. Two years later, on 29 January 1940, Col McKenna was promoted to the rank of Maj. Gen. and appointed as chief of staff with the responsibility, among countless others, for overseeing the fighting efficiency of Maj. Gen. MacNeill's division.

Conclusion

The Irish Military College was established at Keane Barracks in the Curragh Camp in 1930 and came under the command of Maj. Gen. Hugo MacNeill. MacNeill had been head of the 1926 military mission to the United States Army and the director of the Defence Plans Division organised on the return of the mission. The College incorporated the Cadet School, which had begun in 1928 at the ASI and also, in effect, the training functions of the ASI in 1930. Three schools were established within the Military College: the Cadet School, the Infantry School and the Command and Staff School. Throughout the 1930s these three schools, while hampered by inadequate numbers of trained instructors and by an inadequate instructional environment, set about educating a large proportion of the officers of the army. This education was achieved against a background of diminishing unit strengths, which resulted in the Military College being effectively the sole medium of sustained officer education and training in the army. A 1937 Defence Forces regulation codified the format of officer education. By the outbreak of the Second World War, the Military College had succeeded in training the officers of the Irish Army in at least the theoretical aspects of their profession, and in a standardised system of staff duties and command and control of military units and formations. This was not a negligible achievement and was one without which the ensuing expansion and mobilisation of a two-division army would have proven impossible.

4

The 1940s
The Emergency

The Emergency

The Cadet School was founded in 1928 and the Military College in 1930.[1] From then until the declaration of the Emergency in 1939, the Permanent Defence Force (PDF) commissioned 184 young men as 2nd Lieutenants, trained 189 officers to be infantry company commanders, and trained 125 officers as staff officers at battalion, brigade, division and army-headquarters level.[2] A commendable achievement for an organisation that had its origins in guerrilla and civil war, had no experience in conventional war and had to look outside of itself for expertise in contemporary military craft, of which few of its officers had experience. It was also achieved by an institution with limited numbers of experienced instructors, who developed and imparted instruction based on what had been learned by a few of them in the United States, and for an army greatly depleted in numbers, and organised and equipped, however inadequately, along British lines.

The commissioned 2nd Lieutenants and the officers trained as company commanders suffered, however, from one great drawback that was to become dangerously apparent during the early years of the Emergency. Their almost total lack of experience in the tactical and field training of organised units would constitute a serious problem for the PDF. Staff officers trained in the Command and Staff School were at a lesser disadvantage, as the techniques of staff work learned in the syndicate room can be more easily applied at headquarters level than a platoon or company commander who has not had 'hands-on' experience can control troops in action. Nevertheless, it was upon this cohort of regular officers that the PDF and the Irish State depended for national defence at the outbreak the Second World War. This dependency was quickly recognised as being numerically and qualitatively inadequate for the soon-to-be expanded army, and this need for increased numbers of officers almost immediately transformed the focus of the Military College.

Lt Col J.P. Duggan described the Military College during the Emergency as 'a dynamo of efficiency'.[3] He was writing from personal experience having been a cadet in the Cadet School in 1943. He had originally joined the Artillery Corps and served as a gunner before selection as a cadet, and was well placed to observe the Military College at the time. He was also keenly aware of military events on the Continent as he found time to write a letter to the military correspondent of *The Irish Times*, Col J.J. O'Connell, asking him if he could clear up 'some points which were causing controversy in his billet'.[4] O'Connell, at that time officer commanding military archives, enjoyed the confidence of both military and departmental officials. In addition to his role as military correspondent for *The Irish Times*, he was also authorised to broadcast lectures on George Washington and the Battle of the Boyne for the Irish broadcasting service Radio 2RN.[5] J.P. Duggan asked how field artillery was being protected on the march and also, probably with an eye to the future of the Irish Army, what form the British and American armies would take after the war 'seeing that the bulk of these armies, over 90%, is "Emergency". That is if they will not all be killed'.[6] O'Connell's reply is not available, but the question illustrates to some degree the concern of the Irish Military College during the Emergency: that of solving the shortage of commissioned officers needed for the rapidly expanded Permanent Defence Force (PDF) of the 1940s.

While it is by no means accurate to apply Hans Hellmut Kirst's appellation of 'officer factory' to the College, the need to provide officers for the army was without a doubt the keystone to the structure of the recurring paragraph 'Provision of Officers' in the chief of staff's reports from 1940 to 1947.[7] Kirst was an officer in the German Army during the Second World War and wrote his novel *Officer Factory* in 1963. In it, he described the increasingly bizarre and eventually murderous methods employed by a training officer to turn out officers from a training school while under intense pressure from his superiors. While not by any means subjected to such methods, the numbers of officers trained by the College in this period are striking and instructive. There were 1,245 commissioned officers in the PDF on 1 April 1940 only 703 of whom were regulars, and by 31 March 1944, the commissioned officer strength stood at 2,558. More than 1,300 potential officers were trained and commissioned by the Military College in four years.[8] Before the Emergency, the Irish Military College annually conducted courses at the Cadet School, the Infantry School and the Command and Staff School. From then until 1947, only the Cadet School continued with its allotted role, while the other two schools functioned as Potential Officer schools and schools providing courses geared towards the fighting efficiency and administration of the expanded wartime army. The Cadet School continued its annual intake and commissioned 205 2nd Lieutenants between 1940 and 1945.[9] The cadet course was extended in 1942, in order to improve the standard of training to be attained by cadets. The year 1942 also saw a change in the eligibility for cadetships with the examination confined to members of the PDF, who were serving at the beginning of that year. One of those who received cadetship from this examination was J.P. Duggan then serving as a temporary lieutenant, commissioned from a potential officers course run by the Artillery Corps.[10]

Duggan was one of a small number of potential officers who did not receive their training in the Military College since, 'Except for artillery men and personnel with technical or professional qualifications all Potential Officers were posted to the Military College for a short intensive course before being drafted to Units in commissioned rank'.[11] Candidates for these courses were selected from serving members of the army, from reservists, and the Volunteer Force, and also included some civilians with specialist qualifications. One serving soldier who found himself detailed for a potential officers course was Cpl Liam Cosgrave, a future Taoiseach. Recently promoted to the rank of corporal in the Supply and Transport Corps and serving in the Esplanade in Dublin, he went with eight other supply and transport corporals to Clarke Barracks in the Curragh. From there they attended the potential officers course in the Military College with NCOs from other corps and emerged some weeks later as 2nd Lieutenants. The course as he remembers it was tough and intense with much 'drill, marching and lectures'.[12] Ninety-two students reported on the first Emergency Potential Officers Course on 4 July 1940, less than a month after the declaration of the Emergency.[13]

The first course was followed at frequent intervals by courses re-designated as B to H Emergency course (potential officers) and then by the 9th, 10th, 11th and finally 12th pot officers (Emergency) course that formed up on 25 January 1944.[14]

On these courses were trained 1,041 students, a testimony to the capacity and adaptability of a military college conceived, designed and organised for a less frantic and a more academic existence. Col T. Gallagher, the CMC in 1945, shared this view when he wrote of the efforts of the College in training potential officers:

> But in 1940, when the Army had to be expanded out of all proportion to its former strength, the Military College was forced into "mass production". Temporary officers by the hundred underwent a highly concentrated three-month course in small arms techniques, in discipline and administrative training, in tactics and contemporary military history. The College staff, imbued with inexhaustible energy and imperturbable patience, performed a task which even now seems incredible. They trained their never ending "waves" of potential officers with a superlatively smooth efficiency, and the "potentials" responded with a keenness which has been compared to the legendary zeal of Fianna aspirants in the heroic days of Fionn.[15]

It is not clear that the students saw the courses they underwent in the same heroic light. Gallagher admitted that the College became known to many of them as 'a place or state of punishment where some soldiers suffered for a time before being commissioned'.[16] Col Gallagher carried a great responsibility as CMC in providing officers for the expanding Defence Forces. E.D. Doyle, a future director of signals and defence correspondent of *The Irish Times*, attended one of the potential officers courses run by Gallagher in 1943. According to Doyle, 'The aim was to make us capable of leading young soldiers by example and precept. It was intended to ensure that lives were not lost by officers' unfitness or incompetence. Col Gallagher was a man one took seriously'.[17]

The potential officers courses were not, however, in spite of the efforts of the Military College, wholly satisfactory. Nor indeed, given the brevity of the courses, could they have been expected to be so. With at the most three months to train a disparate group of students whose military experience ranged between those of the regular soldier, the reservist, the Volunteer Force member and the civilian, the task must have proven daunting even to Col Gallagher's sterling instructors. Considering that it was necessary to extend the regular two-year Cadet School course in 1942, it is not surprising that the director of training, Col S. McGoran, found it necessary to issue an earlier training directive in October 1940 stating that:

Circumstances connected with the training of recently commissioned Officers, such as the short duration of their course at the Military College and lack of uniformity in their basic standard and in their preliminary training prior to undergoing the College course necessitate special attention being given to the continuation of the training of these Officers.[18]

Commands and brigades provided this continuation training. Another alternative that could have improved the standard of military efficiency of newly commissioned officers would have been the commissioning of regular NCOs. But 'whilst it was desired to put forward a selected number of Regular NCOs for commissions, the Department of Finance would not agree and consequently this desirable source was closed'.[19] A small number of NCOs, seventeen in 1942/43, fourteen in 1943/44 and nine in 1944/45, forty in all, was subsequently commissioned, but this traditional source of commissioned officers tried and tested in many armies in times of mobilisation and expansion was not widely availed of the PDF during the Emergency. Given the seriousness of the international situation and the threat to national security faced by the military authorities, it must have been dispiriting to come to terms with yet another penny-pinching decision. It could be concluded that the Department of Finance was concerned that serving NCOs might in the long term cost more if they were commissioned.

Nevertheless, notwithstanding the weakness of the duration of the potential officers courses and the unequal military experience of the students, training within the Military College was considered to be important because of the instructional standards and methods of the College instructors. During the preceding decade, instructors had usually been selected from among the students who performed best on the courses. It was not a foolproof method as transfer to the Curragh was not an attractive option, as will be seen later for those officers not based there. It was particularly unattractive for married officers living in the south and west of the country. Married accommodation was scarce in the Curragh and accepting a posting to the Military College meant financial hardship with no guarantee at that time of enhanced career prospects. Consequently, the intensive nature of the potential officers courses necessitated finding and posting instructors to the Curragh on a non-voluntary basis. The standing of the potential officers courses was such that in 1941/42, for the course students, 'The results of these Courses were the final determining factor as to whether they should be granted commissions'.[20] But potential officers courses, as vital as they were for the expansion of the PDF, comprised only one element of the contribution of the Military College to its wartime activities.

While the Military College was busy training potential officers, the army had expanded by 1942 from its pre-Emergency strength of 5,915 regulars[21] to a force that could deploy in the field two divisions, commanded by Maj. Gens Hugo MacNeill and Michael J. Costello, the senior members of the 1926 military mission to the United States. The formation of these two divisions called for an increased number of officers to fill command and staff appointments, more than had been previously trained in the now-closed Command and Staff School. Recourse was had to the running of short field officers courses in both divisions for senior commanders and staff officers. As with the potential officers courses, these were necessarily truncated, but as the chief of staff reported they 'went some distance towards replacing the old Command and Staff Course'.[22] Both divisions trained extensively, culminating in major field exercises in 1942 in which they were pitted against each other and which led the chief of staff to report favourably that the 'Two Divisions operated as complete units in the field for the entire period and proved to be effective fighting formations'.[23]

The training in the commands was supplemented with a diverse series of courses conducted at the Military College in addition to its potential officers courses. All of these courses were geared towards increasing the effectiveness of the divisions. The most notable courses were intelligence courses, umpire courses, battalion commanders course, senior officers course and special weapons course for artillery battery commanders. This latter course coincided with the formation of seven new artillery batteries in March 1944 but, as Duggan has recorded, 'without further supplies of anti-tank guns being received; these batteries remained as skeletal cadres'.[24] In all close to 800 students attended these courses during the Emergency period. The Military College also assumed responsibility for conducting courses for the training officers of the local Defence Force, conducting four such courses of three to four weeks' duration. One particular course directly related to the tactical proficiency of the divisions was the battle drill and practice course run for forty-eight officers in 1943. This course responded to troop leaders' deficiencies noted in the divisional exercises. The deficiencies were addressed in two ways: first by conducting the above battle drill and practice course at the Military College, and second by sending twelve officers on battle school/commando and junior leader courses run by the British Army in Northern Ireland.[25] Col James Flynn, who was then serving in plans and operations at GHQ, has stated that attendance on this course came about during meetings between the chief of staff, Gen. Dan McKenna, and Gen. Franklyn, the commander of British troops in Northern Ireland. These meetings, which began in Dublin on 15 August 1941, were authorised by Taoiseach Éamon de Valera and were held to discuss military cooperation, which might become necessary in the event of a German invasion. Flynn noted that Franklyn's 'offer was accepted and in due course some promising young Lts were selected and detailed, mainly on the recommendations of Sean Collins-Powell now at the Military College'.[26] Among the officers selected were two future GOCs, Brig. Gen. Jack Stewart and Brig. Gen. Richard (Dickie) Bunworth, and the GAA hero John Joe O'Reilly. In spite of the divisions proving to be 'effective fighting formations', these courses were considered necessary because 'One of the chief weaknesses apparent during the exercises was the inability of Platoon and equivalent commanders to exercise effective control of their units immediately before and during contact'.[27] This was a fundamental tactical and indeed training deficiency. As it manifested itself at a time when units were at full war establishment, it emphasises how difficult it had been in the pre-Emergency army to provide officers exiting Military College courses with the required follow-on experience that can only be acquired by unit service and by collective training. This deficiency remained to be addressed in the future. Before then, however, the 'dynamo' that was the Military College during the Emergency had wound down somewhat and was due to enter a new phase catering for a different PDF.

Post-Emergency Reorganisation of the Military College

The ending of the Second World War resulted, as with the ending of the Civil War, in the large-scale demobilisation of the PDF. Chief of Staff Gen. McKenna's proposal that conscription be introduced to ensure the swift development of a standing army in the event of future emergency was not acceptable to the government. He was not alone as a chief of staff in having his proposal for conscription rejected. In 1945, Gen. George C. Marshall, chief of staff of the US Army, supported a national service bill introduced to Congress by Secretary for War Henry Stimson. 'In the years ahead, painfully aware of America's initial unpreparedness in two wars, Marshall would continue to fight for some version of universal service for the country's young men.'[28] By 1949, the establishment of the PDF stood at 12,987 but crucially its actual strength was 7,941. Examination of these figures shows a shortage of almost 1,000 NCOs and 3,500 privates indicating under-strength units.[29] This implied limited troop training, ensuring that it would fall to the Military College to provide professional education and training during the difficult low-strength years of the late 1940s, 1950s and 1960s.

The chief of staff was aware of the increased importance of the Military College and re-staffing and restructuring began in 1946 with the Military College being organised so as to consist of three schools: 'Command and Staff School, Infantry School, Cadet School and Potential Officers' Wing.'[30] This reorganisation was short-lived, particularly the potential officers wing, as a Board of Officers was set up early in 1947 to examine 'the organisation and location of the Constituent Schools of the College and the scope of the standard courses to be held there in the future'.[31] The board also considered the question of a divisional organisation as a base for instruction in the College. This question, which will be discussed later in this chapter, was to prove contentious as on it depended the future organisation and missions of the PDF.

The importance of the 1947 board is seen in its members. It was headed by the OC of the Curragh Training Camp and future chief of staff, Col Sean Collins-Powell. Collins-Powell had been a member of the 1926 military mission to the United States and was responsible for the administration, supervision and coordination of the principal army training establishments. Next on the board was the CMC, Col C.J. (Slim) Donohue, who along with Collins-Powell had attended the British Army's 3rd senior officers course from September to December 1946. Also on the board were Lt Col P.J. Hally, a future adjutant general, and Comdt J.J.G. MacCarthy, both graduates of the 17th staff course at the Staff College Camberley, and Lt Col P. Curran, a future quartermaster general and a graduate of the Command and General Staff College, Fort Leavenworth. They also benefited from the periodic attendance of the chief of staff, the adjutant general, the quartermaster general and the director of training 'to give such direction as was necessary'.[32]

Following the board's deliberations, the College was reorganised with the short-lived 1946 potential officers wing wound up. From 1948 to 1951, the annual intake of cadets was to be sixty and the command and staff course would cater for forty students. Wider changes were foreseen for the Infantry School, which was to be relocated to MacDonagh Barracks, the adjoining barracks to Pearse Barracks, which had housed the Cadet School, the Infantry School and the Command and Staff School since 1930. The Infantry School would conduct standard infantry courses for thirty officer students, and also standard infantry courses for NCOs for promotion to the rank of sergeant. Also, standard administrative 'A' and quartermaster 'Q' courses for officers and standard 'Q' courses for NCOs would be conducted.[33] While the Infantry School did occupy McDonagh Barracks, these course proposals seem not to have been implemented since 'A' and 'Q' courses for officers and NCOs are later recorded as being conducted in the General Training Depot (GTD) of the Curragh Training Camp as distinct from the Military College. In addition, the Military College arrivals books only record one NCO course, a battalion sergeant majors course in 1945.

While these matters were being deliberated on, the College set about its first post-Emergency task, the conduct of refresher courses for those temporary officers who had been accepted for regular commissions in the army. Other than the annual intake of cadets, these were the only courses conducted in the Military College between April 1945 and April 1946. It might be considered surprising that it was deemed necessary to train officers who had been in training and in active units for some years, but the objects of the courses were:

> Firstly to ensure that Officers have a sound basic knowledge of military subjects upon which their subsequent higher military training can be based; secondly to ensure that they not only know how to instruct in military subjects, but also to ensure that they can effectively supervise instruction given by others and thirdly to ensure that there is uniformity and a common standard in our methods of instruction throughout the Army.[34]

While it is possible to discern echoes of the 1920s OTC and ASI in these courses, as once again zeal for the demobilisation of the PDF gathered apace, the procedure on this occasion seems to have been less traumatic than after the Civil War. J.P. Duggan, who was no champion of enforced demobilisation, stated that 'On the 1st of November 1945 an Interview Board set about selecting additional officers for the Permanent Force and the First Line Reserve from Volunteer and Emergency officers who were still serving'.[35] 331 officers were selected as suitable for the PDF, and it was these that the College set about training. Undoubtedly, many were disappointed not to be selected, with J.P. Duggan commenting, 'The transition, however, was painful enough for young men who had joined up from school and had got married in a "Sam Browne".'[36] Two courses, designated general refresher officers courses, were run, the first in April 1946 and the second in September 1946. A training managers course followed these two courses in March 1947. While only 95 of the 331 temporary officers attended the two refresher courses, the chief of staff reported in March 1947 that 'The current refresher course is designed to cater for those officers who, as a result of the recent organisation, have been posted to appointments where a knowledge of training management is essential'.[37] It is presumed that the officers who did not complete the refresher and training managers courses were appointed to postings where knowledge of training management was not required.

The Schools

While the 1947 board addressed the future workings of the Military College, it seems not to have considered any change necessary in the roles of the PDF, not that this would have been part of its terms of reference. It seems clear, given the chief of staff's proposals for compulsory national service, that the strategic vision of the general staff for defending the State remained essentially the same as before the outbreak of the Second World War. While cognisance was taken of the overall changed nuclear environment, defence of the State was envisaged as opposing landings of invasion forces, either at or after landings were made. Organisation would remain the same, with or without mobilisation, and available forces would be composed of brigades and divisions with supporting arms. Material and equipment were also considered unlikely to change, nor would procurement difficulties be any less acute. The roles therefore of the officer, both on commissioning and throughout his career, were not seen to have radically changed.

The Cadet School
The Cadet School programme was modified in 1946. The modification resulted in three separate periods of instruction of six, eight and a further six months' duration. The purpose of this modification was:

To ensure that training is put on a more progressive basis with definite standards to be attained on the conclusion of each period with a provision for
adequate revision during succeeding periods so that cadets when being passed
out are revised and brought up-to-date in basic subjects which otherwise
might have largely been forgotten.[38]

While it is possible to understand the concern of the army authorities during
the previous five years that the Cadet School should provide as many officers as
possible for the expanded army, it must be considered that standards may have
fallen if there was a requirement that basic subjects should not be forgotten.
Reports on the Emergency divisional exercises highlighted such failings. Many
of the noted failings related to the duties of junior officers, such as inadequate
fieldcraft and reconnaissance, inadequate digging of slit trenches, neglect of
minor tactics.[39]

The CMC, Col C.J. O'Donohue, proposed changes to the cadet syllabus, following a report he submitted to the chief of staff. He had found on examining
the syllabus that the cadet had to study a large number of subjects but without
the attainment at any set time of any set standard, with the possibility that a cadet
could leave the school on commissioning having forgotten what he had earlier
learned. To overcome this deficiency, Donohue proposed, as we have seen above,
dividing the course into three separate periods while also laying down specific
objectives for each period. The objectives of the first period would be to train
the cadet to the level of a first-class recruit, to give him some experience in
drill orders on the square and to introduce him to some of the other subjects
contained in the regulations, such as military history. The second period would
see the cadet qualifying as a junior leader up to NCO instructor level while
the third period would 'qualify the cadet as a junior Officer suitable for posting
to any branch of the service'.[40] This intention that on commissioning the new
2nd Lieutenant would have the ability to lead, organise, supervise and train in
any branch of the service was later to become contentious. It seems difficult to
understand how the CMC could think that instruction in an infantry environment could qualify a young man for posting to an artillery regiment, or a cavalry
squadron, or a signals company, to mention just a few of the corps. Although
O'Donohue's proposals were accepted by the chief of staff and were applied
for some years, they seem somehow to be tinkering at the edges of what was
required of cadet training. One would have thought that a greater examina-

tion of the failings of junior officers during the divisional exercises might have prompted a more in-depth consideration of what were the essential requirements of a 2nd Lieutenant on commissioning rather than just a restructuring of time periods.

1947, the first full year of these new arrangements, was to see a major exception to the annual intake to the Cadet School when for the first time since 1926 there was no cadet intake. Blame was laid at the door of the civil service commissioners for not organising examinations until 10 November 1947, with results not available until March 1948. Late examinations was not a new problem, as the 1946 intake did not commence training until November 1946, also due to late receipt of results of the civil service examinations. Whether or not the fault lay with the commissioners, their examination was not held until November 1947. The numbers applying for the 100 vacancies were low with only 123 candidates presenting themselves for the examination. For various reasons, only twenty-seven were found eligible and twenty-six candidates from this competition reported to the Cadet School in 1948. Perhaps there was a general Emergency weariness among the young male population of the State and, also, the Interview Board was 'satisfied that the candidates now presenting themselves for examination are not up to the calibre of those frequently in evidence in pre-emergency days'.[41] There was one advantageous result from this 1947 hiatus. The Defence Council decided at its meeting of 10 May 'to discontinue the written examination for the Open Competition and instead invite applications from those in possession of the Leaving Certificate'.[42] It was not to prove a foolproof decision, however, as late notification of Leaving Certificate results would also militate against the aim of starting the cadet course in autumn.

As 1947 was an exceptional year for the Cadet School with no annual intake, so too was 1949, but this time for the opposite reason with two, instead of one, annual cadet intakes. Forty cadets entered the Cadet School on 24 January 1949 followed by a further fifty-four on 3 May 1949.[43] A handwritten note in the arrivals book posed the reasonable question 'Arrived in May. Second group of Cadets. Why extra nos all of a sudden?' The answer is not as reasonable, however, as the question. The second intake was occasioned by what can only be charitably described as political dissatisfaction with the results of the first intake, leading to another competition and selection. This second intake formed the 23rd cadet class and was designated on arrival as the junior 'B' class, a designation that was soon to be colloquially and long-lastingly changed to the 'B' specials.

Rigid supervision was imposed, and twenty of the fifty-four were found not suitable. The remaining thirty-four members of that class were commissioned, with many of them subsequently achieving high rank.[44]

We have seen earlier how, in 1946, the CMC recommended some relatively minor changes to the structure of the cadet syllabus. These were not found to be sufficiently adequate, and the chief of staff instructed the then officer command-ing the Cadet School, the future chief of staff and UNOC Force Commander Lt Col Seán McKeown to consider 'certain changes which past experience and modern development have indicated as being necessary for Cadet training'.[45] In the covering letter to McKeown's subsequent report, the CMC made the surprising statement that 'The policy in the Cadet School since its initiation has been to aim at turning out a finished Platoon Commander, capable at once of taking his place within the framework of a Battalion'.[46] It is a surprising statement when considered against his 1946 contention that the Cadet School aimed to qualify the cadet as a junior officer suitable for posting to any branch of the service. It is an important point as there are significant differences in the demands on a young officer in the different corps i.e. artillery, cavalry, etc. Even given this changed appreciation of the CMC, he admitted that emphasis on military subjects, such as on weapons and the conduct of weapons instruc-tion, 'had resulted more in providing the Army with high grade NCOs'.[47] This quite revealing, if not indeed damning assessment from Col C.J. Donohue led him to suggest that a cadet's basic education on coming into the army should be improved in the Cadet School. He felt that as part of any revision of the cadet syllabus, the corps directors should be asked for their views on what basic requirements they wished young officers to have when being posted to their corps on commissioning. What we see here are the early signs of a reawakening of the 1920s vision of a Military College where the instruction would not be exclusively military.[48] This vision would be advanced in the 1950s with the implementation of certain of the changes proposed by the Cadet Master Lt Col McKeown.

The Infantry School
'Normal business' can be said to have resumed in the Infantry School with the three-month-long 1st standard infantry course, which commenced on 1 September 1947 when thirty-six captains reported to the Military College. This course was later designated as the 13th standard infantry course. It is

not clear why this should have been so as the last infantry course before the Emergency was the 10th such course. Perhaps a need was felt to link into the last of the potential officers courses, the 12th, which was probably conducted at the Infantry School. It took the intervention of the director of plans and operations to have the courses re-designated when he wrote to the CMC asking him 'to look into this as I think we should keep continuity'.[49] In fact, confusion as to what was the accepted class designation continued throughout the decade with the 3rd infantry course being re-designated the 15th infantry course in May 1948.[50] This course seems not to have been included in the chief of staff's report for the period ending 31 March 1949, 'During the period the 14th and 16th Standard Infantry Courses at which 6 Comdts and 65 Junior Officers attended were completed. The 17th Standard Infantry Course, which began in January 1949, was still in progress on 31 March 1949, with 44 officers attending.'[51]

Regardless of the confusion surrounding designation, there was no confusion over the objects of the standard infantry courses, which were clearly laid down in the 1947 instructional circular issued to the students:

> To give advanced training to Company Commanders and Potential Company Commanders in the tactical handling of the Rifle Company, together with Supporting Arms and weapons which normally co-operate with a Company in battle.
> To instruct them in the framework of the battalion in battle.
> To train Company Commanders in Administration and other selected subjects that may come within the scope of their duties.[52]

The 'vocational', as opposed to theoretical, nature of the course is clearly emphasised by the fact that the syllabus is entitled 'Company Commanders Course'. The students were instructed to arrive not only with pen, pencil and notebooks but also with rifle and bayonet, steel helmet, respirator, groundsheet and a complete set of web equipment.[53] They were also advised that the military bicycles that would be issued should be used for military purposes only.

What is also clear is the influence on the Military College of the attendance of PDF officers at British Army training schools. Two officers, both future chiefs of staff, Comdt P.J. Delaney and Comdt C.O'Sullivan, attended a company commanders course at The British Army School of Infantry based at Warminster, Wiltshire in 1947. Delaney and O'Sullivan were obviously chosen for their performances during the Emergency. Carl O'Sullivan for one was appointed second-in-command of the 9th Infantry Battalion as a captain in May 1943 at the age of 24. He was promoted shortly after to commandant in November 1943. The British Army Infantry School has long held an enviable record for testing infantry leaders in as close to actual battle conditions as is possible. A reputation that continues to this day in the present school located at Brecon, close to the Brecon Beacons, the location for qualification tests for the Special Air Service (SAS). The object of the Warminster course very closely mirrored that of the standard infantry course conducted at the Irish Military College in the 1940s. The first two paragraphs are identical. The third paragraph of the British course, 'To assist Company Commanders in the organisation of certain selected subjects of peacetime Training in Infantry Companies and Battalions'[54] is replaced by the third paragraph of the Irish syllabus, 'To train Company Commanders in Administration and other selected subjects that may come within the scope of their duties'.[55] A more striking difference, however, is to be found in the comparative length of the courses, the Warminster course lasting 162 hours while that of the Curragh continued for 397 hours. Most of the disparities are found in the longer time spent on tactical and weapons training. The director of training and the Military College recognised that Irish weapon handling was not as proficient as British. As an example, infantry weapons were allotted ten hours at Warminster whereas on the Curragh sixty hours were required. The explanation is that Irish officers had little opportunity to train tactically with and fire infantry weapons. The pistol, rifle and Bren light machine gun may not have been a problem, but expertise in infantry mortars and anti-tank weapons was limited.

Almost all of the tactical training such as infantry cooperating with other arms, which would have been familiar to British officers, was often allotted double the number of hours on the Irish syllabus. Notable absences on the Irish syllabus were duties in aid of civil power and peacetime training. The Curragh syllabus, however, included individual test talks by students, PT, drill, training management, and thirty-eight hours of administration including tests, which were not considered necessary at Warminster. While the British course syllabus was much modified to cater for the requirements of the PDF, the importance of attending these courses was emphasised in the chief of staff's report:

> We have now got officers of most Corps trained in up to date methods and
> techniques and as a consequence our theoretical instruction in our Schools
> is on a sound basis. It is considered that we should continue the policy of
> sending officers to the principal British Military Schools. This is the soundest
> method of keeping our knowledge and training up to date.[56]

However, the chief of staff's recognition of the value of the British courses was
tempered by his admission that 'theoretical' instruction was on a sound basis
and that 'The value of the courses is to some extent offset by lack of modern
equipment here'.[57] It was an admission that would continue.

For the students on the standard infantry courses at the Infantry School,
an extensive choice of sporting and recreational activities was listed on their
joining instructions, with the proviso that gardening or walking was not classed
as recreational training.[58] During their three-month course, recreational training
may well have been very welcome to the students, as the syllabus comprised
397 hours of instruction including 15 hours of drill and 17½ hours of PT, neither of which were considered recreational. The bulk of the instruction, 263½
hours, was devoted to the main objective of the course, the tactical handling of
the infantry company and its supporting arms. A closer examination, however,
of the syllabus shows that most of the instructional periods were composed
of syndicate discussions, map exercises or demonstrations, with the syndicate
discussions and map exercise being carried on in the classrooms while the
demonstrations would have consisted of passive attendance by the students.
The original vision of the 3rd Infantry Battalion providing troops for practical
exercises was unachievable, although the 14th standard infantry course in 1948
benefited from infantry battalion in attack and defence exercises organised as
regular army unit training and also as demonstrations.

The organisation of these exercises, also arranged for the benefit of the command and staff course, shows the extent to which the wide powers given to the
Chief of Staff Gen. McKenna had been diminished some few years later by the
regulation requiring approval from the minister for defence for inter-command
troop movement. A letter from the chief of staff to the minister effectively
requests permission to move troops from various commands to the Curragh.
The chief of staff informed the minister that:

Arrangements were made as stated in the minutes of the Meeting of the 20th and 21st August for the assembly at the Curragh Training Camp of demonstration units of the Infantry, Artillery, Cavalry and Engineer Corps in connection with the Command and Staff Courses.

This will entail the movement to the Curragh for temporary duty there of 2 Infantry Companies from the Southern Command and 1 Infantry Company each from the Eastern Command and Western Commands together with Artillery, Cavalry and Engineer personnel.

The organisation of these demonstration units is a routine matter provided for in the syllabus of the Command and Staff Course and is referred to you for your approval.[59]

This demonstration unit was organised according to drafts of experimental war establishments for divisional units that were issued to the Military College for instructional purposes. While these drafts updated those issued by the 1948 chief of staff's board on the Military College, their experimental status displays the difficulties experienced by the army authorities in reaching clarity on the future structure of the PDF. It also shows the difficulties surrounding tactical training when the formation of an infantry battalion could only be achieved by moving units from throughout the entire army. These difficulties would continue for decades to undermine unit collective training. The British and American military attachés[60] attended these exercises and demonstrations. One can speculate as to whether their reports included recommendations for or against the continued attendance of Irish officers at British and American military schools. The effort required in organising these exercises and demonstrations must have been considerable when one considers the strength of the Infantry Corps at the time. The establishment on 31 March 1948 was 4,566 all ranks, but the strength stood at only 2,426 all ranks, and by no means were all of these serving in infantry units. These difficulties, which prevented a repeat of the 1948 demonstrations, meant that all of the students who returned to their units after completing their standard infantry course would have little if any opportunity of continuing their 'vocational' training with their under-strength infantry battalions.

The Command and Staff School

Structural reorganisation aside there was a need to consider the instruction to be imparted at the various schools, and this would be of greatest concern to the Command and Staff School. It would not be too onerous for the Cadet School or the Infantry School. The Cadet School's mission continued to be to inculcate young men with loyalty, discipline, leadership and basic military training complemented later in their respective corps school and with their units. The Infantry School's role would be to provide tactical training at platoon and company level and some instruction in the operations of the battalion. This did not mean, however, that pre-Emergency education would suffice. There was a distinct awareness that attendance by officers at foreign courses, particularly in Britain, would be necessary in order to remain abreast of current developments and to learn the lessons of the Second World War. The Command and Staff School, however, would face difficulties in formulating instruction because of rapid demobilisation and lack of clarity on future defence policy.

In August 1944 the minister for defence and the chief of staff submitted a 'Memorandum on the PDF' to the cabinet, followed by a further memorandum on the organisation and equipment of the PDF in April 1946. The cabinet accepted the recommendations of the minister for defence but it 'agreed to the creation of a voluntary reserve instead of a scheme of compulsory national service'.[61] This reluctance of the government to agree to a major component of a defensive plan presented problems for deciding how the PDF was to operate in changing geopolitical circumstances. If the general staff could not formulate agreed defensive plans, the College staff would have difficulties in deciding on a syllabus for the command and staff course, which concerned itself with the operation of the brigade within a division, and indeed with 'war in its wider aspects'. The military authorities were conscious of this problem. The chief of staff recognised 'the necessity for drawing [sic] of a suitable Divisional War Organisation on which problems and other instructional matter could be based'.[62] The board established in 1947 to consider future courses to be conducted in the Military College was also instructed to consider this issue. Drafts of 'Experimental War Establishments for Divisional Units' were issued in 1948.[63] An establishment lays down the units, their strengths and their armaments, for a given formation, in this case, a division. The problem here was that the approved peacetime establishment of the army did not provide for a divisional formation, leading to a reinforcement of the necessarily theoretical nature of instruction, principally in the Command and Staff School.

Theoretical instruction was not, of course, a new problem. Col Flynn recalled an earlier occasion in early 1937 or 1938 when Maj. Gen. M.J. Costello, then assistant chief of staff, informed a conference in the Military College that a recent decision of the Council of Defence had established that College instruction should be based on the peacetime and not the war establishment. This decision upset the College staff as it meant that instruction could not be given above the level of the brigade.[64] While such a decision might be understood in a post-Emergency demobilisation environment, it was inexcusable in 1938. The decision was to stand, but some leeway was given by intimating that a second brigade might become available on mobilisation. The College availed of this intimation by improvising a headquarters that might control two brigades. A pragmatic solution was devised which was to prove important two years later. Col Flynn recognised that 'Strictly speaking it represented a departure from our directive but it was never called in question by Army G.H.Q. who may not have been closely enough in touch with the College to be aware of it'.[65]

Almost all training in military schools is mission-oriented. Students are trained and educated in a procedure sometimes known as 'the estimate of the situation'. This procedure enables them to analyse the situation facing a commander and to formulate an effective plan to fulfil his mission. It is essentially a Cartesian procedure for isolating elements of a problem, which migrated in time from military staff colleges to management education. In its military application, it presupposes two opposing military forces, own forces and enemy forces. Both opposing forces are expressed by the formulation and study of orders of battle, which outline the battle organisation of the forces from corps to platoon and even down to section level. Own order of battle should not pose a problem as it details the standing or mobilised own forces. This was addressed by the chief of staff's board with the drawing up of 'the general organisation and equipment of the following components of the Infantry Division, Infantry, Artillery, Engineers and Signals'.[66] This organisation became known as a 'College' organisation. More difficult to resolve would be the formulation of the enemy order of battle. The armies of NATO membership nations would have no conceptual difficulty with their enemy order of battle: it became that of the Warsaw Pact. Within the Command and Staff School, however, the uncertainty surrounding both own and enemy orders of battle contributed to an enduring emphasis on theory and principles, which in turn required a necessary professional suspension of disbelief, achieved by most students, but with which some struggled. It was not necessarily a difficulty that devalued the course or its objective, as the estimate of the situation provided students on the command and staff course with a solid grounding in staff work and a method of appreciation and problem solving while attempting to keep abreast with wider military developments. This problem of a limited theoretical slant in instruction did not affect students of NATO staff colleges as acutely since, on graduation, they would have frequent training and experience on field exercises. This experience was largely denied to command staff graduates of the Military College whose exercise experience was limited to map and command post terrain exercises (CPTX) carried out on their courses.

The establishment of NATO on 4 April 1949 could have had major implications for the PDF and the Military College. Before the signing of the treaty, there had been intimations that Ireland might be offered membership. An approach was made in Washington DC to Joseph Brennan, 1st secretary at the Irish Embassy, that Ireland should appoint a military attaché to the US, and that more Irish officers should avail of the opportunity to attend courses at US Army schools and colleges. It was noted to Brennan that only two Irish officers, Maj. Gen. MacNeill and Col Collins-Powell, both members of the 1926 military mission to the US, had been trained at Fort Leavenworth. When Brennan remarked that they had officers attending courses in Britain it was put to him that:

> This was all very well, but we must remember that the British were doing as they were told by the US and the US people are the people who will be in command. It would be much more to our interest to have our people close to and familiar with the American Army than the British.[67]

A military attaché was not appointed, and while an official offer was not made for Ireland to join NATO, Seán MacBride, the minister for external affairs in the 1948 Interparty Government attempted to use such a possibility as a means to request the United States to induce Great Britain to end partition. Nationalist special pleading apart, the Irish case purported to offer more security to NATO from a unified than from a partitioned Ireland. This ploy was never likely to succeed, as the Irish high commissioner to Canada, John J. Hearne, reported from Ottawa on 6 April 1949:

> In the opinion of the Governments the Atlantic Pact is not a suitable frame-work in which to discuss such questions as the partition of Ireland which is the exclusive concern of the British and Irish Governments. The situation outlined in the Irish Memorandum is not connected in any way with membership of the Pact.[68]

MacBride underestimated the strength of the British special connection and also did not 'recognise Ireland's low geopolitical and strategic value in the plans of the Western Allies. NATO had sufficient access to facilities in Northern Ireland for defence purposes.'[69] The Irish Government's attempt to link membership of NATO with partition was dropped. Analogous reasoning prevented joining the Western European Union; MacBride later attempted to seek supplies of arms and training in their use from the US, to prevent the country from being at the mercy of Great Britain in the event of a future war. This latter initiative also foundered on the strength of the British connection and on the government's disinclination to enter a bilateral pact with the US.

Membership of NATO would have influenced Irish defence policy and placed increased demands on the Military College. We will read in the following chapter how, in spite of Ireland not joining the Atlantic Pact, discussions were held between the director of plans and operations and the CMC on the necessity to ensure that NATO staff procedures be incorporated into College instruction. This might have had an impact on Irish defence policy in the area of Gen. McKenna's advocacy of conscription. As early as 1950, the NATO Military Committee had tasked its Defence Committee to report on 'the specific areas of inadequacy as regards national military service, mobilisation and training procedures of the various governments'.[70] The report did indeed draw up specific recommendations regarding length of service period, types of mobilisation and training requirements. As regards officer training, the Defence Committee report stated that professional officers are the backbone of any nation and must be capable of training 'those trainees brought into the active armed forces in order that these active units be ready to execute their D-Day mission, and conduct of reserve training outside of active units'.[71] While the Military Committee could only recommend the report to NATO's member states, and recommendations were still being debated in 1955,[72] such recommendations would nevertheless have caused grave difficulties for any Irish government. The matter of NATO centralised or integrated training within the NATO framework also proved to be unsatisfactory. A report initiated by the supreme allied commander Europe (SACEUR) in 1959 noted 'the general unwillingness of national authorities to agree to centralized training'.[73] Institutional difficulties aside, the impact of membership of NATO would have transformed the PDF and its training, but in reality, it was never a serious possibility in 1949.

Instruction therefore at the Command and Staff School resumed without direct input from the wider security developments in Europe. The 10th command and staff course began in November 1947, followed by the 11th in October 1948, and the 12th in October 1949. Each of these courses catered for an average of twenty-five students and the courses differed considerably from those conducted before the Emergency. The main difference was the extension of the course from five to nine months, with a total of 916 hours compared to 361 for the pre-Emergency courses. As was the case with the standard infantry course, which was considerably longer than the corresponding British course, the resumed command and staff course was approximately two months longer than the corresponding course at the Staff College, Camberley. Two Irish officers attended this course from May to November 1946, and a further two in 1949 (the history of attendance at Camberley will be discussed in a later chapter). It seems not to have been the case, however, that extra instruction time was required at the Curragh, but that an extensive series of lectures by external experts and visits to industrial establishments was added to the course syllabus. Instructional methods were also changed, with a move from the lecture-based instruction of the pre-Emergency courses to the syndicate method favoured at Camberley and Fort Leavenworth. In the manner of tutorials, students were required to take an active role in discussions based on supplied texts and overseen by the instructors or directing staff (DS). This syndicate work would then be developed into terrain and headquarters exercises in which students would be tasked with the different responsibilities and duties of commanders and staff officers.

In spite of the rapidly diminishing strength of the army, the instruction was firmly set at the divisional level. A division is typically composed of three brigades each of three battalions, of combat support such as artillery, cavalry and engineers and of headquarters staff, numbering in the region of 10,000 troops. This organisation was inspired at least by the experiences of the two-division Emergencey army, if not by ambitions for a future mobilised army, and based on the experimental divisional establishments drawn up in 1947. That the Command and Staff School staff had benefited from recent Emergency service can be seen by the naming of important exercises with such appellatives as 'spearhead' and 'thunderbolt'. These names not only recalled the two Emergency divisions but also rehearsed their major manoeuvres, spearhead being a division in attack exercise and thunderbolt incorporating a division attack with UISGE, a river-crossing operation.[74] The 1947 syllabus owed much to Irish Army experience, whereas the 1930s courses depended to a great extent on the experiences of officers who attended courses in the United States and Britain. Except for air and naval warfare and armour, the instruction, albeit theoretical, reflected recent training experiences of the army during the Emergency, with the chief of staff reporting that 'the basis of instruction has been considerably widened by our emergency experience'.[75] While national-centered instruction may have been an advantage to the students, the increased length of the course must have caused difficulties for some. Spending eight months in the Curragh is not universally attractive, even though students are relieved from the normal responsibilities of their appointments. It was particularly disruptive for those officers not living in either the Curragh or Dublin, and must have been immeasurably so given transport facilities in the 1940s. Students were advised to avail of leave before coming on the course and weekend leave had to be applied for on the Thursday beforehand.[76]

In addition to separation from families, for many officers, another factor weighed heavily not only on students and prospective students but also on the military hierarchy: that of the age and seniority of the students on the command and staff course. The 10th and 11th command and staff course students were all either lieutenant colonels or commandants with an average service of twenty-five years, and who would already have completed this course if not for the Emergency. These officers were therefore in their middle to late forties and facing uncertain promotional prospects. 1937 DFR CS3 laid down that the command and staff course was 'designed to fit officers of all Corps and Services to hold the rank of Lt-Col and higher rank, to command formations of all components of the PDF and to perform the higher staff work involved in the handling of such formations'.[77] However, the object of the 12th course was stated as, 'To train officers for appointments as commanders and staff officers in the Army'.[78] Albeit that regulation took precedence over joining instructions, neither stated any certainty as to the course being a qualifying course for any particular rank. An indication of the future importance of this situation is found in a letter written on 1 April 1949 by Comdt Eamonn de Buitléar, the personal staff officer to the chief of staff, to the four GOCs and the CMC. Comdt de Buitléar stated that he was 'directed by the Chief of Staff to say that before issuing the minutes of the Conference of 28 March he intends seeing the Minister to ascertain if he agrees with the decisions on policy for future courses at the Military College'.[79] Some decisions taken at that conference caused the chief of staff to delay their implementation. The importance of one of the decisions can be seen in a handwritten memorandum by Comdt de Buitléar on 5 April 1949:

> It has been decided that no officer who on the 28th April 1949 is over 40 years of age will be compulsorily nominated to undergo a Command and Staff Course. Any officer over this age who wishes to volunteer to undergo this course will submit his application to his Commanding officer for transmission to the Adjutant General before 22nd April 1949.
>
> Any officer who does not undergo and pass the Command and Staff Course will only be eligible for promotion to such rank and appointment as his experience and training fit him for.[80]

The decision referred to in the 1 April letter caused considerable upheaval in the Military College throughout the following fallow years of the 1950s PDF.

Conclusion

The Military College had succeeded in establishing a regular pattern of professional career courses during the 1930s, albeit mostly theoretical with practical tactical training hampered by the non-availability of a demonstration battalion. The outbreak of the Second World War and the declaration of the Emergency disrupted this pattern. Except for the annual intake of cadets, the Military College became in effect throughout the Emergency, and until 1947, a potential officers school. While some miscellaneous courses were also conducted, the efforts of the College and its staff were devoted to providing officers for the expanded and mobilised PDF. On demobilisation of this force, the College resumed its pre-Emergency pattern. Some minor changes were made to the cadet syllabus, and an attempt was made to replicate at the Curragh the British Army company commanders course. While well-intentioned, the standard infantry course in the Infantry School suffered again from the pre-Emergency lack of a regularly available demonstration battalion. The greatest change was to the Command and Staff School, which recommenced with the 10th command and staff course in 1947. The school lengthened the syllabus for this and further courses of the decade from five to nine months. While the course aspired to train officers for lieutenant colonel and higher rank, many of the students on these command and staff courses were already of lieutenant colonel and commandant rank.

5

The 1950s

Unease at the College

The PDF entered a period of retrenchment if not of decline in the 1950s. Demobilisation after the Emergency, rejection of any form of National Service and adherence to the chimera of effective military mobilisation in a time of war inevitably resulted in functional headquarters but under-strength operational units. These operational or fighting units – battalions, regiments and squadrons – were dispersed throughout the country in numerous occupied posts and barracks. A battalion, with an establishment strength of 600 all ranks, could often muster no more than 200 personnel. The establishment strength is best understood as the 'on paper' strength, not the strength that the unit can muster and deploy. Its day-to-day activity was largely confined to 'minding' the barracks, with housekeeping administration, shooting and sporting competitions, and essential guard duties predominating. It is true that efforts were made to conduct tactical training, the demonstration exercises referred to in the previous chapter being the main effort. The Artillery Corps also regularly carried out live firing exercises. J.P. Duggan claimed that 'an increased strength of units, supplemented by the First Line Reserve, permitted companies, batteries and cavalry troops to operate independently in the field, thus giving leaders some experience of troop leading and of putting theory into practice'.[1] Judged, however, on the requirements of overall operational capability, the benefits of these efforts were, at best, debatable. The military authorities, struggling with low strengths, lack of equipment, lack of financial resources, exclusion from NATO and the changed nuclear strategic environment, found it difficult to conceive of, and to formulate, a practicable strategy for defending the State against external aggression. Nevertheless, a directive, relating to the content of command and staff, and staff courses, was issued by the chief of staff, Maj. Gen. Liam Egan, to the CMC in June 1954.[2] This lengthy document can be considered as the formulation of military doctrine by the general staff for the employment in a time of war of the PDF, and for the Military College should have been the foundation on which it was to prepare syllabi and instruction.

Military Doctrine

Some officers, particularly some Military College instructors, felt that the general staff had been reluctant to formulate military doctrine, and that this burden fell inappropriately and perhaps unfairly on the Military College. The very explicit contents of the 1954 Chief of Staff's Directive and, as will be seen later, a subsequent 1959 directive, gave the lie to this complaint, at least insofar as the 1950s are concerned. Military doctrine can be a difficult subject, particularly for a small country, and small armed forces where matters rarely if ever moved from the tactical to the strategic level. The United States Army states that doctrine comprises the 'fundamental principles by which military forces guide their actions in support of national objectives'.[3] Odom expands on this definition, explaining that:

> It is the core statement of an army's view of war and serves as a common guide for the conduct of operations. This shared view facilitates communications, enhances flexibility, and fosters confidence throughout the force, and it provides the basis for supporting doctrine, force structure, training, and education.[4]

This definition concerns the United States Army. Maj. Gen. Hugo MacNeill on his return from the 1926 military mission to the United States cautioned against uncritically adopting the American system because of the great differences between Ireland and the US. However, Maj. Gen. Egan, who was one of the officers detailed to work with MacNeill on his return from the United States, went a long way in his 1954 directive to fulfil the terms of Odom's definition. His directive built on the work of the DPD, which outlined the first statement of military doctrine for defending the State'[5], and on the experience of the war years.

The 1954 directive had its genesis in a 1951 memorandum from the chief of staff to the government, and in the work of the director of plans and operations. The memorandum argued that, given the low strength of the PDF, both permanent and reserves, and the lack of success in acquiring defensive material, there was a need to draw up mobilisation plans in the event of war, and plans for expansion of the forces during a war. Paragraph 6 of the memorandum stated that crucial to any planning would be the provision of air defence, early warning radar, anti-aircraft artillery and fighter aircraft operating from airbases equipped from concrete runways. The planners also recognised, however, that:

> In view of the considerable difficulty of obtaining the equipment needed to implement the plans outlined in para 6., it has been decided to base a mobilisation organisation on the equipment that we actually hold – taking into account also those supplies for which orders have been placed.[6]

The director of plans and operations at this time, Col Denis Lawlor, was a particularly active staff officer who worked on this memorandum as the principal planning officer for the chief of staff. He was conscious of the need for close coordination and indeed cooperation with the Military College in the drawing up of a new force organisation. The College was aware of up-to-date military force developments and instructed in their employment. Col Lawlor wrote to the then CMC, Col Dan Bryan, the legendary wartime director of intelligence, on 6 May 1953 suggesting that he might have a meeting with members of the College staff. The letter's first paragraph, unfortunately, indicated an immediate mismatch between his thinking and that of the Military College. Lawlor wrote, 'I have been concerned for some years past that instruction generally in the College has been on a too theoretical basis and that the main cause of this has been lack of knowledge of our Plans'.[7] Lawlor stated that some progress had been made in plans for mobilisation, in the organisation of forces and equipment and felt that both the College staff and students on the command and staff course should be made aware of these plans. He proposed that he should give a talk and have discussions in the College on these matters. His proposal was for a full exposition of the work of his staff section and he would:

> Outline our Scheme of Defence as approved by the Government,
> State our general scheme for employing the forces to be raised on mobilisation,
> and the basis of our Plans,

Give an appreciation of the size and equipment of our mobilised Army,

State the present position in regard to revision of organisation and Establishments,

Give any information sought on equipment problems.[8]

Also, he stated that he 'would be prepared to answer most questions – probably not all – and in some cases, of course, would have to say that we had yet to find the answer'.[9]

It might have been injudicious of him to open his letter with a remark on the 'too theoretical basis' of instruction in the College, as he was constrained to write another letter to the CMC four months later on the same subject. In this letter, he referred to a conversation he had had with Col Bryan who had informed him that his 6 May letter 'had given rise to some discussion in the College and that there had not been agreement as to its value'.[10] Lawlor reiterated his belief that closer liaison with the College was essential, and that the chief of staff and the assistant chief of staff, Col James J. Flynn, also agreed that 'the College Staff should be brought fully into the picture'.[11] On the face of it, the Military College was resisting being brought into the picture, and there is no indication of an acceptance of Lawlor's offer. It does, however, seem that personal relations between the officers were not affected. Brig. Gen. Jimmy Flynn (retd) often recalls seeing his father, the Assistant Chief of Staff Col James Flynn, in the company of both Col Lawlor and Col Bryan, deep in conversation as they walked in and out of the back gate of McKee Barracks, most likely on their way to and from Army Headquarters.

Lawlor's next recorded interaction with the College concerned a proposal he had made to the chief of staff that the PDF should employ a new standardised NATO format for operation orders, which Britain would adopt on 1 January 1954. This reference to synchronisation of staff procedures with NATO is notable for Lawlor's reasoning. Firstly he considered that it would be beneficial for PDF officers attending foreign courses. Secondly, 'it will facilitate operations if we ever have to co-operate with NATO forces and would not be a disadvantage if we were opposed to them'.[12] He was maintaining strict neutrality in his memorandum. Thirdly, in a slight swipe at the College, he considered the NATO format better than that then being taught at the College. The PDF and the College adopted the NATO format in July 1954. Nevertheless, this cooperation with plans and operations did not extend to the more difficult and fundamental matter of coordination of organisation and teaching. The director of plans and operations circulated a provisional draft establishment for the PDF, including the CMC, Col

Bryan, on the distribution list. A letter from Lawlor to the CMC on 3 August accepted that it would be difficult for him to complete his comments on the draft by the end of August and that a reply by 12 September would be acceptable.[13] Much had happened in the meantime, however, culminating with the issuing by the chief of staff to the CMC on 19 June 1954 of the *Directive on the Introduction of revised War Establishments and Recommencement of Long Command and Staff Course*.[14]

Before issuing the directive, the chief of staff held a meeting in the Military College with the CMC and his staff on 4 May. The minutes of this meeting seem not to have survived, but a memorandum on file may well be 'speaking notes' for the chief of staff at the meeting, as a handwritten note describes the document as 'Apparently prepared for Staff meeting at the College'.[15] If indeed these were 'speaking notes' for the chief of staff, he was delivering a direct and uncompromising message to the College. Only the chief of staff would consider addressing the CMC in the following terms, 'Prior to the inauguration of the new Command and Staff Course I have thought it desirable that I should make clear certain matters about which there should be no doubt and which are not open to discussion'.[16] The memorandum reiterated the government's policy of neutrality and the means that the government had provided to apply that policy. It was the responsibility of the PDF to plan and to train with these resources and to defend the State in time of war. The task of the Military College was to educate and to train officers to lead effectively 'and to provide an adequate leadership and efficient employment of the men and material we have got'.[17] The PDF was not alone in wishing for more men and more modern equipment. To make the matter as clear as possible, the author of the document continued: 'So that there may be no doubt I repeat; we will train our officers and men to fight with the weapons we have got'.[18] Any deviation from this norm would require him to inform the government, which the author or the chief of staff was not prepared to do. The College could and should continue to teach students the composition, capabilities and procedures of foreign armies as the PDF may in the future have to face such armies. The document concluded with an appeal to the loyalty of the College staff: 'The staff of the Military College has always been hard-worked and has given loyal and unselfish service. I have no doubt that I can fully rely on its continuing in that tradition.'[19] There is no evidence that this document constituted 'speaking notes' for the chief of staff or that he did, in fact, speak in these terms at the 4 May meeting. Nevertheless, it is reasonable to think that the document fairly reflected the views of the director of plans and operations.

The View from the College

Whether or not the document was used, the meeting on 4 May did not convince the CMC, Dan Bryan. The chief of staff's files contain a lengthy document that the director of plans and operations has notated to the assistant chief of staff on 25 May 1954 as, 'Col Bryan's personal memorandum which he sent up today for circulation. Chief of Staff and Director of Training have copies'.[20] The document is unsigned and undated, and is unequivocal in its disagreement with the view that the Military College should use the PDF's actual strength and equipment as the template for instruction. Its submission as a personal document probably allowed Bryan to circumvent the strict requirements of military hierarchy. It is also indeed possible, given his standing and reputation, that he had been invited to submit the document. Bryan outlines his perception of the problem in his first sentence: 'shall the organisation used in the Military College for "our own forces" be the Preliminary Draft War Establishments or an organisation similar to that used by European armies.'[21] In his view, and most likely in the view of the staff of the Command and Staff School, the war establishment developed by the director of plans and operations was flawed, if not for the PDF then certainly for the instructional requirements and responsibilities of the Military College. In the proposed organisation, the division would be deficient in air support, anti-aircraft artillery, armour and long-range anti-tank protection, in effect the elements that made the difference between 1914 warfare and modern warfare. Bryan then argued that 'a force armed as the Draft War Establishments could not hope to oppose or cope with reasonable prospects of success with a force armed according to modern military principles'.[22]

Whether or not it was his intention, and Bryan cannot be accused of lack of precision, he frequently attended high-level international strategic conferences; this was a blunt statement of the inability of the PDF to defend the State against a modernly equipped and organised aggressor. His intention in making this statement seems, however, to be more concerned with the educational responsibilities of the College. He argued that attempting to teach students how to operate against a modern army with the force as organised in the draft establishment could not be successful. 'If students are not satisfied that the problems used and the solutions given are reasonably likely to be realised in practice, there will not be confidence in the teaching, and without confidence, satisfactory results will not ensue.'[23] He further argued that the only way this might be overcome would be either to limit the armament of an aggressor to that of the PDF or to increase the numerical strength of the PDF, an approach which would be as unreal as 'teaching the employment of weapons we do not possess'.[24]

Col Bryan then articulated the view that continued to be held at the Military College, that by basing its instruction on Ireland fielding a modernly equipped army it would possible then to readjust downward if required. 'In Tactics, Staff Duties, etc., it must be accepted that the greater includes the lesser,'[25] while the success of the contrary case cannot be guaranteed. He then went on to make the telling point that on the early command and staff courses, 'There was criticism because some instruction was given at the Divisional level or that the instruction was in some way at too high a level'.[26] These criticisms were listened to, and the instruction was limited because few could envision the Army fielding divisions and should have been more concerned with guerrilla activities. 'Yet within ten years many of the instructors and students were holding appointments in or directing from other staff posts the activities of Irish divisions.'[27] He insisted that care should be taken that the PDF did not repeat this earlier mistake of limiting instruction at the Military College. The strength of the army might change in ten to fifteen years, and, neutrality notwithstanding, in the case of invasion by Soviet forces, Western forces may well provide Ireland with the arms which were excluded from the draft establishment. 'At a somewhat higher level the question in the eventuality mentioned (invasion by Soviet Forces) could also arrive of the incorporation in Irish forces, or the co-ordination of Irish Forces of formations of troops coming to fight an invader in Ireland.'[28] In this case, it would be essential for Irish officers to be trained in the command and staff techniques of modern armies. In his concluding summary, Bryan reiterated that an army based on the proposed establishment could not hope to defend the State against a modern army, and that students should not be precluded from studying the organisation and techniques of modern armies as had been done in the Military College before the last war. 'It is, therefore, recommended that independent of the question of Mobilisation or "Draft War Establishment", that teaching in the Military College should be based on a full modern war organisation.'[29] The important point in Bryan's paper was that the organisation of the Irish Army to be used in Military College teaching should be that of 'a full modern war organisation'. This point was of course diametrically contrary to the intentions of Denis Lawlor and his staff in plans and operations, and they were not slow to express their opposition to the view from the College.

The View from Plans and Operations

Plans and operations drew up a briefing document for the chief of staff on 25 May 1954, the very day on which it received Bryan's document. Its opening paragraph was as clear as his introduction, 'Should our Establishments be based on the units and equipment we plan to provide? Or should they contain all the units and equipment considered necessary or desirable for tactical reasons?'[30] The section asked if it was sound not to include modern armour, long-range anti-armour weapons, medium artillery and light anti-aircraft artillery in their draft establishments, and decided it was because they were not available and it was most unlikely that such weapons could be purchased in the foreseeable future. It was, therefore, their view that 'the normal teaching of the College should be based on our Plans for mobilisation and we should teach our officers to handle, command and control the units which we intend to raise'.[31] For instruction and exercises in the College, own forces organisation should not include such modern equipment. Again, they asked themselves if this was sound and conceded that close liaison was essential with the College and that no war organisation is final but changes according to changing circumstances. This concession did not affect their view that instruction must be based on what is available as it would be 'unsound to teach one war organisation for instructional or professional purposes and have another organisation on which we intend to fight'.[32] According to plans and operations, the College should, of course, teach how other armies employ such modern weapons. But its instruction should be based on mobile warfare to defend against invasion forces which an enemy could not deploy in great strength until after airstrips or landing fields had been secured. In a veiled retort to Col Bryan's warning against forgetting the lessons of the last war, the plans and operations document insisted that 'We must face up to realities, and, as we did in 1939/45, be prepared to fight as hard and as long as we can with what we have got, or can reasonably expect to get'.[33]

The 1954 Directive

It is clear that there were two diverging views as to how the PDF should face a future conflict. Plans and operations, headed by Denis Lawlor, took the pragmatic 'realistic' view that the PDF should plan to operate with the organisation, forces and equipment that they could reasonably hope to deploy. The College, headed by Dan Bryan, adopted the 'theoretical' view that officers should be taught the methods of a modern European army. Reconciliation of these two views or indeed, as it transpired, acceptance of different viewpoints, was the prerogative and responsibility of the chief of staff, Maj. Gen. Egan. The College staff might have hoped for a favourable hearing from Egan, who had spent some years on its staff and who was also CMC in 1940. It was not to be so, and he favoured his then principal staff officer in plans and operations when he issued his *Directive on the Introduction of revised War Establishments and Recommencement of Long Command and Staff Course.*

The introduction to the 1954 directive states, 'This directive on the conduct of Command Staff Courses and Staff Courses is given [*sic*] you in confirmation of the decisions taken at the Conference held in my office on 4 May last'.[34] The reference to both command and staff and staff courses reflects a different polemic that took place between the general staff and the Military College during the previous four years concerning the command and staff course, and which will be discussed in detail later in this chapter. The directive commenced with the declaration that the 'Defence Forces are raised, organised and equipped for the defence of State territory and have NO obligations or commitments overseas'.[35] The military usage of capitals to emphasise a negative indicates how dominant the Emergency policy of neutrality was and how it influenced military planners then, but some few years later these same planners would embrace deployment on UN overseas missions. The directive followed with a firm restatement 'that the policy of the State, while partition lasts, is to remain neutral in war and that NO alliance or military commitments will be made'.[36] This political stance was immediately followed by the statement or indeed the hope that 'The adoption by the State of the status of neutrality, implies that the State organises the necessary forces to maintain that status and ensures, furthermore, that belligerents are aware that our State territory is defended'.[37] Unfortunately for the chief of staff, his planners and his educators, nothing could have been further from the truth. The necessary forces, except for concrete runways at Baldonnel and six Vampire jet aircrafts, were not provided, thus allowing any potential belligerents to draw the appropriate conclusions.

Nevertheless, the directive proceeded to outline possible future war scenarios and PDF responses to them. There was no ambiguity as to who a potential enemy might be: 'This State is fundamentally and ideologically opposed to communist teaching and communist attempts to world domination. It is furthermore, in sympathy with maintenance of the democratic way of life upheld by Western Powers',[38] Ireland's strategic position between the United States and Europe was recognised and with it the possibility that minor or major enemy raids might be attempted to destroy or to seize installations such as ports, radar stations or airports, followed by possible airborne invasion supported later by seaborne landings. Any such attempts should be opposed by organised forces, excluding specifically guerrilla tactics that 'would only be adopted by local troops remaining in any area which an invader might succeed in generally occupying'.[39] While acknowledging the threat of such airborne attacks, the directive stressed their hazardous nature for the invader. The Military College was to instruct students on how such operations are conducted and on the organisation of such enemy forces. Students should also be tasked on exercises with planning such operations from an enemy perspective to ensure their familiarity with the difficulties associated.

The Directive did not, however, minimise the difficulties facing the defenders: 'It must be assumed that the air situation as far as we are concerned is generally adverse'.[40] An own adverse air situation did not mean that the enemy would have large-scale tactical air support in the early stages as he would have to seize airfields or air strips for this superiority to be achieved. Conversely, own air-to-ground support could not be expected, as whatever air assets Ireland might have would be tasked with attacking enemy aircraft. Nor could the defenders expect to have armour or anything other than light anti-aircraft weapons available to them. The College authorities were to base their teaching on the new war organisation, which 'has been prepared on the basis of the troops which could be organised, raised and equipped within our own resources … The Divisional Organisation does NOT include any armour or anti-aircraft elements. The majority of problems should be based on this organisation'.[41] This did not preclude instruction on the use of armour so that students should become familiar with how it was employed by other armies. Given the accepted difficulties associated with airborne and seaborne landings, and the likely deficiencies in the strength and resources of the PDF, the directive instructed that:

In our strategic situation the initial battles and early campaign are of most importance. Long drawn-out campaigns involving the attack and defence of semi-stabilised positions are considered unlikely to occur here. The problems set in the College should, therefore, be concerned with situations which are considered possible in the early portions of a campaign when warfare will be mobile. Special attention should be paid to the attack on airborne troops during and after landing; to the defence of airfields and the movement of troops to reinforce them, and to attack and defence of hastily prepared positions.[42]

The chief of staff had adopted a pragmatic approach to instruction at the College. It was also his task and responsibility, however, to provide and then to organise the troops and equipment who could carry out the stated defensive operations. The emphasis was on preparing to defend against the early stages of an attack when the enemy would be at his weakest. The planners did not consider what would happen if this defence was not successful, apart from the earlier reference to local guerrilla forces, or perhaps the international support mentioned by plans and operations. The directive also considered the overriding strategic military factor then prevailing, i.e. the employment of nuclear weapons. While their devastating effect was accepted, their potential limitations in an invasion scenario were also recognised. No conclusion was reached, except to instruct the Military College that 'The problems created by the use of such weapons should be studied and, as far as published information exists, included in the College instruction'.[43] The final section of the directive confirmed that 'The Military College is the principal and most important means of educating officers and, in consequence, it is essential that the instructors should have confidence in the tactical doctrine taught and adopt a realistic attitude so that in turn students may have confidence in the realism of the instruction'.[44] The chief of staff did not, nevertheless, give a free hand to the College authorities, as the directive considered it desirable that 'much closer liaison than has existed heretofore, should be established and maintained between the sections of the General Staff and the Military College'.[45] His final injunction was that the directive should be read to all senior instructors of the College and others deemed necessary. This lengthy account should not be considered as merely an argument between two committed professionals, Cols Lawlor and Bryan. It went beyond personalities and considered vital issues of national defence and the training and educating of officers in the implementation of this defence. Plans and operations were closer to the political and economic realities that precluded expenditure on defence, while Dan Bryan, with his wealth of experience, saw it as his duty as CMC to ensure that officers should receive the widest education possible. It also went deeper and asked, albeit in veiled terms, whether or not the State could be defended, and if not, what the purpose of the Military College was. The insistence by the College that own forces depicted in its instruction should be greater than those in actual existence would continue to cloud perception of its connection with prevailing Irish military reality. The Chief of Staff's 1954 Directive, with its insistence on instruction based on the war organisation and on the need for instructors to have confidence in the directive's tactical doctrine, was not welcomed by the College staff. But if it felt aggrieved in 1954, it would be only a few short years later before it had to face greater difficulties. As Odom has written, 'Ideally, doctrine is dynamic, changing to incorporate new capabilities and accommodate new missions'.[46] In 1959, Egan's successor as chief of staff, Maj. Gen. P.A. Mulcahy, issued a new directive that would again impinge on preferred Military College teaching.

The Schools

The Cadet School

While strategic and doctrinal matters were engaging Army Headquarters and the Military College in the early 1950s, changes to the Cadet syllabus proposed by Lt Col McKeown in 1949 were being considered by the chief of staff. While McKeown's recommendations for change were geared towards the aim of equipping the newly commissioned officer to function in any of the army's corps, he also articulated a vision of the purposes of cadet training other than that of producing high-grade NCOs. For him, the aim should be 'To develop in the Cadet the qualities of character and leadership necessary in an Officer and to establish a code of honour and conduct among our future officers worthy of the traditions of our Country and the Army'.[47] The aspiration for all-corps suitability was to be achieved by advancing and broadening 'the general education of the Cadet to fit him for officer rank and particularly to lay a basis of technical knowledge on which future specialist technical training may be based'.[48] McKeown proposed to achieve this by reducing time devoted to purely military subjects such as the Vickers medium machine, mortars, and weapon and tactical training, and by introducing English and elocution, mathematics, mathematical physics, experimental physics, chemistry and staff duties to the cadet syllabus. The social niceties were not to be neglected either, as it was also proposed that courtesy and etiquette, including twenty-six hours of ballroom dancing, which the cadet would be required to undergo in after-duty hours, should be added to the syllabus. These proposed changes would add 550 hours to the syllabus, and with the science subjects being set at first-year university level, McKeown acknowledged potential pitfalls in engaging suitable instructors and in providing laboratory facilities. His proposal to employ officer instructors from the technical corps was eventually to result in multi-year negotiations involving successive CMCs, directors of training and chiefs of staff in attempts to source such instructors. The provision of a laboratory was never to get past the proposal stage.

The chief of staff did, however, engage with the cadet master's proposals for change and established a board of officers on 31 August 1951, composed of members of the College staff to 'consider and recommend what should be the nature and system of Cadet Training. They will study such information as may be available in regard to Cadet training in other forces. They may call into consultation as necessary any officer of the Forces.'[49] The board circulated a questionnaire to selected officers, one of whom was Lt Col Joseph Emphy, a future CMC and adjutant general. Emphy's reply is instructive in its elevated sense of cadet education:

> I am convinced that the initial approach is of the utmost importance. If the cadet is made to feel that he is now something a cut above the average, a selected potential officer, he will react accordingly. On the other hand, if he is told he is a private soldier and treated as such, we cannot complain if he reacts as such.[50]

Unfortunately, a cadet of the period before the proposed changes came into effect remarked that this vision did not apply in his time, and that 'you were never given the sense that you might succeed or that you were training to be an officer'.[51] Emphy was also far-reaching, if not prophetic, in his view of the appropriate environment for a Cadet School:

> The Cadet School should be a self-contained institution situated quite close to Dublin, Cork or Galway to enable it to have close ties with the Universities located in these cities. There is no suitable place under military control in Dublin. In Cork it might be worthwhile taking a look at Ballincollig and in Galway Renmore. I figure we should face up to the problem and build one or else purchase and suitably adapt some place like Carton. We've been improvising far too long on this matter.[52]

While an unidentified handwritten note on the questionnaire disagreed with these proposals, they were to be proven correct, if only partially so, some few years later. Before the board reported, the chief of staff indicated their likely findings in a letter written to the minister for defence on 6 January 1951. In this letter, Liam Archer informed the minister that while the board had yet to report, he felt it desirable to include in cadet training 'subjects which it is now known the Board will recommend for inclusion in the Cadet syllabus'.[53] The subjects for which the chief of staff requested the permission of the minister were mathematics, electricity and magnetism, French and English; these subjects would be taught by serving officers and the only new expenditure would be on textbooks. Nor did courtesy, etiquette or ballroom dancing fall by the wayside either, as the author recalls receiving instruction in 1962 in these essential subjects by serving officers who may now wish to remain anonymous. The board did indeed submit these findings in its report and also recommended that less time be given to weapons training, that an honour and a tutor system be introduced as an experiment and, 'that a grading system be introduced which gives more weight than heretofore to the judgement of abstract qualities while still giving due credit to the military and academic qualities of the cadet'.[54]

Training at the school continued along these lines throughout the 1950s with some modifications, such as the initiative by the Quartermaster General's Branch of increasing the number of hours allotted in the syllabus to instruction on 'Q' matters. The aim here was to qualify a young officer on commissioning for appointment as an assistant quartermaster in a battalion, but it was accepted after some years that theoretical instruction could not achieve this aim. Equitation, motorcycle and driving instruction were also added, eventually developing into a choice between one of each of these subjects to be followed by the cadet. Brig. Gen. John O'Shea found it a completely new and broadening experience as an 18-year-old. As well as the new academic subjects, they studied military history and current affairs. They attended lectures from industrialists, county managers, the future editor of *The Irish Times* Douglas Gageby, and retired military leaders such as Dan McKenna, Hugo McNeill and M.J. Costello.[55] In later years, Gen. McKenna would lecture on 'Policies, Problems and Decisions – the major problems confronting the General Staff in 1940–45' while Lt Gen. Costello lectured on 'Military Reflections'.[56] The transformation of the course from one qualifying the commissioned cadet as a high-grade NCO to one qualifying the commissioned cadet as a young officer was accomplished. The school received added recognition from the military authorities when 'In 1953 the General Staff decided to honour the Cadet School by designating it with full unit status, thereby entitling the School to bear its own Regimental Colour'.[57] The regimental colour, which forms an important part of Cadet School formal ceremonies, also contains the school motto, '*An Ród so Romham*' ('This road before me'), taken from Padraic Pearse's poem '*Fornocht do Chonac Thu*'. This motto is 'taken to signify the highest ideals of loyalty to country and devotion to duty, which the Cadet and the Cadet School must cherish and foster'.[58]

The Command and Staff School

The earlier sequence of addressing the Infantry School before the Command and Staff School must be reversed in this chapter. The Infantry School was so affected by changes in the senior school that developments in that school must be considered first. In fact, the CMC, Col Tom Feely, went so far as to inform the chief of staff in January 1955 that 'the Infantry School has ceased to function as such since September 1953'.[59] In addition to doctrinal matters, the Command and Staff School had to contend with two other important issues: how to ensure that sufficient numbers of officers received staff training and also thereby furthering their eligibility for promotion, and whether or not entry on to the command and staff course should be by competitive examination. When the school re-opened in 1947 after the Emergency, the first four courses, the 10th, 11th, 12th and 13th command and staff courses repeated the pre-Emergency formula. They lasted for eight to nine months and constituted a major commitment on the part of both instructional staff and students alike. However, the next five courses, the 14th in 1951, 15th in 1952, 16th also in 1952 and the 17th and 18th courses in 1953 were designated as modified command and staff courses and lasted for no more than five months. This change was brought about by the imbalanced nature of the officer corps of the PDF, an imbalance that coined in the early fifties the derogatory term 'hump', a term that was to be brought back into use some decades later. The tentative decision by the chief of staff mentioned in the previous chapter, and subsequently approved by the minister for defence, that no officer over the age of 40 would be compelled to undergo the command and staff course, was a product of this imbalance. Many officers over 40, and particularly officers of commandant rank, were unlikely to attain higher rank and unlikely to be suitable to undergo the demanding nine-month-long course.

Senior military officers, as expressed by the then director of training, Col Tom Fox, were convinced that the military authorities had a real responsibility to prepare for war. Fox expressed this conviction in a memorandum to the chief of staff in April 1951, in which he saw the following five years 'as a critical period during which war in Europe may or may not come, and as possible breathing space during which we may step up the tempo of the production of Staff Officers'.[60] The existing system, whereby nomination for the command and staff course was effectively based on seniority and the number of students who could be accommodated yearly, meant that a captain had only a limited chance of being nominated. The chief of staff accepted the recommendation that a modified command and staff course should be conducted and he duly received authorisation from the minister for defence for 'the introduction of a Modified Command and Staff course, as a temporary measure, to replace the full Command and Staff Course. The Modified Command and Staff Course will be accepted as qualifying for promotion on exactly the same basis as the full Command and Staff Course.'[61] It is hard not to see in this decision the desire of the chief of staff to maintain morale among an officer corps that was suffering from very limited promotional advancement. It was also considered important enough for the chief of staff to include the measure in his 1951 'Memorandum on the Statement of Government Policy', which stated:

> The necessity for having available the maximum number of potential commanders and trained staff officers in order to meet requirements on expansion has led to steps being taken to accelerate the rate at which officers are trained in the Command and Staff School. This is being achieved by the introduction this year of a modified Command and Staff Course which will enable the number of Permanent Force officers being passed through the Command and Staff School annually to be doubled.[62]

Between 1951 and 1954, the command and staff school graduated 174 officers on the 'modified' courses. Compared to the 111 officers graduated between 1947 and 1951, this represents more than a doubling per year of graduates. But how different were the courses? Was there a lessening in the professional training of officers even if the general staff's concerns for military preparedness were partly answered? In cannot be said that professional standards were lowered, but the course objectives were changed. The objective of the 13th command

and staff course was to train officers for appointments as commanders and staff officers in the army. That of the modified command and staff courses was 'To train Officers for appointments as Staff Officers, and to give them experience and training which will be of some value in fitting them for appointment as Commanders in the Army'.[63] The emphasis, therefore, was on training staff officers to implement the decisions of commanders with a consequent reduction in hours spent on considering the deployment of battalions and brigades on both map exercises and terrain tactical exercise. The duration of the course was also considerably shortened, with students spending only eighteen weeks in the Military College as opposed to more than thirty on the non-modified courses. Inroads had been made into the 'hump', but not to the satisfaction of all. Particular not to that of the staff of the Military College or the CMC Dan Bryan, whom we had last seen fighting a rearguard action against limiting the scope of College instruction.

To Select or not to Select?

At the same time as the question of training sufficient numbers of staff officers for the PDF was occupying the attention of GHQ, the College proposed that entrance on to the command and staff course should be by competitive examination, a proposal opposed to the perceived needs of GHQ. The College proposal is not available in the archives, but the thrust of its argument can be found in a rebuttal sent from the director of training, Col Tom Fox, to the chief of staff on 26 February 1950. According to Fox, the College case was modelled on British Army practice and aimed, in the Irish situation, to ensure that unsuitable officers did not present themselves for the command and staff course. Fox argued that what held for the British, essentially the need to select no more than 25 per cent of their officer strength for the Staff College at Camberley, did not apply in a small army that needed as many trained staff officers as possible for a future mobilised army. A later document from Bryan gives the rationale behind the College's request for an entrance examination, 'to achieve the best results during the Course, Officers undergoing it must already have attained a good military knowledge, and, in addition developed a military and in particular a tactical judgement'.[64]

The College, apart from possible partiality on the part of members of its staff trained at Camberley, considered that some of the students on earlier command and staff courses, almost all of whom were picked by seniority, were not suitable material for the course. This understandable educator's point of view must be weighed against the prospective student's realisation that passing the course was necessary for promotion to a more senior rank, and this at a time when automatic promotion to commandant did not apply. The debate lasted until 1954 and spanned the years when the College was conducting what it must have considered the imposed modified command and staff courses. GHQ senior staff officers opposed the introduction of an entrance examination. This was hardly surprising given their earlier championing of more officers attending shorter courses. The uncertain nature of examination results, the effect on morale, the promotion qualification nature of the course and the need for an adequate number of trained staff officers were the principal arguments put forward. Col Denis Lawlor sided with Tom Fox's rejection of examination as a means of selection. In a nuanced approach to the College proposal, they both rejected the entrance examination but accepted the need for selection. Fox maintained that selection was required at either command or GHQ level. He favoured the GHQ level with initial selection and nomination by command OCs. Lawlor agreed that 'Vacancies on long Command and Staff be allocated by selection. All officers to have the right to apply for interview'.[65] The decision when it came was, unsurprisingly, a compromise, with its essence contained in Lawlor's reference to a 'long Command and Staff'.

On 26 April 1954, the director of training circulated a confidential document to command OCs and corps directors. The document stated that 'It has been decided to have two types of courses: one a "Long" Command and Staff Course of approximately 9–10 months duration and the other a "Short" Course of approximately 4 months duration'.[66] The College can hardly have been pleased with the rather inelegant titles of long and short courses, although short was later changed to the simpler 'staff' course. Command OCs would nominate candidates to the chief of staff for the 'long' course. They were to be 'Specially selected from the Captains who have successfully completed the Standard Course of their Corps and are judged to have the qualities of character and mind to warrant their selection; they must also be physically fit to undergo this Course'.[67] A list of fifteen considerations was attached to assist command OCs in their selection. The considerations included personal qualities such as keenness, fortitude, initiative and soundness in judgement. The nominations for the short course would be based on seniority and corps requirements. An important element of the new system was that 'It is intended that both courses will qualify for promotion to senior rank, but preferment will be given to graduates of the "Long" Course in filling "command" vacancies and senior staff appointments in Brigade and higher formations'.[68] Albeit a compromise, this was a definite break with previous policy, which relied on seniority for nomination on the command and staff course. It was not a decision that was to last, as by the 1960s the College view had won out and officers were required to undergo a selection examination for entrance to the command and staff course.

The policy of requiring command OCs to select and nominate candidates was modified the following year when captains over 36 years of age were given an option of applying for either of the courses, while a command and staff course would be made available for all officers under 36 years of age. GHQ had a clear preference for captains as students on the course; however, it transpired that not all captains had the same aspiration. A handwritten memorandum from the director of training to the chief of staff noted in January 1956 that 'In the Curragh Training Camp 18 opted for the Command and Staff Course and 2 for the Staff Course. Outside the Curragh, the bulk chose the Staff Course. It is fairly clear that domestic and financial considerations were major factors in influencing officers.'[69] The full figures are more telling, as only fifteen officers from outside the Curragh opted for the command and staff course while seventy-seven opted for the staff course. These numbers and the implied reasons shed a revealing light on the College's aspirations of selection by competitive examination. Nor can it be held that aspirations or declarations of preferment for graduates of the command and staff course for staff appointments were realised. It is most likely that 'natural wastage' on the retirement of older officers meant that the prevailing policy of promotion by seniority continued. What did occur is that, between 1954 and 1960, five staff courses were run by the Infantry School in parallel with long command and staff courses. While they may have addressed the perceived need for trained staff officers, they also severely impacted on the task and primary function of the Infantry School – the training of infantry officers.

The Infantry School

When the Infantry School had re-opened after the Emergency, it had directed its focus to provide what might be called vocational training for infantry company commanders. The courses were titled 'standard infantry courses' and were closely modelled on the British Army company commanders course, which had been attended by PDF officers at Warminster. Three standard infantry courses catering for 120 officers were conducted between 1950 and 1954. While not being able to call on the services of a dedicated exercise battalion for 'hands-on' training was a considerable deficiency, the school did endeavour to restore some semblance of infantry-centred instruction. In addition, it conducted intelligence officers, reserve officers, machine gun and mortar instructors courses, but by 1955, as we have seen above, the CMC, Col Tom Feely, considered that 'the Infantry School has ceased to function as such since September 1953'. This situation had come about by the decision to run parallel long and short command and staff courses, and to task the Infantry School with the conduct of the short or later-named staff courses. Feely considered this to be unacceptable and recommended that the Infantry School should cease conducting staff courses; these should be the responsibility of the Command and Staff School, albeit he did not see a requirement for many more such courses. The Infantry School should return to its proper role of training infantry officers.

His recommendations were accepted, as was indicated in a letter to him from the director of training, now Col T. O'hUigín. O'hUigín noted a GHQ and Command Conference decision that 'The Inf Sch, on the termination of the 2nd Staff course, would revert to its normal role of conducting Inf Courses and special courses'.[70] In a follow-up to this decision, the director asked him 'for his specific proposals'[71] for courses to be run at the school. Tom Feely seems not to have been mollified by this news. In a subsequent report to the director of training he claimed that 'The first sign of decay in the Infantry School was brought about by Directors of Training finding a ready cure for some of their headaches by foisting all types of Courses on the school and gradually diverting it from its proper function'.[72] A handwritten comment described this as 'Nonsense', but did agree with Feely's view that 'A steady pattern of Courses to meet the needs of the Infantry Corps should be gradually incorporated in the annual work of the School'.[73] Nor did the commentator agree with Feely's statement that 'This will take at least two years to effect as the School staff have [*sic*] ceased to function as an Infantry staff over a long period'.[74] That steady pattern did evolve, with the school conducting three standard infantry courses and two new young officers courses in the second half of the 1950s. The CMC identified the necessity of this new course because 'Newly Commissioned Officers posted to the

Infantry Corps require a Platoon Commanders' Course to prepare the Young Officer on subjects which is [*sic*] not covered in the Cadet School and which infantry battalions are unable to train them in'.[75] The inability of the army to conduct even minor tactical training was thus acknowledged once again. Also, the school continued with its allotment of special courses. Among the familiar – intelligence officers, potential NCO and weapons courses – a less familiar, ABC course emerged as a regular at the school. ABC, the forerunner of NBC, stands for atomic, bacteriological and chemical warfare, and the courses were indeed a sea change for a school tasked with providing infantry training in conventional warfare. The Chief of Staff's 1954 Directive to the Military College required that instruction at the College should include all aspects of modern war including atomic warfare. He had, however, directed that 'The extent to which the use of atomic weapons by a foreign attacking force should be included in College problems is left to the discretion of the Military College'.[76] That discretion had now devolved to the Infantry School.

However, this was not the only new development that the Infantry School and the wider Military College would have to face. The final years of the 1950s witnessed the harbingers of different Defence Forces. A reorganisation of the army in 1959 which saw the reserve, i.e. the FCA, integrated with regular formations brought with it a new chief of staff's directive on tactical doctrine. This 1959 directive reiterated the 1954 instruction to the College that 'own forces' must be based on actual organisations, but also went further and laid down 'That the Brigade shall be the highest formation to be used in future studies'.[77] A resurgence of IRA activity on the border with Northern Ireland in 1957–58, which saw armed cadets guarding bridges in County Kildare,[78] presaged the future aid to the civil power (ATCP) duties of the PDF. The first deployment of Irish officers on United Nations duty in 1958, to the United Nations mission to the Lebanon (UNOGIL), ushered in a new international role for the PDF, a role that had been specifically rejected in the 1954 directive. Finally, and arguably of greater influence on the work of the Military College, was the election of Kevin Boland to the Dáil, and his nomination as minister for defence in March 1957. Boland was a fervent supporter of the Irish language and decided to aid its promotion by having it used more widely throughout the PDF. His efforts, which became known as *Usáid na Gaeilge*, were probably more of a hindrance than a help to the Military College in facing or at least in adapting to changing educational requirements for an organisation confronting major new demands.

Conclusion

During the 1950s, the Military College attempted to resume operations by employing lessons learned during the Emergency and by adapting instruction to changing national and international requirements. Significant changes were made to the syllabus of the Cadet School in an attempt to change the focus from purely military instruction to a wider academic focus. While the changes did not prove wholly successful due to a lack of qualified instructors in academic subjects, they did keep alive the vision of some senior officers who saw a need for higher-level education for officer cadets. The wider context saw a dispute between GHQ and the College on instruction, particularly at the Command and Staff School. Increasing Cold War tensions, Ireland's strategic isolation and the inability or unwillingness of the government to countenance increased defence expenditure led the chief of staff and his advisers to issue a 1954 directive to the College. Instruction was to be based only on the forces and equipment which the State would have available to oppose an aggressor. This direction ran counter to the view from the College that this could make instruction both tactically and professionally untenable. The debate remained unresolved. Also, a modified staff course was introduced with the objective of having sufficient staff officers available when, as was widely considered likely by the general staff, war broke out between the Western and Eastern powers. A consequence of conducting these courses in the Infantry School was a decrease in the number of trained junior infantry officers. The last year of the 1950s saw additional challenges for the College. The Defence Forces were reorganised and the chief of staff issued a new directive on tactical doctrine. Officers of the PDF deployed on overseas duties with the United Nations, and the minister for defence introduced instruction through the medium of the Irish language to the Military College.

6

The 1960s
Moving from the Old to the New

After thirty years of existence, the Military College had become a permanent and recurring institution in the careers of the officers of the Defence Forces. With the notable exception of 'technical' officers, those who had entered the Defence Forces with degrees for the Medical, Engineer, Ordnance and Signal corps and the School of Music, all army officers had been commissioned from the Cadet School. All infantry officers and many from the other corps completed standard courses at the Infantry School, and almost all senior officers had graduated from the Command and Staff School. In addition to catering for officers from the army, officers from the Naval Service and from the Air Corps also completed command and staff courses. Although attendance was not consistent and at times caused dissatisfaction on the part of some Naval Service and Air Corps officers, their commanders understood the importance of this course in spite of its army-heavy content. The ubiquity of the College extended not just to individual careers but also to the status of the College within the structure and institutional life of the Defence Forces.

While on the one hand being 'other', insofar as it existed apart from the daily unit life of the PDF, and it was a place to which officers went, it was the one entity that provided the only stable focus of institutional professional training and education. Other corps schools provided training in specifics; artillery, signals, ordnance, cavalry and so on, but it was to the College that not only individual officers but also the military authorities looked for the 'College solution', that often-pejorative understanding of how things should be done tactically and operationally. Infantry units seldom exercised in the field, a function of the by-now endemic and almost institutionalised low strength of the Defence Forces. The College staff had taken on, often quite justifiably, something of an aura of infallibility; after all, they had been selected to devote their careers, whilst posted to the College, to studying and to imparting sound professional education to the officer body, who had little opportunity to practise their military craft either in battle or in exercise situations. This 'setting apart' of the College instructor was subtly reinforced by a minor change in dress regulations with the introduction of small orange tabs beneath the rank markings of the DS. These tabs mirrored in status and in symbolism the red tabs worn by officers posted to Army Headquarters and the blue tabs worn by officers posted to Command Headquarters. Red, blue and orange tabs all indicated that their wearers were occupying functions of greater importance than those occupied by other officers, be they in subordinate staffs or in line units.

The Military College operated in the 1960s in a changed, structural and organisational system than had applied since 1946. A new Defence Forces organisation and establishment was introduced in 1959. The chief of staff, Lt Gen. Patrick A. Mulcahy, a younger brother of Gen. Richard Mulcahy, considered that the year 1959 'was a vital one for the Army as a whole; the new organisation would take effect in October and priority must be given to it'.[1] Six brigades were established and were composed of regular units and of units of the reserve, the Fórsa Cosanta Áitúil (FCA). The defence of the State was to be achieved by the mobilisation of these six brigades and other units designated for protection of installations. At this remove, but also considering the lengthy mobilisation and training experiences of the Emergency army, it is hard to see how the responsible military planners imagined that this new organisation could be trained and mobilised in time to face and oppose a foreign invasion, a fact that became disappointingly obvious after a few years. The most favourable assessment is that their intention was to create a sustainable cadre of officers and NCOs that could survive a period of limited investment in the Defence Forces. The new organisation was accompanied by a 1959 directive from the chief of staff to the CMC detailing how the College was to instruct students. Although the directive was issued in 1959, it will be considered in this chapter as the College had little opportunity to address its implications for instruction in the 1950s. The main message delivered by the directive was that College instruction should be based on the understanding that any defence of the State must be undertaken with the forces in existence. Given that a large portion of these forces would be relatively untrained reservists, an obvious disconnect existed between this understanding and the new organisation.

Instruction in the three schools of the Military College emphasised the deployment of lightly armed infantry formations supported by artillery, light cavalry and engineers, in opposing equally lightly armed invading forces. Isolation was not complete, however, as the military authorities continued their policy, albeit with difficulty due to financial restraints, of selecting officers for attendance at foreign military schools, who then returned to serve as DS in the Military College. However, this situation was about to change. By 1960, a contingent of officers had been deployed to serve as United Nations observers with UNOGIL in Lebanon, an operation that was to develop into large-scale overseas deployment by the PDF on peacekeeping and peace enforcement missions with the United Nations. Later in the decade, unrest on the island of Ireland would demand a re-evaluation of doctrine and tactics in internal security. The standard of education of officers within a national community that saw the introduction of free second-level education demanded a radical revaluation of the Cadet School objectives and syllabus. All of these developments were taking place within the wider context of the major reorganisation of the Defence Forces, which saw the reserve, FCA, integrated with the PDF in an organisation composed of six brigades. But before these modernising tendencies could impact on the stable status of the College, it was to be faced with another, less welcome, unprofessional and unfortunately backward-looking if patriotic crusade, the imposition of Irish as the medium of instruction in the Irish Military College – *Usáid na Gaeilge*.

Usáid na Gaeilge

Kevin Boland was elected to the 16th Dáil and appointed minister for defence in March 1957. Boland, a son of Gerald Boland, a founder member of Fianna Fáil, held staunch republican views and was committed to the restoration of the Irish language to national life. His appointment as minister for defence presented him with an opportunity and a vehicle for advancing his commitment. The vehicle, the Defence Forces, may not have been a wholly willing one, but it was an obedient one. On 24 October 1957, Boland instructed the adjutant general, Col Patrick Hally, that 'The time has now been reached when the great majority of officers in the Defence Forces have sufficient knowledge of the Irish language to be able to converse about, or carry out, their work in that medium'.[2] Patriotism aside, the minister might have been expected to have more regard for the effectiveness and the efficiency of the Defence Forces than for promoting a sectional interest. The minister's intention was, unfortunately, more than patriotic, as he required that commanding officers should 'submit to G.H.Q. a return of those officers who are prepared to use whatever Irish they know in conversation with other officers who are prepared to respond'.[3] The minister also proposed that these officers should wear a distinguishing insignia on their uniforms. The chief of staff responded to the minister's initiative by issuing a directive that emphasised that 'It is a fundamental part of An t-Aire's policy that An Coláiste Míleata be an Irish Military Academy in every sense'.[4]

The seriousness of what he proposed cannot be understated. All courses at the Military College were to be translated into Irish and then taught through the medium of Irish to students whose ability to absorb the instruction through Irish was at best uncertain. The breadth of this change of policy was also immense. From basic instruction in musketry, through the tactical deployment of an infantry company in attack up to the detailed staff work required in commanding a brigade – all these were henceforth to be taught through Irish. Translators were to be found, texts and manuals were to be translated, syllabi were to be rewritten, instructors qualified to instruct in Irish, including NCOs for the Cadet School, were to be found. Most critical of all, students who qualified through Irish would then somehow have to find a means of imparting their hard-gained learning to units and soldiers through English. Clearly military efficiency was not the guiding principle of the policy of *Usáid na Gaeilge*.

Application of the policy to the Cadet School provided a suitable beginning. Irish was part of the instruction and a pass in Leaving Certificate Irish was an eligibility requirement for a cadetship. The minister raised this entry qualification to honours Irish and a 50 per cent mark in an Irish interview as part of the selection process. He issued a direction in late 1957, which decreed that the Cadet School:

Should become an Irish-speaking Coláiste.

The use of the English tongue for instruction be progressively eliminated.

The instruction of Cadets will be through the medium of Irish only except in the case of specialised instruction where it may NOT be possible to so arrange.[5]

The minister's sights were set not just on the Cadet School, and a memorandum from the director of training, Col Tom Higgins, to the chief of staff in February 1959 showed just how rapidly the military authorities had moved to implement the new policy. In addition to the application of the policy at the Cadet School since January 1958, a weapons refresher course and a young officers course had been conducted in Irish between February and April 1958, and a standard infantry course was being conducted at the Infantry School. This course had been postponed from the previous year, and the 3rd command staff course was also postponed from September 1959 until September 1960. Tellingly, a nuclear biological and chemical warfare instructors course had been postponed indefinitely.[6] This short memorandum reveals the imponderables behind the ideological decision of the minister. Two essentially technical courses, a weapons and a young officers tactical course, were conducted through Irish, a company commanders course was postponed until translation could be achieved, and the most senior course in the Defence Forces, the command and staff course, was postponed for a year. This expedient is unsurprising given the amount of translation required for a nine-month-long course. These difficulties did not just apply to the command and staff course, as there was also a fear that officers who might fail the standard infantry course because of inability to assimilate the instruction through Irish would be unjustifiably disadvantaged. While the task of translating the nuclear biological and chemical course, was postponed indefinitely, this did not stump the translators, as it was eventually run but with one officer who failed the course complaining that he was given only twenty-four hours' notice that the course was to be conducted through Irish.

The technical difficulties did not deter the minister. After a meeting in the Military College in February 1959 to review the progress of running courses there in Irish, the minister decided that the scope should be extended and that 'standard courses in Corps schools should be run through Irish as soon as possible'.[7] The ambition here, if that is the correct word, is far-reaching. Artillery fire control, engineer bridge-building and demolition, radio transmission, supply and transport and mine-demolition became just some of the subjects that were to be instructed through Irish. It is an absurd claim that such instruction could not be in Irish. It would have been necessary if the Defence Forces had been an Irish-speaking organisation. The crucial point is that instruction given to officers is for the purpose of that instruction being passed onwards to NCOs and soldiers to ensure the proper efficiency of the Defence Forces. Insisting that officers be instructed through the medium of Irish resulted in an attenuation of the benefit of such instruction, a lowering of the receptivity of some officers towards the instruction and an increase in the 'otherness' of the Military College.

The 1959 Directive on Tactical Doctrine

The minister's language policy for the Defence Forces constituted a significant distraction for the chief of staff, Lt Gen. Patrick Mulcahy, not that language difficulties in military affairs were new to him. The chief of staff had served in the British Army Royal Engineers during the First World War with a signals liaison unit attached to the French Army. His focus and that of his headquarters staff at this time was on the structural reorganisation of the Defence Forces, which eventually became known as 'integration'. The general staff had reached the conclusion that Ireland, as a neutral State, fourteen years after the end of the Emergency and the rejection of the defence plans then proposed by Gen. McKenna, would 'at the commencement of an Emergency be virtually militarily defenceless'.[8] In 1958, it had reached this stark conclusion for the following reasons:

> It has NOT been found possible, for instance, to maintain the Permanent Force at the figure originally fixed; it has NOT been found possible to raise a First Line Reserve within measureable distance of the target of 45,000 proposed; it has NOT been possible to accumulate the weapons and equipment for a field force of larger than six brigades; and, finally, as regards the foreseeable future, realism suggests that any radical improvement in the position, either as regards manpower or material, is NOT to be expected.[9]

Given such realities, the general staff proposed to government a reorganisation that would see the 20,000-strong FCA assume the role of the first-line reserve and be integrated with the PDF into six trained brigades capable of being immediately mobilised. The proposal was approved in principle by government in July 1958.[10]

The previous chapter recounted discussions between the CMC and the director of plans and operations, which resulted in the issuing of the 1954 directive stipulating that instruction at the College should be based on the then organisation of the Defence Forces. This approach was reinforced following the 1959 reorganisation with the issuance on 27 April 1959 of the 'Directive – Tactical Doctrine'.[11] The directive was 'issued primarily for the guidance of the Ceannfort and Staff of An Coláiste Míleata in the preparation and conduct of future courses for officers in An Coláiste Míleata'.[12] It was also issued to command OCs for their guidance in any courses or periods of instruction that may be carried out in the commands. In a probably unintended but nonetheless important comment on the language policy, the directive was written entirely, with the odd exception of titles and institutions, in English. While the 1959 directive built on its 1954 predecessor, it was much more explicit and indeed prescriptive in its directions to the CMC.

The directive re-emphasised that the prevailing strategic situation of neutrality, likely invasion threats coming from Communist powers albeit not excluding attempts by Western powers to seize facilities, and unfavourable air situation remained, and that the Defence Forces 'are raised, organised and equipped for the defence of the State territory'.[13] There was to be no doubt, however, that the chief of staff intended that the College should base its instruction on the new six-brigade organisation and that the 'Brigade should be the highest formation to be used in future studies'.[14] As we saw earlier, this difficulty also arose in 1954 when the College insisted that the brigade could not be taught in isolation. Higher command coordination was provided for in the 1959 directive by stating that if one or more brigades were to operate together, although this would be highly unlikely and dangerous given the air situation, existing territorial Command Headquarters would ensure command and control. Furthermore, divisional and brigade administrative structures would no longer exist and 'units will be supplied from within command areas'.[15] The CMC and his staff were to understand that the directive was based on the existing Defence Forces organisation:

This organisation is the result of a realistic approach to our manpower and equipment problem. Having regard to the continued low strength of our permanent and first line reserve forces, and to the major difficulties experienced in the procurement of adequate war equipment, and realising that compulsory national conscription is unlikely in the foreseeable future we must acknowledge that in the event of being involved in war we shall have to depend upon the manpower and equipment already available at the outbreak of war.[16]

This emphasis on 'fight as we are' tactics would require officers to be instructed in more flexible thinking and quick decision-making and taking. Static defence would be inappropriate as would be set-piece attacks, and more instruction should be provided in withdrawal operations. Troops should move and operate at night, large-scale movement by motor transport would be unlikely and even guerrilla warfare should be studied at the Command and Staff School. Authority was given for instruction at higher level on the types of forces that may be employed by other armies, but any reference to external aid must be referred to the Chief of Staff's Branch before it could be included in instruction. It was recognised in the directive that such instruction posed difficulties but that 'a realistic approach must be made to the problem posed by an overall situation in which we find ourselves confronted by an enemy superior in numbers and equipment and enjoying air superiority'.[17] Little concession was given to Dan Bryan's earlier warning that both staff and students should have confidence in the feasibility of the instruction given at the College. In what could have been seen by some as a criticism of existing College instruction, the directive enjoined that 'Emphasis in all tactical studies must be on the developing of the mind of the student to face given situations under realistic conditions, rather than on solving, what might be termed, purely academic problems'.[18] In conclusion, emphasis was placed on 'facing facts' and, in his covering note to the copies issued to the CMC, the director of planning and operations, Col Thomas Gray, a worthy successor to Denis Lawlor, had no doubt that the CMC 'would arrange to have instruction in the Col Mil [*sic*] brought into line, where necessary, with this new directive as soon as may be practicable'.[19] How this directive was addressed by the Military College will be reviewed in the following section on the Command and Staff School, the school most concerned with the instruction concerning formations higher than the battalion.

A Dissenting Voice – Col Eóghan Ó Néill

Col Eóghan Ó Néill, more commonly known throughout the army as Eugene Ó Neill, a native of Lisronagh, County Tipperary was born in 1918. He entered the Cadet School in 1938 and served in the 13th Infantry Battalion during the Emergency. He commanded the 34th Infantry Battalion serving with the UN in the Congo before being appointed as cadet master in the Military College, where he was considered somewhat of a martinet, commandant of the Command and Staff School and later CMC. While Ó Néill was considered by some an intellectual when such a term was not necessarily complimentary in Irish military circles, his opinions and writings were valued and appreciated by the members of a Defence Review Board established in 1965. He submitted a detailed and comprehensive set of documents to the head of the Review Board, Col Joseph Emphy. The documentation, which extends to some 130 pages, provided clear-sighted analysis of defence issues facing the State and the Defence Forces in the 1960s, and is in the main critical of the officer training and education then being provided.[20]

Ó Néill maintained that there existed no clear-cut or independent assessment of the standard of Irish officers. There was, however, 'a highly dangerous tendency to generalise and say "The standard of the Irish officer is the best in the world. We proved it in the UN."'[21] He provided a counter-opinion from Col Jonas Waern, a Swedish officer who commanded Irish units in the Congo. Waern, Ó Néill stated, 'was both popular with Irish officers and was highly respected by them for his courtesy, intelligence, leadership, courage and ability'.[22] An extract from a secret report from Waern, which Ó Néill appended, claimed:

Officers are exclusively regulars yet discipline is defective … Field exercises have been practised only theoretically, and almost exclusively defensive warfare is practised. Nothing in the way of longer exercises has been done before. The officers have a relatively satisfactory standard in matters of education and theoretical training. The three officers on my staff (all instructors in the Military College) can be taken as skilled even by Swedish standards … Seen against this background, it is natural that the Irish had great difficulties and their actions were not so brilliant.[23]

Ó Néill was not completely in agreement with Waern's assessment as he said that, 'not all officers are bad. The majority are good. Some are superb. A minority which we cannot afford are bad.'[24] It should also be noted that the training in conventional war received by Irish UN officers in the Military College enabled them to lead their troops in a successful battalion attack in Elisabethville and in a heroic defence of their positions at Jadotville. Military College and Artillery School training also enabled the sustained and successful attachment of a heavy mortar troop in support of an Indian brigade. Nevertheless, Waern's opinion would have been difficult for the Review Board to accept, but Ó Néill proceeded to give his own examples of defects in the prevailing system of officer education. He believed the educational entrance standard of cadets was too low. Higher educational standards on entry, a more scientific selection procedure, and eventual third-level education were necessities. The absence of unit training inhibited officers' development to such an extent that officers arriving on a command and staff course 'spend so much time LEARNING fresh knowledge that the time spent APPLYING that knowledge to problems, which is the real purpose of a higher Course is reduced'.[25] Analysis of defects was followed by a plan for officer education, which recommended a five-month young officers course with the aim of producing 'an infantry officer capable of commanding a platoon and taking over from his Company Commander if necessity arises'.[26] This would be followed by a standard infantry course, also of 5 months' duration, which would produce 'an officer capable of commanding a company and of taking over from his battalion commander or unit or brigade staff officers in the field, if the necessity arises'.[27] These changes emphasised the combat role of the officer over and above the theoretical and administrative. The command and staff course should continue to qualify officers for the rank of lieutenant colonel, and courses should be provided for officers of this rank and higher. It will be seen that Ó Néill's recommendation for the young officers course were not accepted, but two other far-reaching recommendations were eventually acted on and introduced. He recognised that there was a need to train both officers and NCOs in the Infantry School as their roles in combat were inextricably linked. His lasting legacy, however, as shall be seen below, was to Scoil na nDaltaí.

The Schools

Scoil na nDaltaí – The Cadet School

Previous chapters have recounted changes to the cadet syllabus, which resulted in a two-year programme aiming to widen the cadet's general education, in addition to transforming him from civilian to young officer. The training regime at the Cadet School was rigorous; cadets were inculcated with a sense of separateness if not of specialness. While the approaches of different cadet masters and class officers had differing influences over the regime, with some favouring a martinet-like approach over a paterfamilias type, at no time did cadets lack appreciation that their career selection was a demanding if rewarding life. They were aware that they were being placed in a situation of stress and were constantly under observation by the senior cadet class, if they were first-year cadets, by their class officers and by the cadet master. Their NCO instructors also had a great influence over them in the early months, when foot-and-arms drill were the main vehicles for turning the young civilians into young soldiers, most of whom had no military experience, in spite of a Fianna Fáil Árd Fheis motion that membership of the FCA should be a requirement for a cadetship.[28] Schedules were tight, free time was limited, physical demands, including a strong emphasis on sporting activities by all cadets, alternated with academic demands. Cadets progressively assimilated the overriding influence of the school, the importance of teamwork and mutual support not only for individual success and survival but also for future success in their chosen military career. Most graduates of the Cadet School will agree that loyalty to comrades was the single most enduring aspect of the training they received at the Curragh.

Minister Boland's language policy had the most influence in the Cadet School with its emphasis on transforming it into an all-Irish speaking environment. Translation difficulties existed, particularly in weapons instruction, but by and large all instruction and activities in the school were conducted through Irish. This did not mean that the instruction was assimilated equally by all cadets. Nor can it be claimed that all discourse, while not under supervision, was conducted through Irish. Weapons instruction was increased on the syllabus through a rare intervention from one of the commands. The Southern Command pointed out to the director of training that with the new 'integration' organisation FCA units were equipped with mortars and medium machine guns, and that the young officers who were responsible for training these FCA units were not trained in their use. The command recommended therefore that 'The Cadet syllabus should in future include sub-courses on Mortar and M.M.G., so that each Officer commences his service with a good foundation in these weapons'.[29] It seems not to have occurred to the Southern Command that such a foundation would have been of equal benefit to a young officer not only in an FCA unit, but also in a PDF unit, a fact borne out a few short years later in the Congo. Since much of the weapons training in the Cadet School was delivered by NCOs, instruction through Irish made the selection and indeed the sourcing of Irish-speaking NCOs an ongoing and difficult task. This difficulty resulted in 1963 in the unsatisfactory expedient of posting newly commissioned 2nd Lieutenants to perform NCO duties at the Cadet School. Fortunately, this ill-conceived experiment was quickly discontinued. The stalwart, committed and humane Irish-speaking NCO instructors of the Cadet School were by-and-large unsung heroes, but deeply respected and liked by the cadets who learned from them. Other, more successful activities of the Irish-speaking environment of the Cadet School were the summer camps in Gaeltacht colleges. Cadets marched to Falcarragh in County Donegal and cycled to Ring, County Waterford, set up camp and enjoyed Irish language and dancing classes, albeit that hob-nailed army issued boots and 'bulls-wool' uniforms were not necessarily appropriate dress for the environment.

Such bucolic delights obscured stresses affecting the delivery of the syllabus. It became increasingly difficult to find officers from the Engineer, Ordnance and Signals corps to instruct on the scientific subjects on the syllabus; one class of cadets alone seeing three officers rotated through this task in one half-year. Col Emphy, who had earlier commented critically on the location of the Cadet School and was now, in November 1960, CMC, informed the chief of staff that a critical situation existed in the Cadet School concerning its academic programme. Consequent on the non-availability of a suitable instructor he had 'found it necessary to cancel for a while a considerable portion of the academic syllabus'.[30] Given that academic subjects counted for 536 hours of instruction over the two-year course, and that the posting of properly qualified officer instructors to the Cadet School had failed, Emphy concluded that only the appointment of a suitably qualified civilian instructor could solve the problem. But the chief of staff, now Maj. Gen. Seán McKeown, former cadet master and CMC, who had overseen the introduction of the academic subjects, was facing a related but different problem, the shortage of junior officers in the PDF. J.P. Duggan considered that the 1959 reorganisation that saw FCA units integrated into an overall force structure of six brigades had not been a success, and that 'The steadily declining officer establishment was grossly understrength in junior officers'.[31] A steadily declining officer establishment also had to provide officers for the units deployed to ONUC, which was commanded by Maj. Gen. McKeown from January 1961. Maj. Gen. Sean Collins-Powell replaced McKeown as chief of staff and addressed the shortage of officers at the source, the Cadet School. He proposed two solutions to the problem: conducting three cadet classes instead of two at a time or reducing the length of the Cadet School syllabus. Accommodation and instructor resources made the first option unrealisable, so the solution adopted was to shorten the length of the cadet syllabus. Certainly, the officer shortage needed to be addressed, but expediency led to the retrograde removal of academic – in particular, scientific – subjects from the cadet syllabus.

During the 1960s, the Cadet School conducted twelve cadet classes and commissioned 342 cadets as 2nd Lieutenants.[32] The 36th and 37th cadet classes witnessed and participated in some of the most iconic events in Irish and international history of the twentieth century, such as the 1963 visit by President John F. Kennedy to Ireland and his state funeral to Arlington Cemetery after his assassination in Dallas, Texas, on 23 November of the same year. The 36th cadet class under the command of Lt, later Brig. Gen., Frank Colclough provided the guard of honour at the wreath-laying ceremony in Arbour Hill by President Kennedy. The performance of the cadets impressed the president, and he can be seen on film speaking to Lt Colclough; he told Lt Colclough that 'it was the finest Honour Guard he had ever seen'.[33] On his return to the United States, President Kennedy requested a film of the ceremony. It had been excluded from the official record of his visit and was re-recorded but, this time, by the 37th cadet class, as their senior class, had been commissioned. President Kennedy continued to be impressed by the ceremony and according to Col Cyril M. Mattimoe, the cadet master at the time, showed the film to visitors to the White House.[34] Mattimoe has also recorded that, 'it was because of his great interest in the Cadets that Mrs Jacqueline Kennedy decided to have them present at his funeral'.[35] It was an extraordinary request and an equally extraordinarily positive response from the US military to afford a contingent from a foreign army the most prominent military ceremonial position at the graveside. The 37th class, mostly 19-year-old and younger, was commanded again by Lt Colclough and accompanied by Lt Gen. Seán McKeown, the Cadet Master Col Cyril Mattimoe, and the Officer in Charge of the class Capt. and later Maj. Gen. and Quartermaster General Kevin Duffy. The cadets performed their daunting task with distinction and to the acclaim and praise of many, bringing international recognition to the Defence Forces and Ireland. It is unfortunate that because of the vagaries of timing, the 36th cadet class did not receive the same praise. They had made the initial impression on President Kennedy and would, without any doubt, have performed as impeccably at Arlington as their junior class, the 37th.

International notice of the Cadet School took an entirely different course four years later when six young Zambians were enlisted as cadets at the Cadet School. An agreement had been signed by the Irish and Zambian governments which resulted in four classes, three between 1967 and 1973 and a fourth class between 1995 and 1997. In a later debate in 1997, the minister for defence informed the Dáil that the Zambian cadets were being trained in

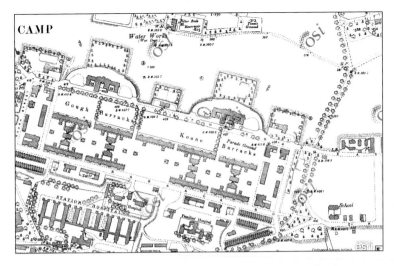

British Army map showing Keane and Gough Barracks, future home of the Military College. MATTHEW MCNAMARA COLLECTION

From the left: Col Dunphy, Gen. Michael Collins, Commander-in-Chief, National Army and initiator of the Irish Military College, Maj. Gen. Emmet Dalton, Comdt Gen. Peadar McMahon and Comdt General Diarmuid O'Hegarty, at the Curragh Camp, August 1922. LT NS (RETD) MALACHAI O'GALLAGHER COLLECTION

An t-Óglác

Vol. II. No. 6. (New Series.) (Registered as a Newspaper). APRIL 26, 1924. Price TWOPENCE.

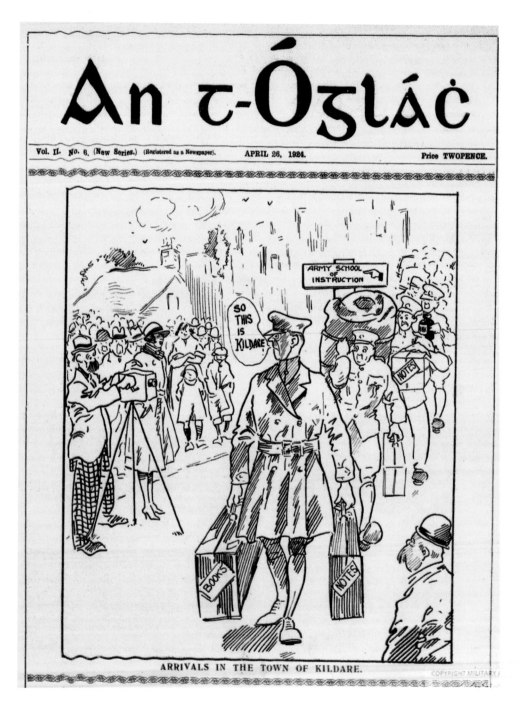

ARRIVALS IN THE TOWN OF KILDARE.

The arrival of the Army School of Instruction in Kildare in 1924. MILITARY ARCHIVES

The 1926 Military Mission to the USA. From left to right, seated: Col M.J. Costello, Maj. Gen. Hugo MacNeill, Maj. Joseph Dunne. Standing: 2nd Lt Charles Trodden, Lt Sean Collins-Powell, Capt. Patrick Berry. MILITARY ARCHIVES

The 1st Cadet Class commissioned in 1929. MILITARY ARCHIVES

Commandant of the Military College, Col T. Gallagher, Minister for Defence Oscar Traynor and Chief of Staff Lt Gen. Dan McKenna attend a commissioning ceremony at the Curragh in 1943. LT NS (RETD) MALACHAI O'GALLAGHER'S COLLECTION

DUBLIN UNIVERSITY

OFFICERS' TRAINING CORPS

FINNER CAMP, 1932

Dublin University Officer
Training Corps Camp, 1932.
MILITARY ARCHIVES

President Seán T. O'Kelly
inspecting a cadet guard
of honour during the
inauguration ceremonies
of the Republic of Ireland
in 1949. MILITARY ARCHIVES

The Minister for Defence Kevin Boland addresses a
military audience, c. 1957. MILITARY ARCHIVES

Training was not always realistic enough. Mortar training, c. 1958. MILITARY ARCHIVES

RÚNDA

SECRET   COPY NUMBER _____

OPERATION - SARSFIELD

HEADQUARTERS 36 IRISH BATTALION - E/VILLE.

36 IRISH BN OPERATION ORDER NO. 2

REF MAPS: E/VILLE - 1,20000.
            E/VILLE - COLOURED.
            SPECIAL OPERATIONS SKETCH.

GENERAL

1 Bde plan to implement overall Kat Comd Plan for destruction of
Gendarmerie resistance in E/Ville Area.

SITUATION:

1. Enemy Forces.

   (a) Air. Cannot op except after darkness due to Air superiority
       of friendly forces in daylight.

   (b) Ground

       TUNNEL area three Coys plus.
       CAMP MASSART two MP Coys.
       MT ENT CAMP MASSART a strong point.
       BCK - Camp Enemy recce Sqn.
       ATHEE School has a large number of Europeans.
       KEN SUPPLY DEPOT is MG location.
       RLY YARD - Enemy OP.
       Gen at Presidential Palace: One Para Coy at LIDO: One MCR
       Unit at UNIONMINIERE.
       Reserve Coy in Town on AVE DROOGMANS.
       Reserve Coy in AVE LOUVAIN.
       Reserve Coy in ETOILE.
       One Coy (-) two mortars and two Armd Cars at RLY ROUNDABOUT.
       Sixty men 600 yards EAST OF TRANSMISSION STN.
       MCRS on ridge of GOLF Course.

2. Friendly Forces.   12/14 Swedish Bn on left to take Camp MASSART.
                         35 Bn in rear.
                         One Sec Indian Hy MCRS under Comd.
                         3 Gurkha Bn cleared STANLEY AVE, and THEATRE AREA.

3. Mission.

   36 Irish Bn will:-

   a. Seize and hold area of rd junc KASENGA - LUXEMBOURG rd (Point C)
      to secure RIGHT flank of Swedish attack.

   b. Be prepared to seize and hold the TUNNEL.

4. Execution

   General Outline.

   Attack will be in two phases.

   Phase 1 - Capture of area rd junc - Point C.

   Phase 2 - Seize and hold TUNNEL area.

RÚNDA

36th Irish Battalion Operation Order for Operation Sarsfield,
Elizabethville, Congo, December 1961. MILITARY ARCHIVES

3ú Cúrsa Caighdeánach I.G.M., 1959

(An Céad Cúrsa I.G.M. Tré Gaeilge)

Tul Rang : S/C. M. de Roiste, Capt. P. O Siochfhradha, Lt. Cor. S. O Cuinn, Cor. S. MacEoin, Lt. F. O Connaill, Cor. Emfi S-P., Cft. T. O Riain, Capt. B. O Casaide, S/C P. O Tiomanaidhe.

Meadhon Rang: Sair P. S. O Ceallaigh, 2/Lt. T. MacCormaic, 2/Lt L. O Ruaire, 2/Lt. M. Aingleis, Lt. L. O Cadhlaigh, Lt. P. MacMathuna, Lt. S. O Raigne, Sair P. O Laithbheart.

Cul Rang : Lt. F. O Muirin, Lt. S. de Siuin, 2/Lt. O Ceafarcaigh, 2/Lt. A. O Murchadha, 2/Lt. de Nortuin, 2/Lt. MacEil, Lt. C. O Gogain.

Vickers machine gun training through Irish in 1959. MILITARY ARCHIVES

36th Cadet Class Guard of Honour at Arbour Hill during the visit of President John F. Kennedy, 28 June 1963. THE IRISH TIMES

37th Cadet Class Guard of Honour at Arlington Cemetery during the funeral of President John F. Kennedy, 25 November 1963. ASSOCIATED PRESS

Cadet Seán Duggan, Cadet Captain of the 36th and 37th Cadet Classes parades the Cadet School colour on to a College Commandant's parade in 1963. The colour is escorted by junior cadets Hodson and McMahon. AUTHOR'S COLLECTION

The author is commissioned as a 2nd lieutenant in 1964. The officiating officers are future Brig. Gens John G. O'Shea and Patrick F. Monahan. AUTHOR'S COLLECTION

Zambian cadets, 1967. MILITARY ARCHIVES

Chaplains Seminar, Infantry School, Military College, July 1972.

Back Row L. to R. Rev's. P. McCabe, E. Dunne, D. Kehily, N. Molloy, G. Keohane, F. Moriarty, C. Mathews, E. Dermody, L. Fleming.

Front Row L. to R. Rev. G. Byrne, Canon F. Knowles, C.I., Comdt. D. O'Carroll, Comdt. C. Cox, Very Rev. P. Duffey, Lt/Col. J. Coyle, Rev. G. Brophy, Comdt. C. Kelleher, Rev. R. Neville, Very Rev. L. Breen P.P.

Chaplin's Seminar in 1972, yet another task for the Infantry School.

Cadet intake 1970s. MILITARY ARCHIVES

Commissioning of the first female officers in April 1981. MILITARY ARCHIVES

First two female cadet classes. MILITARY ARCHIVES

Commissioning of a Zambian cadet, 1997. *THE IRISH TIMES*

Cadet intake 2009. *THE IRISH TIMES*

Graduates of the Command and Staff School graduate with the National University of Ireland Maynooth Masters Degree in Leadership, Management and Military Studies. *THE IRISH TIMES*

Ireland, 'because first, we were requested to do so by the Zambian Government and, second, there is a formal agreement in place'.[36] The minister's terse reply to former 1970s Minister for Defence Bobby Molloy hides much diplomatic activity needed to bring about this inter-governmental agreement. Prior to independence, Ireland had afforded training to a number of Zambian officials in government departments and in the Institute of Public Administration. Dr Kenneth Kaunda, the future president of Zambia, also had discussions with the Minister for Defence Mr Gerald Bartley in June 1963 when 'the question of training officers for the Northern Rhodesian forces was discussed'.[37]

The first follow-up to these discussions was a visit on 25 July 1964 to the Irish ambassador in London by Brig. Gen. C.M. Grigg MC, commander of the Northern Rhodesian Army, with a request for assistance from Ireland for the loan of 'subaltern officers of infantry to help officer the two battalions of infantry of the Northern Rhodesian Regiment which are at present completely without subalterns and will be until such time as African officers have completed their training in the United Kingdom'.[38] A follow-up visit by a Col Slater showed how Defence Forces officers were making an impact overseas when Col Slater remarked that 'he knew Col Delaney of ONUC well when the latter was stationed in Katanga, that they had worked together across the border between Katanga and Northern Rhodesia'.[39] While Grigg's request could not be acceded to by the Irish Government, the next stage in the diplomacy was a private visit by a friend of Dr Kaunda, Fr Walsh SJ, to Taoiseach Seán Lemass with a request this time that officers of the Defence Forces and the Garda Síochána would serve as members of the Zambian security services in a special-branch role. President Kaunda's handwritten note to An Taoiseach, delivered by Father Walsh, noted that 'it is not possible for me to write all I would like to in this note but I am sure Father Walsh will explain'.[40] This initiative resulted in eleven officers of the PDF retiring and taking up positions in Zambia, albeit their service there was relatively short-lived. Further contacts between intermediaries, such as Mr T.J. Barrington, director of the Institute of Public Administration, and Mr Skinner, an Irish-trained barrister and then Zambian minister for legal affairs, finally led to an offer to train cadets for the Zambian Army, and the signing of the agreement between the two governments. The training provided must have been of benefit to the Zambian authorities who were understandably anxious to lessen their dependence on the United Kingdom. It was also another example of Defence Forces contribution to Irish foreign policy objectives. Its benefit to the Military College can best be described as mixed, insofar as while it occupied scarce resources it also introduced several classes of Irish cadets to the wider world where many of them would later serve.

Beyond the exotic, however, the quotidian demands of the Cadet School were in transforming young Irish civilians, all males at this stage, into equally young and largely inexperienced officers. Cadets from the 1960s were the first cadets who could reasonably expect to serve overseas as junior officers in command of platoons, or their corps equivalents. Units drawn from the army were regularly deployed in the 1960s on overseas missions with the United Nations, first to the Congo and then to Cyprus. While the Cyprus mission UNFICYP was relatively calm, troops and officers fought and died in action in the Congo. As cadets, these young men were being trained using what was rapidly becoming an outdated syllabus. Inability to provide officer instructors for the academic and science subjects resulted in an almost exclusively military-oriented syllabus. In the 1960s a cadet's training consisted of turning the civilian into a soldier who could march, drill, handle small arms weapons and direct and control his classmates in rudimentary infantry tactics. Training was of course given in leadership, the organisation of the Defence Forces, the officer's responsibility to his troops, physical culture and the many other essentially 'in-house' military subjects considered necessary to enable the young officer to take his place within a unit of the regular army. The military authorities recognised the deficiencies of this almost unique and isolated regime. It could have been compared, not wholly inaccurately, to that of an Irish seminary, although the cadets, in spite of compulsory religious instruction, did not see themselves or behave in this light. On 11 August 1961, the director of plans and operations, Col Edward Shortall, circulated a paper on cadet training to the adjutant general, quartermaster general and director of training. The paper was prepared by direction of the chief of staff, Lt Gen. Collins-Powell, who surprisingly did not task the director of training with its preparation. The paper is neither signed nor dated but may have been drafted by Col Joseph Emphy, as he had made many of the arguments in the paper in earlier submissions.

The paper stated that the aim of cadet training was to 'produce a commissioned officer of good character with a good education and whose qualities of leadership are developed to the maximum extent in the time available'.[41] As something of an afterthought, the author conceded that the cadet 'must also acquire some basic military skills'.[42] The paper was highly critical of the location of the Cadet School, its status as being just one and, at that, the least of the schools at a single institution. It criticised its recreational – and particularly its educational – facilities. The author is unequivocal in his view that the level of education of newly commissioned and eventually of all officers should be raised to university level. He cited the example of the British and American armies in ensuring this level for all, or increasing numbers of their officers. He proposed three options that might be considered to achieve this major change in the education of cadets: relocating the school to a university city where the cadets could attend evening courses, having all cadets complete third-level education, or selecting the best cadets from each class to go forward to university. Each of these options had advantages and disadvantages and would need much consideration, but the author concluded that the existing Cadet School 'is unsuitable from the point of view of instruction and environment and that more emphasis on the academic education of the cadet is necessary'.[43]

The Advent of Third-Level Education to the Cadet School

Col Emphy, if indeed it was he who authored the paper, considered no future option for cadet education other than the acquisition of third-level qualifications for some if not all cadets. This was not a universally held view among senior officers then or later, as can be seen in the case of a junior officer who requested permission to defer his attendance on a standard infantry course for domestic and educational reasons. The then director of training was of the opinion that the officer's stated reasons were purely private, and in his view 'a serving officer must be prepared to put army matters first and such arguments as getting married and improving his educational qualifications must take second place'.[44] In any case the officer was too young, at 24, to be married and the director of training could not 'see such grounds for exemption being accepted in any army of the western world'.[45] The chief of staff, Lt Gen. Seán McKeown, did not accept these arguments and the officer was exempted from the course on the understanding that he would attend the following standard infantry course.

The 1961 paper circulated by Col Shortall should be seen within the context of the establishment by the government of the Commission on Higher Education in March 1960. In a Dáil debate, the minister for education, Dr P.J. Hillery, outlined that the members of the commission had been directed to 'inquire into and to make recommendations in relation to university, professional, technological and higher education generally'.[46] These terms of reference could not have been more helpful for those members of the Defence

Forces who had the vision to recognise the necessity, if not the inevitability – although that will be shown not to be a given – of third-level education for its officers. One of the members of the commission was Lt Gen. M.J. Costello, previously head of the Irish Sugar Company. Costello had of course been a member of the military mission to the United States in 1926, and had been an influential member of the Military College staff before commanding the First Division during the Emergency. He wrote a memorandum to Judge Cearabhall Ó Dalaigh, chairman of the commission, on 14 February 1961, some months before the paper circulated by Shortall. In his memorandum, Costello argued that third-level education was necessary for cadets and future officers, though he emphasised the need for officers to be 'pre-eminent in their understanding of the religion, language, history and traditions of our people'.[47]

He was in agreement with the previously quoted paper that academic education was equally if not more important than military education, and that the present Cadet School was an unsuitable location. His recommendation on location was that the Cadet School should be transferred to Renmore Barracks and that cadets should study for an Arts degree at University College Galway (UCG). Military training could be provided during a short course before commencing the degree course and during term breaks. Cadets, while attending the College in uniform and as a military unit, should take a full part in non-curricular university life, which 'would be a better preparation for their future life than the somewhat monastic life without opportunity for a suitable social life'.[48] Costello saw much benefit to be gained by the Defence Forces from university-educated officers, given their increasing international duties. The State also had much to benefit from those officers who would eventually retire and enter civilian life as graduates, also thereby improving promotion prospects for officers remaining in the forces. Nor could he resist suggesting that 'army officers who would have proved their ability at a University would have a better chance of terminating the discrimination now practiced against them in favour of Civil Servants'.[49] Costello's viewpoint that the military education of a cadet should be secondary to his academic education is important in that he had been renowned as a particularly demanding field commander who insisted on the highest standards of military performance from his divisional officers.

Barry O'Brien, who has studied the early stages of third-level education in the PDF, credits the development of the Defence Forces submission to the commission to Col Eóghan Ó Néill. He considers that it was 'Generally accepted that it was he who gave the necessary inspiration, direction and drive to the initial discussions, which led to a well thought-out case being compiled in advance of the Commission's visit to the Military College'.[50] Another crucial figure in what was to be the major change to date in the Military College was the Chief of Staff Lt Gen. Seán McKeown. Both these officers had returned from service in the Congo and the intellectual drive of Ó Néill combined with the commitment and leadership of McKeown would be required to see through this important initiative. The first military submission was one from the Military College 'which outlined the history of each of the three Schools that constitute the Military College, and described the courses conducted at each in turn'.[51] The submission made proposals that two of the schools, the Cadet School and the Command and Staff School, should be associated with university education. Concerning the Cadet School, the arguments put forward seem almost nowadays as axiomatic, 'Firstly it was felt that the better the education an officer received the better he would be able to carry out his job. Secondly the requirements of the modern military profession demanded officers of high mental and technical calibre'.[52] The case for the Command and Staff School was that it conducted courses of benefit to civilians as well as to military officers, that no other schools afforded comparable education and that the school 'should be affiliated to a professional institute and that its courses gain recognition comparable to that of university post-graduate'.[53]

This submission led to a visit to the Military College from members of the commission on 26 June 1964. The visit was reported on in the press and prompted favourable correspondence from members of the public. But it was not until 1967 that the commission issued its report and recommended that 'the training of military cadets be associated with university studies at University College, Galway'.[54] The commission made no recommendation regarding the Command and Staff School. The chief of staff, with the approval of the Minister for Defence Mr Michael Hilliard, engaged with the president of UCG, Dr M. Ó Tuathail, who expressed himself as being favourable to the commission's recommendation. The commission had recommended that the Cadet School be associated with UCG 'as it had a special commitment to the Irish language, as had the Cadet School at that particular time'.[55] The recommendation was not to be acted on for some time, however, as opposition became apparent from the civilian branch of the Department of Defence. Such opposition was to be expected as the military authorities had been given an opportunity to deal directly with the commission, extra finance would be required and the scheme did not extend to civil servants. The Department of Defence attempted to delay if not to derail implementation of the commission's recommendation by referring the matter to the Higher Education Authority through the Department of Education. The extra cost involved also led to opposition from the Department of Finance. It was at this period that the leadership of Lt Gen. McKeown became paramount. If he had not been fully committed to the proposal that university education should be the future norm for officers of the Defence Forces, bureaucratic opposition might well have prevailed. He made Hilliard's successor as minister for defence, Jim Gibbons, aware of the difficulties being raised, with the result that the government agreed in principle to the proposed scheme on 22 July 1969.

The military proposal envisaged that the educational entry for cadetship would be raised to matriculation standard and that, after one year of training at the Cadet School in the Curragh, cadets would then complete a first-year undergraduate course at UCG. Success in first-year university exams either in summer or autumn repeats would see the then commissioned cadet continue his studies until he received his degree. Failure in the university exam would see the 2nd Lieutenant, if he had been recommended for commissioning, posted to a unit. This proposal was of course experimental; it was decided not to relocate the entire Cadet School to Galway, for reasons of cost but also because it had been decided that attaining a third-level degree would not be compulsory for commissioning. The delay in implementing the commission's recommendation meant that it was not implemented until 1969, one of the most demanding years in the modern history of the State and of the Defence Forces. Sectarian tensions were worsening in Northern Ireland and would shortly lead to major increases in the PDF and to the need for increasing numbers of cadets and junior officers. The military authorities were determined to proceed with the scheme 'and the necessary administrative arrangements were immediately made so as to enable the 14 members of the 43rd Cadet Class who had reached matriculation standard, to be sent to Galway for the academic year commencing October 1969'.[56] Inevitably there were difficulties in the implementation of the experimental scheme; difficulties that could have been obviated if the commission's recommendation had not been delayed. An important initiative, conceived some years earlier by officers of vision, had been implemented, one that would have profound lasting effects on the Defence Forces, the Military College and the officers it educated. From 1969 onwards, increasing numbers of officers of the PDF would be educated to third level and many older officers pursued third-level education independently of the UCG scheme. It was a development that would eventually lead to a raising of the level of instruction in the Military College.

An Scoil Coisithe – The Infantry School

The 1960s was a decade in which the Infantry School conducted its courses almost entirely through the medium of Irish. It was an imposed policy and one that militated against effective instruction in the acquisition by infantry and other corps officers of some of the essential elements of their trade. In addition, a recurring factor during this decade will be the almost total absence of infantry training for officers in their home units, except in those units formed up for overseas service, leaving the Infantry School as the only available source of this necessary training. The reduction in the length of the cadet course led to a consequent reduction there in military training, and to the military authorities' realisation that a young officers course was necessary for newly commissioned infantry officers. Young officers courses were being conducted at the corps schools outside of the Military College. Junior officers were expected to lead platoons on overseas missions without having experience in this basic requirement. That the courses originally lasted five weeks but were extended to eight and then to twelve weeks in 1965 showed how necessary they were in compensating for the lack of unit training. The designation of the course as a 'young officers' course was doubtful in 1965 with 23 being the average age of the students.

The earliest of these courses caused some difficulties as the CMC was to report in his annual report for 1965 that, 'there is a change to be seen in the diligence and attitude of the students to the course. This is due without doubt to the fact that several students failed the previous course.'[57] Nevertheless, the CMC reported that in spite of the improvement of the students' attitude it was 'very difficult to provide modern infantry battalion training to students on the Young Officers Course because of a lack of qualified instructors'.[58] The extent of this lack can be measured by his recommendation that an officer should be sent on a general-purpose machine gun (GPMG) instructors course the following year. It also became apparent at this time that there was a need for a weapons wing at the Infantry School to instruct students in the handling of basic infantry weapons. There is a particularly telling, even poignant tone in the report's statement that 'there is a great lack of Irish speaking NCO weapons instructors required to train young officers at the School'.[59]

Standard Infantry Course

The young officers course had been introduced at a stage in the infantry officer's career between commissioning and his attendance at the standard infantry course, also taught at the Infantry School. This course had become necessary for career advancement and lasted for four months. Designed in the 1950s to mirror the British Army company commanders course attended by Irish officers at Warminster, it had by the 1960s incorporated an increasing amount of instruction in staff duties and had become effectively an academic course with most instruction given in the lecture hall, syndicate rooms or on terrain map exercises. All of this instruction had been translated into Irish, although students had not fully adapted to the change; they were given an option on the 27th course in 1962 to submit their military history lectures in either Irish or English, and two out of twenty-six students opted for Irish. In the following year, five students from a class of twenty-four opted for Irish. Again, the necessary emphasis on theoretical work was caused by the absence of a demonstration battalion, which would have given students practical experience in the command and leadership of troops. The resident Curragh-based 3rd Infantry Battalion was no longer able to provide even company-level demonstrations, and several courses were required to travel for tactical exercises with troops to Clonmel, County Tipperary, where two companies of the 12th Infantry Battalion were based. Annual reports from the CMC mention the often low standard of military knowledge of students coming on the course, a situation which led to an increase of seventy-three hours of tactical and twenty-five hours of staff instruction on the 31st standard infantry course in 1966. The school introduced a preliminary examination at the start of the course to assess the often disparate level of military knowledge of the students. Attendance at the young officer course raised the military knowledge of students on the standard infantry course as the decade progressed. Given that the Infantry School had no control of unit strength, it cannot be faulted on the instruction imparted on the course. Students were given solid, albeit theoretical instruction in the techniques of deploying, directing and administering an infantry battalion in all phases of conventional war. Comparable courses in other armies carried out the same function, but students then had the opportunity of putting theory into practise in their home units.

The College's reputation, allied to the four courses run for Zambian cadets, was such that the Zambian Army requested that Ireland train a number of their senior captains and junior majors at the Infantry School. This resulted, ironically, in instruction being translated back into English when a combined class of six Irish and six Zambian officers attended the 3rd standard infantry course in 1969. Preliminary discussions on the attendance of the Zambian officers saw the Zambian military attaché to the United Kingdom, Lt Col McGill, indicate that 'he would NOT object to demonstration of weapons but he would be satisfied if the students were instructed in the capabilities and employment of weapons in battle'.[60] No doubt the CMC, Col Bill O'Carroll, would have been happy to provide such instruction, and not only for Zambian officers, but it was not in his power to fulfil such a request.

The Infantry School continued its traditional role of conducting miscellaneous but necessary courses such as intelligence and weapons courses during the decade. In 1962 it commenced a series of potential officers courses that saw ninety-three NCOs commissioned to fill, though not exclusively, administrative appointments in the Defence Forces. Another, more high-profile undertaking was the conduct of *Fianóglach* (ranger) courses. Modelled on the US Army ranger course first attended by Capt. Harry Johnson, followed later by other Irish officers, this course was intended to raise the level of leadership and tactics of junior officers. It was originally planned for 1968, but difficulties in purchasing inexpensive yet necessary items of equipment such as combat uniforms and sleeping bags saw it postponed until 1969. Twelve officers completed the first course in July 1969, and following the deteriorating situation in Northern Ireland were quickly recalled to the College to instruct on two further courses that trained 36 officers, 79 NCOs and 186 privates, to a level of infantry training which few of them had previously attained. The Infantry School's *Fianóglach* courses eventually facilitated the establishment of the Army Ranger Wing (ARW).

An Scoil Ceannais agus Foirne – The Command and Staff School
The Command and Staff School commenced the 1960s with having to run an unwelcome course, the 5th staff course, another of the short courses considered necessary in the previous decade. The course became a requirement following two ministerial decisions; firstly that courses in the College should be conducted through Irish, and secondly 'that, in future, an officer will not normally be considered for promotion to or within senior rank unless he has completed a Command and Staff Course, a Staff Course, or a course acceptable in lieu thereof'.[61] The first of these decisions had meant that the school was given

permission to defer the 23rd command and staff course until October 1960 to enable the staff to undertake the considerable task of translating all course documentation from English into Irish. The adjutant general, Col P.J. Hally, recognised that this course deferment was 'of immediate concern to officers over 40 years of age and who have not successfully completed a Command Staff Course, a Staff Course or other acceptable Course'.[62] Conflicting decisions meant that the school staff was constrained to run one course while simultaneously translating texts for the next course. Even without such distraction, the staff was faced with assimilating the 1959 Chief of Staff's Directive on Tactical Doctrine, a directive that, as we have seen earlier in this chapter, instructed the College that 'the Brigade should be the highest formation to be used in future studies'.[63] Also, only existing units and formations of the 1959 reorganisation were to form the basis of instruction at the school. This caused difficulties, as the staff of the Command and Staff School saw its role as training staff officers not only to brigade level but to brigade level within a divisional organisation. These difficulties seem, however, to have been surmounted, as a briefing document produced in 1964 by the College for visiting members of the Commission on Higher Education stated that the school, 'conducts Courses to develop characteristics of leadership and to train captains in the tactics and techniques of all arms to a standard where they should be capable of commanding a brigade group or functioning as a Chief of Staff or head of section on a division staff'.[64] The document also stated that the command and staff course 'touches on the command and tactical employment of a division and deals with both in the context of nuclear as well as conventional warfare'.[65]

There were a number of reasons that may have facilitated the Command and Staff School in holding fast to its long-held preference for instruction above brigade level. The issuer of the 1959 directive, Lt Gen. P.A. Mulcahy, had been succeeded as chief of staff by Lt Gen. Seán McKeown. McKeown, along with other staff members, had completed a staff course at Camberley where instruction was not limited to the brigade. He had instructed in the Command and Staff School and had been CMC from 1957 until his appointment as chief of staff. It would have been completely understandable for him to have shared the views of the College staff and not to have insisted on the restrictions of his predecessor. McKeown, who was appointed as commander of UN forces in the Congo (ONUC) on 1 January 1961, may well have looked askance at one of the opening assumptions of the 1959 directive which claimed 'that na Fórsaí Cosanta are raised organised and equipped for the defence of State territory and have NO obligations or commitments over-seas'.[66] This was a particularly egregious claim given that research has shown that the government may have earlier considered changing the Defence Act 1954 to allow service with the United Nations, and that 'In June 1958 Ireland responded positively to the United Nations (UN) secretary-general's request to provide personnel for an unarmed, military observer mission in Lebanon'.[67] McKeown would also have been aware of the significance of the deployment in August 1960 of Col H.L. Byrne, also a CMC, as OC 9th Brigade. This brigade staff was to serve as part of the wider military organisation of ONUC, emphasising the need for staff officers trained to operate above brigade level, amply evidenced by the appointment of Col Justin McCarthy as ONUC deputy chief of staff and chief of operations.

Domestically also, the 1959 reorganisation on which the 1959 Tactical Doctrine Directive was based proved not to be a suitable foundation for defending the State, as low strengths of PDF units would have required full mobilisation of the FCA to enable brigades to carry out their missions. Inspections showed the unlikelihood of effective mobilisation. Even more critically, the general staff had lost confidence in the likely effectiveness of its plans for defending the State. In 1964, Plans and Operations had provided answers to questions formulated by students on the command and staff course. One of the questions raised the issue of foreign military aid in a time of invasion and whether in default of such aid guerrilla tactics should be adopted. Plans and Operations replied that 'the General Staff does not consider that present plans are adequate for the defence of the country, neither is it satisfied that adoption of guerrilla tactics would improve the position materially'.[68] Plans and Operations also noted that:

> It is General Staff opinion that present plans, which provide for the utilisation of only a small part of our manpower, are inadequate to resist the threat of a future war. The supply position in relation to armament and equipment is also a cause for concern. Nevertheless the General Staff considers that a policy of decentralised warfare (guerrilla warfare) should not form the basis of our defence policy. Initially at least, the Defence Forces such as they are must be prepared to defend with or without foreign aid, what are considered to be primary invasion objectives.[69]

In spite of these GHQ reservations on the success of the 1959 reorganisation, Mulcahy's intention that officers should 'face facts' and be trained to face an invasion with the means available was admirable in its honesty. It was not, however, sufficient to convince the College that it limit officer education and training to that of the brigade, if only theoretically. UN service would show that its aspirations were not just theoretical.

In the 1960s, Command and Staff School education was essentially twofold; firstly, officers were trained in the techniques of solving problems concerned with the tactical employment of all-arms formations from brigade upwards, and secondly in the techniques of ensuring, as staff officers, that the tactical decisions arrived at by commanders are translated into orders and directions which enable subordinate commanders to implement the higher commander's intent and decisions. Most of the tactical problems presented to students on the command and staff course were based on invasion scenarios where a fictitious state, Invasia, made either airborne or seaborne landings in Ireland. Addressing these problems requires practise in situation assessment, logical thinking and the application of military principles. The students are taught to consider specific defence scenarios, within wider national and international contexts, supplemented by lecturers external to the College staff. While the school was generally successful in its invitations to lecturers in areas separate from defence, the contrary was the case with matters of defence policy. In 1963 the CMC and future chief of staff, Col Carl O'Sullivan, requested that the minister for defence might address the 25th command and staff course on 'The Future Development of the Defence Forces'. He also requested that the minister for external affairs would address the course on 'The Role of Ireland in International Affairs'. He based this request on the reasonable case that such input 'is considered a very important feature of this, the senior post-graduate Course in the Army, that officers undergoing it, who are being prepared eventually to take on the duties of some of the highest offices in the State, should be addressed by members of the government'.[70] The chief of staff, however, was not in favour of inviting the minister for defence and was 'doubtful if Minister Aiken's schedule would allow him to undertake this lecture'.[71] Nor was the CMC any more successful with the Department of Defence. He seemed to have reached agreement with the secretary of the department for a symposium to be held in the College on the responsibilities and duties of the Department of Defence. Col O'Sullivan forwarded suggestions on how the symposium might be organised, with the telling if perhaps provocative observation that:

It has been pointed out by officers of the College staff who have attended such courses abroad that our officers are neither as well briefed nor indoctrinated as to the policies and methods of their country as are the students of other countries. Indeed, they sometimes return from these courses much better informed about the policies of their host country than they are about our own.[72]

It may well have been too provocative as there is no record of the symposium occurring and in its place the secretary of the department nominated the department's Establishments Officer Mr B.A. Tréanlámhach to give a lecture 'on the civil side of the Department'[73] to the course.

Most of the education on the command and staff course was conducted through syndicate work and discussion, based on texts, précis, lectures and demonstration provided by the College staff. During the sixties, this model was hindered by the policy of instruction through Irish, with the CMC reporting that, during the 23rd command and staff course, the first course conducted through Irish between October 1960 and July 1961, 'free and easy discussion and particularly the informal argument, which normally characterises a Command and Staff Course, are very circumscribed'.[74] This difficulty applied not only to students but also to instructors. Prospective students were required to attend pre-course instruction in their home commands and to pass a military and an oral Irish test some months before coming on the course. There is no evidence available as to whether or not any prospective student was denied entrance to a course following such tests.

A recurring comment from CMCs in their Annual reports was the mediocre level of military knowledge of most students arriving on the course – this in spite of the fact that 75 per cent of the students up to 1964 had had field experience during the Emergency and had attended courses conducted by their commands. The comment is understandable insofar as the school staff preferred to know that students would arrive with a broadly comparable level of military knowledge that would not require 'remedial' instruction. In the case of the 26th command and staff course, which reported to the school in 1965, the CMC reported that in addition to having little experience in field tactical-map exercises, the students, before coming on the course 'needed revision in message writing, voice procedure, orders, map marking, field administration, organisation and basic estimate of the situation'.[75] This situation continued with the following course, and it was found necessary to call on the staff of the Infantry School to instruct the students on battalion-level tactics, with disappointing results in a follow-on test. Nevertheless, the CMC felt that 'given that there is so little tactical training done up to now outside of the College it is clear that there has been a big improvement'.[76] In spite of this surprisingly upbeat opinion, little change was to be seen in the students' level of knowledge coming on courses during the 1960s. The school recognised that there was 'a continuing requirement for research, review, revision and preparation of new exercises'.[77] A request that the next course be delayed until 1970 to allow for this work was not granted and the next report saw the CMC request that texts then being drawn up be allowed stand for the following five years. The dominant impression from reports of the decade is that of a school staff attempting to educate officers to a level of military competence someway above the level which the under-strength PDF was in a position to utilise at home. The recurring demands of overseas UN service also understandably saw College officers in much demand to occupy command and staff appointments at national battalion headquarters and at higher UN Headquarters.

Neglect of the Military College Infrastructure

A lack of instructional staff was but one of a succession of obstacles with which CMCs were faced. For all the respect the College achieved, it was an institution that suffered from serious resource starvation. This must of course be seen within the context of overall resource starvation for the entire Defence Forces. Since the chief of staff had no budget control, it followed that the CMC had no influence over expenditure either. Expenditure was in the control of the secretary of the Department of Defence. The department resisted all expenditure where possible, and its guiding principle was that savings should be made from within submitted estimates. This determination can best be seen in a 1949 progress report from the Department of Defence to the Department of Finance, in which the first paragraph almost proudly asserted:

> The progress made since the change of Government in February 1948, mainly consisted of efforts to effect reduction in expenditure. The Defence Estimates for the financial year 1948/49 as originally framed provided for a net expenditure of £4,532,460 and, although this sum was voted by An Dáil, the Minister, when presenting the Estimate, promised that a saving of £744,000 approxi-

mately would be effected in the course of the year through various economies. Accordingly, throughout the year every effort has been made to keep expenditure within the limit set and, if possible, to effect an even larger saving.[78]

Explanation and understanding, while helpful, do not necessarily ease frustration. Frustration is the main attitude to be seen in the recurring requests for the allotment of adequate resources contained in the reports of successive CMCs to the chief of staff during the 1960s. In addition to a lack of qualified officer instructors, which could be considered a matter internal to the military authorities, qualified non-commissioned administrative staff was also lacking. Stationery, paper, writing materials, reproduction facilities, maps, map markers, replacements for blackboards – plywood painted black by the Corps of Engineers – chalk, erasers, files, paper clips, drawing pins, talc, manuals, library books: all were lacking and had to be requisitioned through endless, bureaucratic, Kafkaesque channels. Transport was often unavailable in spite of the efforts of the Supply and Transport Corps in the Curragh. Students often had to travel long distances to and from exercise locations in canvas-covered trucks. On other occasions, until eventually they declined to cooperate, staff and students were obliged to use their private vehicles to travel on exercises. The spectacle of often no-longer-young officers clad in walking-out uniforms and encumbered with large map boards riding army-issue Emergency-era bicycles was a frequent if bizarre sight throughout the countryside. Significant though these difficulties were, they were relatively unimportant compared to the main obstacles to proficiency in the delivery of effective instruction, appropriate living accommodation for students, appropriate office accommodation for teaching staff and appropriate lecture rooms and halls.

In the 1960s, living accommodation for cadets was spartan with cadets at times sleeping in eight-bedded converted lecture rooms. Mess facilities were completely unsuitable with improvised unsanitary kitchens and no toilet facilities. This was eventually alleviated in 1963 when the cadets' mess was relocated to the evacuated officers' mess in the adjoining McDonagh Barracks. While the move was welcome, the CMC was forced to note in 1966 that 'while there were no longer any rats in the Mess they have been replaced with wild cats'.[79] Students throughout the three schools were often confronted with wandering sheep in the corridors. Hot and cold running water was not available in students' rooms, nor were showers conveniently available. Office accommodation was cramped and insufficiently lit, and lecture rooms were lacking not only in pedagogic aids but also in comfortable seats and desks. A restrained but accurate resumé of the College's inadequacies was given by Col Thomas L. O'Carroll, CMC and soon-to-be chief of staff, in his 1968 report:

> A special board has been set up to examine the current needs of the College in lecture hall, theatre and other accommodation for all purposes. It is not unreasonable to state that for a seat of learning the College even compared with a country national school in these matters is ill prepared for its task. There is not even a comfortable chair for a student to use. In comparison with an institution equipped for higher learning it is sadly lacking in all departments. The existing accommodation is inadequate for the diversity of Courses and numbers of students at present being handled.[80]

Col O'Carroll had little improvement to note in his following report and his attention on his appointment as chief of staff in 1971 was diverted from the College to the more pressing problems of the Defence Forces' role in aid to the civil power operations. His 1969 assessment of the College's facilities would remain valid for at least another decade.

Conclusion

During the 1960s, the Military College contended with several conflicting influences as it attempted to fulfil, with inadequate resources, its role in educating and training cadets and officers of the Defence Forces. Facilities at the College were outdated. The ministerial policy that instruction in the College should be through the Irish language was detrimental to its overall raison d'être of educating officers so that they, in turn, could train their largely English-speaking troops. The level of military knowledge of students reporting on the command and staff course was insufficient. A reorganisation of the Defence Forces brought with it a tactical directive that attempted to circumscribe the scope of College instruction. Involvement of the Defence Forces and College instructors in overseas UN missions went a long way towards limiting the impact of the directive. But by far, the most far-reaching influence was the decision by the State, and the implementation of that decision, to provide third-level education for cadets and officers. The effect of that decision was to prove, in time, groundbreaking for the future path of the Military College.

7

The 1970s
The Board Years

Changed Contexts of Defence Policy

The Military College, in spite of not having a founding charter, nor an assigned overall mission, must reflect the actuality of the Defence Forces in its instruction training and education. The actuality of the Defence Forces during the 1970s was its intense involvement in aid to the civil power (ATCP) consequent on the deteriorating security situation both north and south of the island. Chapter 4 showed how the outbreak of the Second World War led to the effective suspension of College activities except for the training of potential officers and their commissioning. This chapter will examine whether or not a comparable change occurred in the College in response to the changed role of the Defence Forces.

While by no means as traumatic as the 1940s, the 1970s produced an upheaval in the roles, organisation and activities of the Defence Forces that were at odds with the prevailing College preference for training in conventional warfare. During the 1970s, militant republican activity required a re-alignment of defence policy and consequent re-investment by the State in defence, this time against an internal and not an external threat. In 1972, the government re-evaluated threats to the State in the light of the international strategic environment and the security situation on the island. Internationally, it was assessed that the greatest threat could come from the collateral damage of a conflict between the major nuclear powers. In such a situation, where Ireland might remain neutral or become a willing or an unwilling belligerent, invasion of the State was considered a lesser threat than nuclear fallout and the effects of continuing internal unrest.[1] International strategic developments would have occasioned such a lessening of focus on invasion regardless of the internal threat to national security; the probability of a neutral Ireland being embroiled in an East/West conflict had greatly diminished. The establishment and success of NATO as a bulwark against the Soviet Union in Europe and the post-war economic rebuilding of Europe made a military advance westward by Soviet forces unlikely, thus greatly diminishing the possibility of a hostile invasion of the State whose geopolitical location mattered less in a nuclear age. In spite of these changing geopolitical circumstances, defence planning since the Emergency had emphasised the function of the Defence Forces as being an anti-invasion force, and attempted to structure and train the forces to oppose such an invasion, while at the same time contributing troop contingents to United Nations peacekeeping operations.

But continuing armed civil unrest on the island of Ireland required that the Defence Forces be re-focused to fulfil an ATCP role, with a lessening of focus by military planners on defence against invasion. As occurs in many States in peacetime, the pendulum of defence commitment had swung from the necessity of the Emergency back to indifference, and had now swung, albeit reluctantly, to awareness again of the need to address defence deficiencies. Over time, between 1972 and 1976, the hastily concentrated ad hoc infantry groups deployed to the border with Northern Ireland were replaced by three new Infantry Battalions: the 27th based in Dundalk, the 28th based in Donegal and the 29th based in Cavan/Monaghan. These units and, in fact, the entire Defence Forces were employed in the essential gendarmerie roles required of ATCP. To paraphrase Dag Hammarskjöld's comment on peacekeeping, ATCP is not the preferred function of troops trained for conventional warfare, but only the legitimate armed forces of the State could carry it out. Some senior officers who had experience of the Katangese Gendarmerie did not appreciate this gendarmerie role. Veterans of the Congo viewed the Katangese Gendarmerie in an unfavourable light and feared that ATCP operations could diminish the Defence Forces' conventional role and persuade the government to limit it to such operations. As it transpired, a not unwarranted fear.[2] Nor was government commitment to UN missions unequivocal, as a contingent to UNEF II, originally deployed to UNFICYP in Cyprus, was withdrawn from the Sinai

Desert during a particularly difficult internal security period in 1974. In the same year, the government also considered the question of greatly increasing the Defence Forces and what effect such increase would have on political attitudes in Northern Ireland. While it decided that any major increase in the Defence Forces would send a negative political signal, it nevertheless considered the military implications of a greatly deteriorating situation that might see the withdrawal of Britain from Northern Ireland and a possible intervention by the UN. Military planners noted that if there were to be intervention by the Defence Forces, it would be conducted by 'formed military units' but that their missions 'could hardly be described as warfare in the sense that we know warfare from what we have seen of warfare in Europe in this century'.[3] Here, again, can be seen a recognition that possible Defence Forces missions had moved away from conventional warfare.

Evidence of a divergence of opinions on the primary role of the Defence Forces – which could have had consequences for Military College instruction – emerged in 1978 in correspondence concerning a Department of Finance proposal that the strength of the Defence Forces should be reduced to comply with a government intention to review public expenditure. The Tánaiste and Minister for Finance George Colley requested the 'Government to approve his proposal that over the years 1979 and 1980 the strength of the Defence Force be reduced to 12,000 from the present 14,800'.[4] Fortunately, this proposal was resisted by the Department of Defence and by the Taoiseach's department on the grounds of the threat to the security of the State that would be posed by such a reduction, given the continuing demands on the Defence Forces from the still-unresolved internal security situation. In the event, the Department of Finance's proposal for a reduction in the strength of the Defence Forces was withdrawn. Not, however, before a divergence of opinion on the future primary role of the Defence Forces emerged between, on the one hand, both branches of the Department of Defence, and on the other the Taoiseach's department. A Department of Defence memorandum, which outlined its objections to the finance proposal of reducing the strength of the Defence Forces, articulated the defence establishment view of the primary role of the Defence Forces:

It may be stated that the success of the Defence Forces in fulfilling their main secondary task since 1969 – that of providing assistance to the Civil Power – has been due in the main to the emphasis placed in recent years on the provision of the essentials for a "gendarmerie" type force i.e manpower, mobility and communications. This emphasis has of necessity been at the expense of equipment needed to permit the Defence Forces to train for their primary objective, viz., that of providing a deterrent against and resistance to external aggression … accordingly the time must be awaited when the internal security situation has improved to the extent that (possibly through a lesser involvement in aid to the civil power) a reduction in strength might have to be contemplated in order that funds so released could be applied towards effecting further desirable improvements in equipment required for proper training for the primary role of the Defence Forces.[5]

In the absence of any direction from government to the contrary, this was the correct and indeed the only responsible approach to be taken by the minister for defence and by the chief of staff. It was not, however, an approach that received unambiguous support in the Taoiseach's department. In an internal memorandum, Frank Murray, a future secretary to the government, queried as to whether:

At this stage one might, I suggest, reasonably question whether the primary objective of our Defence Forces is as set out in the memo "that of providing a deterrent against and resistance to external aggression" … indeed it is hard to visualise the primary role of the Defence Forces being other than one of responsibility for internal security, in all its aspects, for the future.[6]

Mr Kirwan, who forwarded Murray's memorandum to the Taoiseach, agreed with his comments on the likely future role of the Defence Forces.

A divergence of opinion on the primary role of the Defence Forces is apparent between, on the one hand, the Departments of Defence, which opposed reducing the Defence Forces, and, on the other, the Taoiseach's Department, which eschewed defence against external aggression. These discussions were important for the functioning of the Military College, because whatever roles government allots to the Defence Forces, it is the main task of the College to contribute to the education and training of its officers so they can effectively carry out those roles. Military authorities looked forward to a time when ATCP duties would diminish, and the Defence Forces could return to, in their view, its primary role of defence against external aggression. It is not, therefore, surprising that no instruction was given to the Military College to lessen its focus on training for conventional warfare, and to re-focus on training for ATCP operations. The chief of staff, however, was not content to leave the College to its own devices.

The 1972 Board on Officer Training

Col Thomas Leslie O'Carroll was appointed CMC in February 1968. He served in that appointment until he was promoted to major general and appointed as chief of staff in July 1971, an appointment he held until his retirement in July 1976. Given these two appointments, he was in a position to appreciate the role that the College had to play in educating the officers of a rapidly expanding and changing Defence Forces. O'Carroll's time as chief of staff was dominated by the changing role of the Defence Forces. New battalions were established, and increased numbers of cadets were being trained, while at the same time cadets and newly commissioned officers were attending third-level courses at UCG. Such developments inevitably called into question the relevance and the function of existing officer education at the Military College and prompted the chief of staff to establish two boards to examine officer education.

O'Carroll recognised that examination should go further than existing courses and that it should also encompass 'School establishments and essential facilities to cater for course requirements' and also the more difficult question of 'course requirements relative to promotion'.[7] In keeping with this view, he nominated one of his senior staff officers, the Director of Training Col Daniel Fitzgerald, as president of the board. Remaining members of the board were Col P.J. Dempsey, a future adjutant general, and future GOCs Lt Cols P.J. Carroll and K. Nunan. Comdt C.A. McGuinn, also a future adjutant general, was the only 'College' officer on the board. Capt. Seán Norton, a DSM-recipient for action during Operation UNOKAT in Elisabethville in December 1961, was secretary. The omission, intended or otherwise, of a more senior College membership of the board was probably the cause of early friction between the CMC, Col Feardorcha Lee, and the president of the board.[8] It is not possible at this remove to judge whether or not such friction was warranted except to record in its favour that the board fully recognised the responsibilities and prerogatives of the College when it stated that they would not be 'listing subjects or levels to be attained in detail for any particular course or school. Syllabii [*sic*] as such should be prepared by An Coláiste Míleata or the school concerned, and approved by An Ceann Foirne (Chief of Staff)'.[9] However, while deciding not to encroach on pedagogic terrain, the board quickly completed its work and submitted a comprehensive two-part report. Part I examined courses and Part II examined the delivery of these courses. Implementation of the board's report could have provided a clear, if eventually contested, system of courses, and would have supplied the Military College with the means to deliver these courses.

Before addressing its terms of reference, the board considered that attention should be given to the wider context of the future likely operational environment, within which the officer would be operating. It, therefore, examined:

What standard of performance may be required of the officer of the future, at various levels.
What type and level of education is necessary to meet this standard.
What structure can best cater for this education.[10]

Nor was the board satisfied with such considerations. It understood that any such education must have regard to a changing environment. Its understanding in 1972 of this changing environment was prescient:

The widening spectrum in the forms of war
The varied settings in which an officer may have to operate e.g. Internal Security, United Nations, Civil Defence, Conventional Warfare, Nuclear Warfare
The effects of entry into EEC, on our military role
The rapid development in Military Technology
The complexity of many military problems, containing as they do Political, Economic, Social, Religious, Psychological and Financial elements
The ability of the communications media to effect problem areas[11]

All of these environmental elements have since proven to be relevant. The implied priority of missions and tasks outlined in subparagraph b did not, however, reflect accepted priorities in the Military College nor indeed in the wider Defence Forces of the time. The board surprisingly placed conventional warfare after internal security, United Nations and civil defence tasks. Its approach, however, did mirror that of the earlier-mentioned views from the Taoiseach's department. This divergence from the heretofore-accepted priority of instruction in the College created difficulties for the implementation of the board's recommendations.

The board expressed its opinion that while educational courses for officers should 'in general terms be broad, progressive and continuous',[12] they nonetheless felt that courses should constitute only part of his – at the time – education, which should be complemented by unit training. This was an abiding deficiency, although increased recruitment meant that unit strength had increased, bringing with it greater scope for the training of officers by the unit commanders. It recommended an overall scheme as follows: a two-year cadet course followed by third-level education for some, a captains course, an all arms course, a command and staff course and finally a national defence course. While the board was convinced that third-level standard should be the future norm for officers of the Defence Forces, it did not exclude non-university educated officers and found fault with the then-existing system whereby officers only attended third-level courses at University College Galway. The present system, it argued, resulted in the commissioning of cadets after a shortened period in the Cadet School, which saw them unqualified to lead or to train platoons in an emergency. This grave defect should be rectified by all cadets completing a two-year course before embarking on a university course. This approach would qualify them as platoon commanders and obviate the need for a young officers course at the Military College. It also took the view that, as the period before an officer was promoted to captain was decreasing, it was necessary that the cadet receive a solid military indoctrination before commencing third-level education.

The proposed captains course, which was to qualify an officer for that rank, was to be preceded by an entrance examination, 'failure in this examination will automatically impose a deferment to the next Course, with the possibility of a loss of seniority'.[13] Officers of corps other than the Infantry Corps would be required to complete also a standard course conducted at the relevant corps school. The next step in the educational chain was the completion of an all arms course considered as an essential intervening course before the command and staff course, where the age of the students continued to rise. The all arms course would be the qualifying course for promotion to commandant and would also require a candidate to pass an entrance examination. In keeping with the same formula, the command and staff course, which should be completed before the student had reached the age of 36, would, on completion, qualify for promotion to higher ranks. However, no officer over the age of 40 should be compelled to attend the course, and only recommended officers should be allowed sit a competitive examination for entry to the course. Completing the system of courses was an ambitious proposal for the establishment of a national defence course. The rationale behind this proposal was that senior officers of the Defence Forces are called on to act in emergencies at the highest level of governmental and civil service agencies and should not, therefore, be educated in isolation from these other actors. The course, modelled on similar courses abroad, would also be attended by senior non-military officials. It 'would produce a body of senior officers of the army and civil service, who would be capable of holding high command and key appointments in the structure of National Defence in both peace and war, and be in a position to advise the government in policy making and planning'.[14] In addition to this high-level course, the board recommended the establishment at the Military College of a full-time doctrinal board, composed of one lieutenant colonel and two commandants with previous experience as instructors (DS) of the Command and Staff School. Its task would be to provide 'the research, analysis and study necessary to produce worthwhile recommendations with regard to training and operations in relation to Army Policy'.[15]

These proposals for a reformed system of educational courses for officers formed the core of Part I of the board report. In concluding remarks, concern was expressed regarding the existing officer profile of the Defence Forces. The board noted that 'approximately half the officers serving presently are over 40 years of age' and more critically, therefore, were 'not fit for operational duties with troops'.[16] It further noted that 'operational capacity is dependent on the physical and mental state of all its leaders to operate in combat conditions. Age is a vital factor.'[17] While straying somewhat from its terms of reference, the board felt that age had an impact on education and recommended the setting-up of a resettlement scheme that would facilitate a lowering of the age profile of officers and a speedier access to higher ranks. Again, its recommendation in this area was prescient.

The final section of Part I of the report constituted a severe criticism of the policy of *Úsáid na Gaeilge*, then in force for more than twelve years. This criticism was important, coming as it did from a board whose president was the director of training, Dan Fitzgerald. In the opinion of the board, the policy of conducting courses in the Military College was flawed because, 'Irish is not the normal everyday language of Instructor or Student, and in consequence discussion in depth is inhibited'.[18] In this area, Norton, as the member of the board closest to unit training and operations, felt he made a contribution beyond his secretarial duties with the inclusion of the following observation:

> Military Education suffers because:
> The value of instruction is diminished to varying degrees depending on Instructors and Students competence in Irish.
> It is difficult to apply the results of courses to normal unit activity.[19]

The board concluded Part I of its report with the opinion that the policy, in addition to having a deleterious effect on military training, had also failed in its aim of advancing the Irish language.

Part II of the report put forward a detailed plan for the implementation of the proposed system of courses. It envisaged that with full implementation of this system, the Military College would have to cater for 200 students per annum, but that it would take up to five years for the system to be fully in operation. The role of the CMC required modification with more emphasis on his academic responsibilities, while the administrative functioning of the College should become the responsibility of a camp commandant with an increased staff. The parlous position of the educational facilities of the College was recognised, and the board conducted a comprehensive review of required facilities and their cost. The members of the board were satisfied that their proposals would, if accepted, 'best accomplish the education of the Defence Forces Officers of a small country recently admitted to membership of the EEC'.[20]

While it must be assumed that the chief of staff discussed the report with its president, the director of training, the board's overall concept of officer education and its recommendations were not fully implemented. There are some factors that can be advanced for this lukewarm reception. Its proposed system of courses, while logical, was also radical, and, being based on the principle of qualifying entrance examinations, required a fundamental change to the system of officer promotion. While the existing regulations laid down that certain prescribed courses would qualify an officer for promotion to a higher rank, this was only one of several criteria laid down in DFR A 15. The proposed new system would go further and require an officer to qualify for attendance on a course, with consequent failure rendering him ineligible for promotion. The lengthy lead-in time before the system would be fully integrated also probably militated against its acceptance. Given the demanding employment of the Defence Forces in ATCP operations, the chief of staff was unlikely to have been amenable to lengthy educational experimentation. It is also possible to speculate that the College authorities did not favour the board's recommendations. In particular, the relegation to a lower tasking priority of conventional warfare would have caused a major upheaval to the existing Military College *modus operandi*.

While the board's full recommendations were not immediately acted upon, some of with them were adopted. A captains course was substituted for the standard infantry course in 1975, and four commandants courses were substituted for the command and staff course between 1974 and 1978. The chief of staff subsequently directed that these four courses, the 1st to 4th commandants courses, 'be equated to Command and Staff Courses'.[21] The courses were also renamed as the 34th, 35th, 36th and 37th command and staff courses.

The 1976 Board on Officer Education and Development

The partial adoption of the recommendations of the 1972 board was probably the worst of all solutions, and the concerns that prompted the board's establishment were by no means alleviated, leading to the establishment of another board in 1976. The terms of reference of this second board give some indications as to why the chief of staff considered a second board necessary. The board was required to re-examine the 1972 report, to assess the new courses consequent on that report, to consider a submission made by Col Eóghan Ó Néill and also two submissions made by the CMC to the chief of staff in 1975.[22] It is clear that the College authorities were not satisfied with the results of the 1972 board.

The composition of Maj. Gen. O'Carroll's second Board on Officer Education could not have been more different than that of his first. This time, the sole members were the three senior officers of the Military College. They were the CMC, Col Pierce Quinlan, the commandant of the Command and Staff School, Col William (Bill) O'Carroll, a future CMC and GOC the Southern Command, and the commandant of the Infantry School, Col Dermot Hurley, a future director of operations. Surprisingly, the board did not include the commandant of the Cadet School. While all three were, in fact, senior officers of the College, it is not clear that they had served there previously as instructors, thereby giving a less-than-full College slant to their deliberations.[23] The three school commandants appointed Comdt Donal O'Carroll, a future commandant of the Infantry School, as the board's secretary. The convening order tellingly required its members to, among other considerations, 'assess and report on the practical experience gained from the new-type courses so far run at the Military College'.[24] The courses referred to were a platoon commanders course, which had replaced the traditional young officers course in 1971, and the captains and commandants courses introduced following on the 1972 board report. Why the 1976 board membership should have been so completely given over to the College is not clear, except perhaps for the fact that the CMC had made his submissions to the chief of staff on 23 May and 4 October 1975. Not having sight of these submissions, it is not possible to be certain, but it is quite likely that he was critical of these 'new-type' courses, a likelihood borne out by the board's deliberations.

In its opening remarks, the board went to great lengths to make the point that it did not consider performance on academic courses to be the most important element in the assessment of an officer's capabilities and suitability for promotion or command. In the opinion of its members, 'a more fruitful and accurate source of information on an officer's character, general demeanour and usefulness should be the opinions of the various commanding officers under whom he has served'.[25] Commanding officers also had more responsibility than the Military College for the education and training of officers:

> The importance of on-the-job training cannot be over-stressed, particularly now that unit strengths are high. If any deficiency exists in officer instruction it is suggested that it is far less likely to exist in formal education by way of courses than from a lack of on-the-job training in command and important staff appointments.[26]

The board could be accused here of somewhat disingenuous self-pleading, as while it was true that unit strengths had improved, this was a relatively recent development and most of those units were employed in personnel-heavy ATCP operations. It made early criticism of the 1972 report by contradicting its view that courses can qualify an officer for promotion or render him fit for a particular appointment or command. In the opinion of the board, the aim of career courses should be 'to provide the administrative, academic and tactical instruction which would help to prepare a (rank) for promotion to a (rank).'[27] However, it went on to more damning criticism of the two courses introduced as a partial response to the 1972 recommendations. In its view:

The Captain's Course except in emphasis, is very little different from, and is geared of necessity to the same level as the Infantry Course. The Commandant's Course is geared to the same level as the Command and Staff Course but is of shorter duration and of somewhat less educational value because of the total omission of certain areas of instruction which were included in the Command and Staff Course … the net result of these changes is that, apparently, for the sake of a small number who would undertake a new-type Command and Staff Course – the content of which is as yet undetermined – the vast majority of officers would, in the future, get less military education than they would have got under the old system.[28]

This was a valid criticism, bearing in mind, however, that these two courses formed just part of a proposed wider system of officer education. That system, as was seen above, had recommended the introduction of an all arms course between the captains and commandants courses, which would qualify the officer to command at the battalion level. The 1976 board's comment on this recommendation was that it 'should not comment further on this matter other than to say that it agrees with the decision not to put it into effect'.[29] Criticism was also levelled at a perceived elitist trend of the earlier board, which was felt to be leaning towards selecting a small number of officers who would compete for attendance on the new-type command and staff course. Selection would, if adopted, 'drastically reduce the morale of the vast majority of captains/commandants by depriving them of hope at too early a stage in their careers'.[30] This was not a new argument, but it was a change from previous Military College arguments that had advocated selection and entrance examinations for the command and staff course.

Unsurprisingly, the 1976 board recommended a return to the system operating before 1974. In its opinion, this system, 'had produced officers at both junior and senior level, who despite the shortcomings at home in practical experience, were in a more than favourable position in competing with foreign officers in United Nations service both at command and staff work.'[31] This opinion was and probably still is a commonly held belief, but it was not, as we have seen earlier, a universally held one. The 1976 board's conclusions were not, however, a simple atavistic yearning for an earlier status quo, insofar as, while proposing a return to the traditional system of cadet course, young officers course, standard infantry course and command and staff course, it also recommended important, qualitative changes to these courses. It agreed with the 1972 board that the cadet course should revert to a two-year course for non-university-attending cadets and also for university-attending cadets if possible. The board did not wholeheartedly favour the UCG third-level scheme, which will be covered in detail later, but recommended instead that 'a separate study be undertaken by suitably qualified persons of the whole question of third level education in the Army'.[32] The board recommended that after commissioning, officers should complete a young officers course before they became eligible for promotion to captain. This course would comprise approximately four weeks at a corps school, the Infantry School for corps officers who did not have a separate corps course and four weeks at the School of Administration. The board did not consider these courses as career courses qualifying an officer for promotion to captain. In the opinion of its members, 'if an officer's general performance and conduct of his duties are such that he is not considered suitable for promotion to captain serious consideration should be given to the question of his retention as an officer'.[33]

The next career course that the officer should attend would be the standard infantry course; the board strongly recommended ending the captains course. Officers attending the standard infantry course should be captains or senior lieutenants, and the course would be the academic qualification for promotion to commandant. On this course, they would be trained to be company commanders or the equivalent corps appointment, and as staff officers in a battalion. The Board took the view that since 'all formations in the Army are infantry formations' all officers regardless of their corps appointment should, therefore, complete the Standard Infantry course, in addition to their corps courses.[34] All officers regardless of their corps appointment should, therefore, complete the Standard Infantry course, in addition to their corps courses. This recommendation was a limited recognition of the existing ATCP operational requirements of the Defence Forces. At the next level of career course, the board again strongly recommended the ending of the commandants course. The command and staff course should be re-instituted as a year-long academic course and as the academic qualification for the rank of lieutenant colonel. Here the board recommended an important change in that officers should apply to attend the course and, if recommended, would be allowed attend. Such a change, they considered, would be a better system than the often-proposed entrance examination, insofar as it would limit the courses to those who had a genuine interest in career advancement and who were prepared to commit themselves to a lengthy course away from home. Finally, the board acknowledged that there was a need for refresher courses and further and continuing education for senior officers. However, it advanced no clear proposals other than the creation of a 'Centre for Advanced Studies' at the Military College, which would 'research the whole relevant area of advanced studies and come up with a report and recommendations'.[35]

Overall, the board's recommendations tended towards re-instituting the status quo that prevailed before the 1972 board. It was successful insofar as the standard infantry and command and staff courses were quickly reinstated after the board reported to the chief of staff. The young officers course took longer to reappear as the Infantry School continued to conduct platoon commanders courses into the 1980s. It was to be some years before the important recommendation of officers applying to attend the command and staff course was introduced. What is noteworthy concerning the deliberations of the three most senior officers of the Military College is that they conceived the work of the College almost exclusively in academic terms. While they maintained that the unit had the primary role in training officers, they also acknowledged the difficulties experienced by units in providing training for their officers in leadership and command. The board showed minimal recognition of the actual roles performed by units, and did not seem to consider the College to be in a position to provide anything other than predominantly class-oriented education in its schools. Nevertheless, the board's work was influential as it established or re-established the format of education in the College for some years to come. This point is apparent in a briefing given by the staff of the director of training to a command and staff course in the mid-1980s. The briefing drew heavily on and quoted liberally from the 1976 board report, emphasising the board's conviction that 'No course of instruction will in itself train an officer to command a unit or formation'.[36] The 1972 and 1976 board reports were, in part, occasioned by the major change that had been brought about by the decision to introduce third-level education for cadets, and to a much lesser degree by the changing roles of the Defence Forces. To consider the effect of the 1972 and 1976 boards and of the introduction of third-level education for cadets and officers, it is necessary now to look at the individual schools of the Military College, beginning as before with the Cadet School.

The Schools

The Cadet School
The previous chapter detailed the introduction of the third-level educational scheme for cadets and officers. In its deliberations, the 1972 board had expressed

concern that an important and traditional element of the cadet programme – the inculcation of identity – was eroded by the attendance of cadets and junior officers at UCG. The new system meant that 'tradition and continuity in the Cadet School no longer exist. The incoming cadet class has no senior class; each class starts from a new beginning'.[37] This was indeed a serious problem. Most if not all graduates of the Cadet School will acknowledge that the defining and enduring influence of their time at the school was the sense of loyalty to the State and to the Defence Forces engendered by the shared experience of their being members of a unique, numbered cadet class. They formed lifelong friendships that facilitated their shared progression throughout their careers as commissioned officers. Each officer is an individual, but to be effective must operate as part of a team, a skill and an attitude imparted during the Cadet School experience. Contrary, however, to the concerns of the board, it was not the nascent UCG involvement that threatened the traditions of the Cadet School, but the rapid and increased intake of cadets demanded by the expanded PDF. During the 1960s, the average number of cadets in each class was thirty-three but during the 1970s, cadets per class numbered fifty, sixty, seventy and more. In all, between October 1968 and November 1975, 472 cadets entered the Cadet School, and '204 were never actually to attend university'.[38] In addition to this, the amount of time spent in the Cadet School was greatly reduced. It is almost as if the Emergency experience was repeating itself, except insofar as the Emergency expedient of awarding temporary commissions was not availed of,[39] and it is to the credit of the Cadet School instructors, both officers and NCOs, that all of these cadets benefitted from the traditions enjoyed by their predecessors. This increased intake lessened as the decade progressed, and the 54th cadet class, which was commissioned in 1979, consisted of the more normal thirty cadets. The 1970s also saw the regular amalgamation of Aer Corps and Naval Service cadets with army cadets. The cadet register[40] records that in 1974 the 49th cadet class also included seven cadets of the 8th Aer Corps cadet class and three cadets of the 12th Naval Service cadet class. The Aer Corps and Naval Service cadets did not complete the full course but reported to their respective headquarters for completion of training and eventual commissioning. This pattern became standard practice. With the return to more normal class sizes, a defining and continuing aspect of the early education of officers newly commissioned from the Cadet School was attendance at the newly established Defence Forces unit, the University Student Administrative Complement (USAC).

Third-Level Education – University Student Administrative Complement (USAC)
It has been earlier remarked that the rapid inception of the third-level educational scheme for cadets and officers was fortuitous as it could well have been derailed by the new, continuing and increased ATCP demands placed on the Defence Forces in 1969. Because of its rapid inception, the scheme was inevitably introduced on a somewhat ad hoc basis and would require modification. While competing academic and military training requirements took some time to be appraised, administrative requirements demanded early attention. The first pressing requirement was for suitable accommodation for the student cadets. Capt. Barry O'Brien, who graduated from UCG, served with USAC and later transferred on retirement to the National Council for Education Awards (NCEA), and completed a master's degree on the early USAC scheme. He described how, as with the early days of the Military College, an opportunity was missed not only to accommodate students at UCG but also to acquire an appropriate location for the Cadet School itself, although this would have separated the school from the Military College:

> As regards accommodation, it was noted at an early stage in discussions that St. Enda's College in Salthill was up for sale. A military hospital during the Emergency, St. Enda's had operated as a Preparatory School for candidates seeking entrance to teacher training colleges up until 1963. With spacious playing fields, sizeable dormitories, and with easy access to the University, it could very well have proven an ideal location for a Cadet School.[41]

St Enda's had, however, been handed over to the Galway diocese in 1963 at, as noted by O'Brien, a time when discussions on the university scheme were at a very early stage. The first fourteen cadets who entered UCG and some cadets of subsequent classes found themselves housed in two hotels, Flannerys and Ryans in Galway city, ample evidence for those who had forebodings of the death of the Cadet School ethos. Mellows Barracks, Galway is a small self-contained establishment that had little scope for accommodating and messing the increasing numbers of cadets posted to Galway, even though the attached brigade HQ yielded up office space as living accommodation. It became apparent that such arrangements could not suffice and, probably to the annoyance of the Departments of Defence and Finance, a decision was made to construct an accommodation, dining and recreational facility on Department of

Defence lands adjoining Mellows Barracks. The complex was officially opened in September 1974 by the Minister for Defence Mr Paddy Donegan TD and a new unit of the Defence Forces, the 'University Student Administrative Complement', was established. Its acronym, USAC, became for some years the eponym for the Defence Forces policy of cadets and officers, and eventually officers only, pursuing third-level education as part of their training. Comdt Tom Quinlan DSM, later Brig. Gen. and GOC Southern Command, was appointed as the first officer commanding USAC, having earlier been in charge of the cadets before the establishment of USAC.[42]

Modifications to USAC

Given the somewhat precipitate inception of the USAC scheme, and its controversial modification of a 40-year long tradition of cadet training, it is understandable that it would come under considerable and early scrutiny. Col O'Carroll, the CMC under whose authority the first cadets entered UCG in October 1969, reported in April 1970 that 'all were progressing well'.[43] A statistical examination carried out by Barry O'Brien in 1978 of officers and cadets who enrolled at UCG between 1969 and 1974 showed that their academic performances were on a par with those of civilian students who enrolled at the same time.[44] Some senior officers, including the then Chief of Staff Maj. Gen. O'Carroll, did not appreciate this parity. They considered that the obvious material advantages enjoyed by the military students should have resulted in a better performance than that of their civilian counterparts. O'Brien made the counter-argument that many of the military students entered the university with lower Leaving Certificate results and could be considered to have therefore outperformed their civilian co-students. Inevitably, however, a board was called for to review USAC. Preliminary work was carried out by an early champion of the scheme, Col Eóghan Ó Néill, who worked out the parameters of the board while undergoing his annual reserve training. The board was convened on 25 September 1976 under the presidency of Col Redmond O'Sullivan and submitted its report on 3 February 1977. The board endorsed the concept of the scheme and the provision of university education for officers and made two important recommendations for modifications to the scheme. Firstly, the shortening of the Cadet School course, with the second year spent in university, had many disadvantages, and it was recommended that the cadet course be lengthened to eighteen months of predominantly military training, followed, after commissioning, by a period of five months posting of the officer to a military unit. The purpose of this recommendation was 'to give the young officer an increased understanding of himself and his men, of the Army as an organisation, of its place in society of today and of its relationship with the world'.[45]

The implementation of this recommendation would mean that commissioned officers only would attend university, eliminating the potentially unsatisfactory practice of mixing cadets and junior officers in USAC. It would also ensure that the junior officer would receive a complete inculcation into his chosen military career. The second recommendation was that the university education of officers not be limited to that provided by UCG but that the scheme should be expanded to include other third-level institutions such as the then Thomond College of Physical Education and Bolton Street College of Technology. Both of these recommendations were acted upon and resulted in third-level education being the educational norm for all commissioned officers in the Defence Forces. Other board recommendations led to the raising of cadet educational entry standards and consideration of how courses provided by the Military College might in future be formally recognised within the State's educational system. The board confirmed and vindicated the vision of the early supporters of the scheme, Lt Gens Seán McKeown and M.J. Costello, and Col Eóghan Ó Néill to name just three. Theirs was not a new vision, as previous senior officers had envisioned close cooperation between the Military College and the universities. But from them came the impetus, drive and timely awareness that have ensured that an officer corps, educated to a standard that places them in the forefront of the nation's institutions, now lead the Defence Forces. The scheme also encouraged many officers to pursue third-level education in their own time and with financial support provided by the State.

The Infantry School

The Standard Infantry Course

The Infantry School continued to see its principal role as that of training senior lieutenants as qualified company commanders and as staff officers at battalion level with the emphasis placed on conventional operations. The advent of USAC with a consequent shortening of the cadet course made it necessary to conduct yearly platoon commanders courses to supplement the deficit in young officer tactical training. Officers not attending USAC became more and more involved with ATCP and border duties, which made it difficult for some units who had to release officers for courses. The Infantry School did, however, acknowledge the experience gained by officers both on ATCP and overseas service. The report on the 38th standard course noted that:

> Thirty nine students had served with Border Units and thirteen had United Nations service before coming on the course. Consequently the standard of Man Management and troop leading was of a high standard and students were better able to relate theoretical instruction to tactical problems.[46]

It is interesting that the school saw the actuality of operations as assisting it in carrying out its allotted function of training for war. Without direction to the contrary, it cannot be faulted for this approach. Nevertheless, the school included training for ATCP, with exercises, demonstrations and lectures and the amending and updating of existing instruction by college DS. Except for the two captains courses — instituted on the recommendation of the 1972 board — the school conducted a standard infantry course annually.

As had been reported by the 1976 board, these two captains courses bore little difference to the standard infantry course, and the reversion was justified. Early in the decade, many students coming on the standard infantry course had not attended a young officers course, a fact that greatly inhibited tactical instruction at the company level and above. This difficulty eased with increasing numbers of students who had completed a platoon commanders course and, as has been shown above, had gained greater experience at platoon and company level. The school endeavoured to extend the tactical as opposed to the purely theoretical nature of the syllabus and benefited from cooperation with NCO and recruit courses being conducted at this time in the General Training Depot (GTD), again a factor which is discussed more fully below. While some exercises were conducted with troops, the course emphasis was on the theoretical exposition of conventional and, increasingly so, internal security operations, up to battalion level. The instruction imparted on these courses, except for an increasing emphasis on training for ATCP operations, had not changed greatly from that imparted in previous decades. Infantry tactics had changed little, except for the introduction of armoured personnel carriers (APC), and students continued to be tested theoretically in company attack and defence, with the school remarking on the students' lack of tactical proficiency on arrival. A change was appearing, however, in school instruction on the junior course.

Platoon Commanders Course

The 1st platoon commanders course conducted for twenty-nine officers in 1971 was composed of officers who had attended a two-year cadet course and also of those who had completed one year before attending third-level education at UCG. The school commandant's report that 'the difference in training observed between the students who had completed the two year Cadet syllabus and who had completed one year's training was minimal,'[47] might seem surprising except that the course content was mostly theoretical with, as an example, only ten hours of practical internal-security training. The school commandant also felt that 'it would be impossible to provide tactical training for the students in the handling of troops'.[48] Three years later, the situation had changed when seventy-seven officers reported on the course, a number that could have been expected to overwhelm the school's capacity. Paradoxically, this increased number, a consequence of the earlier-increased cadet classes, led to an emphasis on tactical instruction at the level of the platoon commander. Increased cadet numbers had also been matched by increased recruiting in response to the internal security situation. Many of these recruits were at that stage in training on advanced 3-star private and potential NCO training in the General Training Depot (GTD) in the Curragh, next door to the Military College. Cooperation with the GTD made it possible for the Infantry School to provide realistic training, insofar as the training moved from the classroom to a requirement for the students to command, lead and manoeuvre troops on the ground up to full-company strength and equipped with armoured personnel carriers (APCs). Added, and necessary, improvements to the course were as follows:

> Instruction by outside instructors was done in English.
> Some instruction by the staff of the Infantry School was also done in English either because:
>> It was traditionally done in English.
>> Personnel from the GTD were involved.[49]

This improvement had to be sought from and approved of by the chief of staff, an indication that the school authorities still had to contend with the policy of *Úsaid na Gaeilge*.

The platoon commanders course continued to benefit from cooperation with GTD courses throughout the decade and to provide much-needed 'hands-on training' to young officers, most of whom were by the end of the decade university graduates. All course reports commented on the enthusiasm of the students but also that, 'throughout the conventional tactics stage it was apparent that a number of students did not fully understand the application of fire and movement techniques and in applying movement techniques to terrain over which they attacked'.[50] The Infantry School became convinced of the importance and the necessity of the more realistic tactical training which it was able to provide to young officers and had reservations concerning a return to the traditional young officers course as proposed by the 1976 board report. In 1978 the school commandant, Col Pat Lavelle, himself a Cavalry Corps officer, ended his report on the 14th platoon commanders course with the following recommendation:

> In its present form the Young Officer's Course syllabus is heavily test oriented, and by nature of this fact, is NOT geared towards practical exercises with troop participation. Should the policy of phasing out the Platoon Commanders Course be implemented shortly, it is recommended that a close study be made of the Young Officer's Course syllabus with a view to including a greater content of exercises therein and perhaps with a lessening of emphasis on the formal test aspect.[51]

While it seemed as if the classroom was beckoning again for the young officer, parallel young officers and platoon commanders courses were conducted in 1980/81. The report of the 12th infantry young officers course indicated in 1980 that a new syllabus with more tactical training and fewer tests had been drawn up for future such courses. Paradoxically, the Infantry School had benefited rather than suffered from the demands placed on it by the increasing numbers of young officers coming on courses. Supported by GTD courses, it was able, arguably for the first time since the Emergency years, to consistently conduct tactical training with full-strength sub-units up to company level. Still lacking, unfortunately, were facilities for introducing the live firing of weapons during this improved tactical training.

Potential Officers Courses

The Infantry School was also tasked with continuing the general staff policy of providing courses for NCOs, to qualify them for commissions. Some NCOs had completed such courses during the Emergency, as distinct from promotion directly from the ranks, but the policy had fallen into abeyance until a course was conducted in 1962 for eighteen army and two Naval Service personnel. The military authorities had sought and received political and financial approval for this course; their justification was that continuing low officer strength could not have been remedied by the then-prevailing low annual intake of cadets. The intention was that successful candidates would 'be appointed to commissioned rank in order to fill vacancies as store officers, administrative officers and assistant quartermasters'.[52] Given their proposed future employment, those selected for the 1962 course had considerable administrative experience and their average age was 40. Subsequent courses in 1970 and 1975 saw student numbers increase to thirty-one and twenty-two respectively and the average age drop to 31 and 34. Promotion prospects also increased with the possibility of reaching the rank of commandant and lieutenant colonel.

Attendance on these courses was relatively onerous with the course lasting for twelve months and successful candidates being required to serve in any appointment selected, and to vacate married quarters, where occupied, on commissioning. Take-up was satisfactory and achieved the objective of providing experienced administrative officers. As the decade progressed, the original focus of ameliorating low officer strength lessened, and it was recognised that the courses achieved another equally important function: that of 'improving and contributing to the morale of NCOs by providing an opportunity of advancement to NCOs of ability and character'.[53] Notwithstanding the somewhat patronising tone of the letter, it was decided not to confine successful candidates to administrative appointments. Also, for a course scheduled for 1978/79, 'Generally officers will be intended for Adm appointments but will not be necessarily debarred from operational appointments'.[54] In recognition of this changing aspiration, the minimum entry age for the course was lowered to 22 and corporals became eligible to apply for the course. The object of the 4th potential officers course, conducted over fifty weeks between 1978 and 1979, was to 'train selected NCOs to the standard required to fit them to take their place as commissioned officers of the Permanent Defence Force'.[55] Successful candidates were not limited to administrative appointments. Nor was the syllabus, which covered weapons training, general studies, command and staff, tactical operations, internal security, administration and quartermastering, communications and character development, leadership, all arms and catering management.[56] This demanding course was not limited to the classroom as the students were required to complete three weeks' tactical training in the Glen of Imaal in coordination with the 54th and 55th cadet classes. The value of the course, not only to the Defence Forces but also to the students, can be gauged from the concluding remarks of the students' report on the course:

> If variety, challenge, retention of interest of the student and ability to extract a high work-rate are indications that a Syllabus had been successful in achieving its objects, then we, the students of the 4th Potential Officers Course can only say with hindsight, that it did.[57]

The commissioning of ninety-three NCOs to commissioned ranks between 1962 and 1979 is indeed a low figure, but it must be considered against the relative educational standards required for a cadetship at the time, and the considerable upheaval both domestic and professional which was required of candidates for these courses. For the staff of the Infantry School, these courses provided a particularly satisfying and rewarding task that led the officer in charge of the 4th potential NCO course to record that he 'was proud to have been associated with you and will follow your future careers as officers with interest'.[58]

The Command and Staff School

The Command and Staff School maintained its efforts of imparting higher-level instruction, with the aim of preparing senior officers for command and for service as senior staff officers in higher formations. The unequal military experience and education of students and the attitude of some students attending the course posed difficulties for the school staff. The thirty-one students who reported on the 30th course in 1970 presented the following profile:

> The average age of the course was 40 years. The oldest student was 42 and the youngest 34. The majority of the students had held staff and administrative appointments for many years prior to the course. Very few had experience in command of troops except as commanders of sub-units in UN contingents. None had had experience as a senior staff officer in formation HQs at home. The class as a whole displayed exceptional interest and enthusiasm throughout the entire course. From a disciplinary point of view they were very well behaved.[59]

While it is hoped, if not indeed expected, that officers of 40 years of age would be very well behaved, it could be questioned if officers with at least twenty years' military service should be required to complete such a lengthy course in the hope of gaining promotion. The 1972 board had also reached this view. The assessment by the commandant of the command and staff school, Col Crowe, of the students' experience is somewhat confusing, insofar as experience with UN contingents did not seem to rate highly. Confusion, if not disinterest, in UN operations seems also to have been the majority view among students on a later course, the 33rd command and staff course in 1974. Comdt Patrick Maguire, a DS and future CMC and GOC Curragh Command, circulated a survey among the students requesting their views on the three hours allotted to UN operations on the course syllabus. Introducing the survey Maguire felt that the time was inadequate for 'coverage of the subject, considering the wide spectrum of UN experience which most Command and Staff classes now contain, and the contributions which students could make to our pool of direct knowledge in this particular field'.[60] It seems that not all students shared his view as only eleven of twenty-nine returned the survey. All, however, of the eleven felt that the time allocated was inadequate, but only one felt that 'War Stories' should be preferred to lectures as a method of instruction. Perhaps the somewhat derogatory term used by the student was an indication of a lack of confidence in actual UN experiences compared with College instruction.

By the end of the 31st course in 1972, Col Crowe had become much more critical of the ability of the school to fulfil its functions given the disparity in the experience and ability of the students. He was of the opinion 'that a small proportion of the students might not be considered suitable to undergo the course, if more stringent requirements and conditions were applied.'[61] While individual personalities may have played a part in this contention, it was also a reiteration of the earlier debate in which Col Dan Bryan championed a qualifying examination to attend the command and staff course. Crowe went further and suggested 'a system of recommendations, confidential reports and qualifying exams somewhat on the lines used for Camberley qualification'.[62] He was also aware that the stumbling block of such a suggestion would be the need for a 'revision of the regulations concerning promotion to senior rank'.[63] This confusion of aims led Col Crowe to the unusual admission concerning the 31st command and staff course that 'the fact that all succeeded in passing the course is no indication of the real merit of some students and I would be reluctant to classify some of the students as suitable senior commanders and staff officers'.[64] It cannot be fully assumed that this situation was peculiar to the 31st course, and it illustrates a continuing dichotomy of requiring officers to attend courses without a clear understanding of their end result. The fault should not be found only with students, who were considerably put upon by the inadequacies of the school and its administration. The school commandant appreciated these inadequacies. He remarked in his report that he and the chief instructor carried out much of the daily and personnel administration, and that 'it is hard to imagine a 9 months course being properly administered without a proper administration element'.[65]

The provision, or rather the non-provision of transport, while not the direct responsibility of the school, presented one of the greatest difficulties. On a course on which much of the instruction is terrain-oriented, a guaranteed facility to move out from the school is a *sine qua non* for effective instruction. Crowe's report to the CMC presents an almost farcical, but sadly accurate, situation where resort to students' and instructors' private transport became necessary. Command post terrain exercises (CPTEs), an important instructional technique in which HQ staffs simulate the operations of a full formation while moving across the exercise area, were particularly badly affected. Crowe reported that:

> The supply of transport for outdoor CPTEs has been so difficult in latter years that we are inhibited from producing more CPTEs, however desirable such exercises may be. During the two CPTEs organised for the 31st Course many student officers were obliged to use their private cars as reconnaissance and HQ vehicles and to carry radios and radio operators.[66]

It was at the very least unedifying that the senior instructional establishment in the Defence Forces should have had to resort to such contingencies.

The perceived linkage between the command and staff course and promotion continued to cause difficulties. As successful completion of the course was deemed necessary for promotion to the rank of lieutenant colonel, most officers felt it incumbent on them to attend the course. At the beginning of the 1970s, officers attended the course with limited possibility for further promotion, while towards the end of the decade officers who completed the course could have to wait fifteen years before promotion to lieutenant colonel. A more discriminating system for student selection was needed. The course syllabus continued to emphasise conventional operations against an invading force, although both staff and students realised the unlikelihood of such an event. Qualified suspension of belief was required on both sides. Increasing attention was paid to the internal security role of the Defence Forces with students required to address the senior planning functions of this now predominant role. Modern management techniques began to appear on the syllabus, influenced by officers returning from Fort Leavenworth, with most of the emphasis given to the perceived dichotomy between leadership and management. There was an increasing if gradual realisation in the Command and Staff School that the focus on instruction on conventional warfare was more a means than an end in the training and education of senior officers.

Conclusion

During the 1970s, the chiefs of staff recognised a need for reflection on officer education in the Defence Forces and convened two boards to do so. The first board in 1972 saw a need for change that proved to be too radical, while the 1976 board effectively restored the status quo of the traditional system. This status quo gave limited recognition to the main function and activity of the Defence Forces during the 1970s – aid to the civil power. The 1976 Board cannot be solely faulted for this as the general staff, without any contrary direction from government, was required to see defence against external aggression as the primary role of the Defence Forces. Consequently, less instruction on ATCP than on conventional warfare was to be found in Military College syllabi. ATCP had a wider impact on the activities of the College because of the increased numbers of cadets trained in the Cadet School consequent on the expansion of the army.

It can and has been argued that conventional war training, which is aimed at qualifying officers to lead and command, and to function as staff officers, also trains them to conduct ATCP operations. While there is validity in the argument, the College could have adapted earlier and recognised the need to align its teaching more to the reality of current Defence Forces roles and private official understanding of those roles. Dropping conventional war instruction would not have been necessary, but training and education for ATCP operations could have been given more attention in the 1970s, thereby preparing students more for their day-to-day activities. This option could also have lessened a perceived impression of the 'otherness' of the Military College. That this would have been well within its capabilities is clearly illustrated by the fact that it was largely former Military College DS who formulated and developed the hugely important and influential CO (current operations) documents that defined and regulated how the Defence Forces conducted their ATCP operations.

The same argument – conventional training fitting all – is advanced for another defining mission in the history of the Defence Forces, which occurred towards the end of the 1970s – the deployment of an infantry battalion as part of the United Nations interim force in Lebanon (UNIFIL) in 1978. It is not hyperbolic to consider this deployment as a defining moment for the Defence Forces. They were committed to this mission for a continuous period of twenty-three years, suffering forty-seven fatal casualties during this time. As with ATCP operations, the Military College, while introducing some instruction on UN missions, relied on its traditional concepts of education and training. Except insofar as leadership and tactical awareness are concerned, operations conducted in UNIFIL bore little resemblance to the conventional war operations taught at the College. Much demand was placed on privates, NCOs and junior officers being able to handle dangerous situations with tact, courage and situational awareness rather than with the application of fire. The College could have done more to include this changed operational environment on its courses. Nevertheless, as in the Congo, training in conventional warfare proved its worth when A Company of the 46th Infantry Battalion, commanded by Comdt Dave Taylor, later Brig. Gen. and GOC Southern Command, mounted a successful, conventional company-in-attack in At Tiri, South Lebanon.

A decisive change did occur in cadet and officer education in 1969. While USAC eventually administered it, the Cadet School of the Military College was originally responsible for the third-level education scheme. This scheme eventually provided a generation of officers who would oversee a renaissance not only of the College but also of the wider Defence Forces.

8

The 1980s

Anticipating Change

While the College maintained its traditional instructional focus in the 1970s, towards the end of the decade the Defence Forces underwent a major reorganisation. The military authorities accepted that the 1959 'amalgamation' had not been a success, and requested approval from government in 1975 to separate the Permanent Defence Force (PDF) from the FCA. If approved, the PDF would be 'organised with four highly mobilised infantry brigades with some extra operational administrative repair elements and support personnel' and the FCA would 'be limited to local defence in an infantry role'.[1] The government, which was probably concerned with a negative reaction from the FCA, did not immediately grant approval. The proposal was resubmitted in 1977 with the recognition that 'Care will have to be taken to ensure that, organisationally and with particular reference to officer appointments, the F.C.A. (a volunteer force) is not down-graded in the eyes of the members and the public'.[2] The government finally approved the proposed reorganisation on 29 June 1979.[3]

The relevance of this decision for the Military College lay in the fact that in addition to the four highly mobile brigades, whose mobility would, unfortunately, remain aspirational, the reorganisation provided for a 'Field Force drawn exclusively from the Permanent Defence Forces of four Brigades and an Eastern Command Infantry Force'.[4] This latter force, which came to be known by its acronym ECIF, was commanded by a colonel and had a headquarters staff based in Gormanston Aerodrome. ECIF had operational control over the two Eastern Command Infantry Battalions based on the border, the 27th in Dundalk and the 29th in Monaghan. The changed structure meant that the College could continue to instruct above the level of the brigade by employing the field force as a controlling tactical headquarters. The earlier chief of staff's directive limiting instruction to brigade-level formations need not now be adhered to, not that the College ever showed much enthusiasm for it. A later aspect of this reorganisation saw the raising of command OCs and the CMC College to the rank of brigadier general. Raising the rank of the CMC was to be of some importance to the College, insofar as it retained parity of rank between the now GOCs and the CMC, even though the GOCs had greater command and administrative responsibilities. The CMC did, however, have to face evolving responsibilities particular to his appoint-ment: proposals to redesign the College, the training and education of female cadets and officers, effective utilisation of the policy of sending officers to attend foreign staff courses and initial cooperation with the National Council for Education Awards (NCEA). Each of these issues will be dealt with in this chapter in addition to activities at the schools.

Redesigning the Military College

The previous chapter explored a decade of board reports into the working of the Military College. This chapter will also deal with reports, not as many as in the previous chapter, but with one potentially more far-reaching when considered in the light of other structural changes externally imposed on the Defence Forces. During this period, the Defence Forces were occupied with continuing ATCP operations, the training and six-monthly rotation of infantry battalions to UNIFIL and the considerable administrative demands of securing and maintaining up to thirty separate posts and barracks. As seen earlier, this more than occupied its decreasing strength, which remained under critical scrutiny by the Department of Finance. Although the 1976 board had stabilised the course structure within the schools of the Military College, the provision of these courses was made more difficult by the large intake of cadets during the previous decade. This large cohort of now-commissioned junior officers had widened the bottom of the inherently pyramidal shape of the officer corps and had created a requirement for courses without which these young officers could not effectively progress in their chosen career. In 1975, there were 520 officers who had yet to complete the standard infantry course, the academic qualification for the rank of commandant, and the director of training estimated that it could take twenty years at the existing tempo of courses to cater for all these officers. Also, the average age of officers attending this course, which the 1976 board had recommended should be 28, was then 30 and rising.[5] It followed naturally that the same difficulties would eventually arise for the command and staff course.

Such difficulties were not confined to the education and training of officers. The operational experiences of ATCP duties and most especially operations in UNIFIL had highlighted how the success of these operations often depended, particularly in the early, critical phases of conflict prevention, on the ability and efficiency of NCOs and in many cases on private soldiers. It was imperative therefore that NCO training should not only be raised to a higher level, but also be integrated with the training of junior officers. This concept was not, of course, new. Many Irish officers who had attended courses at the British Army School of Infantry had trained in this way. The concept had also been advocated for the army by Col Eóghan Ó Néill, at least as early as 1965. Ó Néill had then written that:

> The Infantry School is where the majority of officers undergo their minor tactical training and their weapons training. These are two important subjects in the NCO Course and it is important that the system taught should be the same. Indeed, a basic wing of the Infantry School might well undertake the tactical and weapon training Courses for junior officers and Senior NCOs.[6]

It would be some years before such an eminently sensible proposal was adopted. In the case of weapon training, it would require the catalyst of a tragic mortar training accident in 1977, in which five soldiers of the 4th Infantry Battalion lost their lives, to promote the cause of a dedicated infantry weapons school for officers and NCOs.

The military authorities were neither unaware of, nor were they ignoring these problems. In 1978, the then Director of Training Col P.J. Barry asked the officer commanding the Curragh Command and the CMC to examine proposals to establish a weapons wing at the Infantry School, and also to move the Senior NCO School from the General Training Depot (GTD) to the Infantry School.[7] It is to his credit that a short five years after a major report on the

Military College, P.J. Barry's successor as director of training, Col Brendan Cassidy, instructed a study group to examine the structure and organisation of not only the Military College but also of the GTD. The GTD conducted NCO courses and had in the past conducted centralised recruit training for the PDF. This recruit-training function had been transferred to the commands during the 1970s, leaving the GTD with responsibility for NCO training and some weapons training. Also, the training ethos of the Curragh had been somewhat diminished when the Curragh Training Camp had been organised into an operational command. A new infantry battalion, the 30th, was established in Kilkenny and the Curragh Command assumed increasing ATCP responsibilities, most notably the securing of Portlaoise Prison.

The director of training's study group was a close-knit group composed of Lt Col Frank Stewart of the director's staff, Comdt Michael Mullooly of the Military College and Comdt Seán Burke of the GTD. They submitted a concise report on 10 November 1981 and outlined the problems facing both institutions as follows:

> The immediate necessity to devise structures which can cater for the large influx of officers into the Permanent Defence Force (PDF) in the last 10 years during which time the officer strength increased by 33%.
>
> The necessity to rectify a perceived deterioration in the overall efficiency and authority of NCOs, at a time when most small unit operations, both at home and abroad, are commanded by NCOs.
>
> A near complete lack of weapons expertise and a shortage of NCO and Officer weapons instructors in the Infantry Corps.[8]

The authors underlined the gravity of the last of these three problems by referring to 'the necessity to appoint an Arty Officer to take charge of the last 81mm Mortar Course run in the Infantry School'.[9] Their report led the Chief of Staff Lt Gen. Louis Hogan to convene a further study group on 23 June 1982 to report in greater depth on a redesign of the Military College. The retention of the study group format was a change from previous practice insofar as it differed from the more formal convening of a board of officers, with the intention, presumably, of accelerating the process. Col Charles McGuinn, a member of the 1972 board on the Military College, originally chaired the study group. Shortly afterwards Lt Col Frank Stewart became chairman. The study group was instructed to submit its report to the chief of staff within three months, and its deliberations would eventually lead to the first major institutional changes to the Military College since its establishment in 1930.

Redesigning the Military College, in the way and for the reasons advanced by Lt Col Stewarts' study group, would prove to be a difficult and very lengthy process. Resource limitations quickly confronted utilitarian objectives, which were also attenuated by the inherent weaknesses of the 1930s compromise structure of the College. This compromise structure, as has frequently been alluded to, attempted to accommodate disparate educational and training requirements in one institution. In the institution, 18-year-old civilians were trained as 2nd Lieutenants. Infantry officers learned their trade. Middle-ranking officers were educated in higher-staff work and command, and senior officers were to be given some awareness of the function of the Defence Forces in wider national and international affairs. While two of the problems considered by the group – inadequacies of NCO and weapons training – had not been considered by previous investigations, the third – the College's difficulties in dealing with increased student numbers – had been faced in the past. The proposed redesign now being envisaged would introduce into the Military College common tactical and weapons training for junior officers and NCOs. This development was not universally welcomed. A small number of officers thought that the Military College's academic aspirations and limited resources in staff and facilities should not be diluted by the introduction of weapons and NCO training. Their intentions had some merit insofar as they considered that a combination of both officer and NCO training, without the necessarily increased resources, could dilute career-officer education. In the event, resource provision would prove to be a major factor in delaying the implementation of the proposed redesign. Those opposing the scheme were, however, a minority, and most officers, including the CMC, and subsequent chiefs of staff recognised the validity of the arguments put forward by the study group. The actual make-up of the redesigned Military College will be covered in the following chapter, as it was not achieved until 1993. In the meantime, concern still existed for the inadequacies of infantry weapons training. The chief of staff, Lt Gen. Louis Hogan, directed on 15 December 1981 that 'a Weapons Wing be set up in the GTD'.[10] The wing was renamed the Infantry Weapons School in March 1982 and was initially commanded by Comdt Desmond Travers, a future CMC.

Attendance at Foreign Military Academies

One of the mainstays of officer education was and is the regular attendance by Irish officers at foreign military academies. It has been seen that the dispatch of the military mission to the United States in 1926 had a seminal influence on the organisation of the Defence Forces and the Military College. This chapter, considering developments some fifty years after the foundation of the Military College, is an appropriate point to examine the development and operation of this practice. While there have been previous references to the attendance by Irish officers at foreign courses, what is intended here is an examination of attendances at foreign-command and staff-level institutions. There is no intended or implied downgrading of the importance of attendance at other lower-level schools. These courses constitute an essential function in keeping abreast with developments at the tactical and technical level of military training, be it in infantry tactics and weaponry, or in the specialised functions of other corps such as artillery or ordnance to mention just two. Non-attendance at foreign courses at this level would have seen the Defence Forces retreat to the earlier situation of near professional ineptitude. The demand for foreign courses of this kind became acute before and during the Second World War and was supplied by the British Army. Command and Staff schools, on the other hand, aim to educate officers in the techniques and procedures of employing all-arms formations. They also educate officers in doctrinal changes occasioned by strategic choices and imperatives, and on the role of military forces in wider society. By the 1980s, the original choice of the Command and General Staff College at Fort Leavenworth had been widened to include the Command and Staff School at Camberley UK, École Supérieure de Guerre in Paris, and Führungsakademie der Bundeswehr, Hamburg. During the period covered by this work, and beginning with the 1926 mission, forty-seven officers attended command and staff courses at foreign military institutions. This attendance was less than one officer per year and less than 0.5 per cent of the officers commissioned during the period.

The motivation for the 1926 mission was a realisation and awareness that the embryo Defence Forces born in revolution and civil war had extremely limited knowledge and experience of the actuality of a conventional army under civilian control. The year-long mission to the United States successfully laid the foundations for such an Irish Army and established the precedence for seeking individual education and experience for selected officers, and external knowledge of military affairs from foreign sources. It has been seen, in Chapter 2, how on his return from the United States Maj. Gen. Hugo MacNeill stressed that its army and systems could not provide the only model for the Irish Army. The need to examine other systems was re-emphasised by the visits of MacNeill and other senior officers to British Army educational institutions in 1928. The 1928 visit to the British Army did not, however, immediately result in Irish officers attending at the British command and staff course at Camberley. On the contrary, it was followed soon afterwards by high-level political discussions between, on the one hand, the British service chiefs, and on the other hand the Dominions Office, mediated by the Cabinet Secretary Sir Maurice Hankey and the Prime Minister Ramsay McDonald.

These discussions were occasioned by a request from the high commissioner of the Irish Free State for the dates of a number of Royal Air Force (RAF) courses, including the dates of the staff course at the RAF College Andover.[11] It was quickly recognised by the UK authorities that this was a matter that would eventually concern all the armed services, and Marshall of the Air Force Sir Hugh Trenchard suggested to the Cabinet Secretary Sir Maurice Hankey that the question of Irish Free State officers attending staff courses should be considered by all the chiefs of staff. Trenchard was not new to military policy decisions concerning Ireland. He had been a member of the British delegation to the Defence Committee of the Treaty negotiations in Admiralty House that faced the Irish delegation of Michael Collins, J.J. O'Connell, Diarmuid O'Hegarty and Emmet Dalton.[12]

His recommendation was quickly acted upon and the chiefs of staff came down very firmly against Irish officers attending staff courses. They had three main objections, the first of which, that Ireland was not a dominion like the other dominions, was based on a speech by the Minister for Justice Kevin O'Higgins at the 1926 Imperial Conference, in which he expressed the independence of Ireland's defence policy.[13] Secondly, they foresaw the possibility that Irish officers who might attend a staff course would have participated in the War of Independence and would find themselves alongside British students 'who were actually engaged in this bitter conflict or who have actually suffered bereavement or loss of property from the unhappy events that preceded the settlement of 1921'.[14] If this were to happen, the chiefs of staff feared 'that the intermingling of Irish Free State officers with the other students at the higher educational establishments will almost certainly tend to check rather than to advance the healing of wounds for which the passage of time can be the only remedy'.[15] Finally, the service chiefs noted that students attending the staff colleges had progressed through various stages of their careers gaining much experience along the way, whereas:

> The officers of the Irish Free State Army have not yet had these opportunities: they were created as it were, *ad hoc*, and it would hardly be fair to thrust them into schools of advanced learning for which they would pay proportionately large sums and in which they would be inevitably out of their depth.[16]

Condescension and financial concerns aside, there was some military justification in these objections. These were not, however, reciprocated by the Dominions Office, which favoured a more conciliatory approach to the request from the Irish Free State, and which asked in a draft memorandum, 'what is to be the basis of our policy with regard to that Dominion? Is it to be one of trust or not'.[17] They favoured a compromise proposal whereby, 'only Officers should be admitted to our senior training establishments who were not actively identified with the recent troubles'.[18] While being conciliatory, the Dominions Office was also clear that any attendance by Irish officers at senior courses, 'is with a view to the gradual development of cooperation between the United Kingdom and Irish Free State forces on the same lines as that between the United Kingdom and other Dominion forces'.[19] Maurice Hankey, who substantially supported the stance of the chiefs of staff, arranged with the approval of the prime minister a meeting between the Secretary of State for Dominion Affairs Lord Passfield and the chiefs of staff. The report of that meeting, while restating the views of both sides, also affirmed that the secretary of state agreed to secure from the Irish Free State an understanding that when Irish officers were admitted to senior courses, they would not be actively identified with the recent troubles and would do so on the same terms and conditions as other Dominions officers.[20] Such conditions appear almost unthinkable today, but a measure of how important cooperation was viewed by the Irish defence authorities can be gauged by remarks made by Lt Gen. Peadar McMahon, secretary of the Department of Defence and former chief of staff, during a meeting which he shortly after requested with Sir Maurice Hankey. In his report of the meeting, Hankey informed the prime minister that, after frankly outlining the background to the issue, 'General McMahon took this in very good part and did not dissent from anything I had said, and remarked that at the present time there was no intention of applying for these Higher Courses. At the same time he did evince a considerable desire for cooperation.'[21] Both sides held to their positions: Ireland did not request attendance at Camberley until 1938, and the UK did not accede to the request until after the end of the Second World War.

Nonetheless, increasing international tensions highlighted the need for further Irish officers to be trained at foreign staff colleges, and Fort Leavenworth saw the return of Irish officers in 1939. The intention of broadening foreign educational experience beyond the UK and the USA continued and was restated and re-articulated in a case presented by the general staff in 1938, just a year before the outbreak of the Second World War, when it was proposed that two Irish officers should attend a course at École de Guerre, Paris. This proposal came fifteen years after the visit by the Chief of Staff General Seán McMahon to the French Army in 1923. We have seen how Gen. McMahon was impressed by the manner in which the French military authorities realised 'the great necessity for training officers in order that they will not only know how to handle their men but also that they may be able to use judgement and discretion when opposed by difficulties in the field'.[22] Difficulties in the field had become an increasingly likely eventuality in 1938, but the choice of France proved contentious. In his case to the minister for finance, the minister for defence, Frank Aiken, supporting the military proposal stressed that 'the necessity for keeping abreast with modern military theory and practice, particularly with reference to the effect thereon of the introduction of new weapons and methods, means that reliance cannot solely be placed on the military doctrine of any particular nation'.[23] This view was not appreciated by Walter Doolin of the Department of Finance, who presented an opposing view based not solely on the financial aspects of the case, but on an argued view that 'it looks as if, that in any international flare-up to be anticipated in the immediate future, our pressing problem will be to fit our special Defence plans with the scheme adopted by the British to provide for their own security'.[24] Also Doolin insisted that apart from the risk of not fully assimilating information in French, 'French aims and methods which will be mainly based on their peculiar land-frontier and Mediterranean-Colonial problems are to us of far less immediate consequences'.[25] Nor were financial considerations ignored by Doolin, who maintained:

that as the bulk of our Rearmament equipment will come from British sources it is essential that our understanding of the application and most effective employment of all this costly equipment should be studied by the best qualified officers in the countries best qualified to give instruction without any loss of time.[26]

Somewhat surprisingly, Seán McEntee did not agree with his departmental official on the grounds that 'we have so much lee way to make up',[27] and sanction was given for two officers to attend the War College and to be attached to French Army units for a period before reporting on the course. In the event, the French authorities could only provide a place for one officer, and Comdt Denis Lawlor – who as we have seen was later to engage in spirited discussions with Col Dan Bryan – departed for France in June 1939. Comdt Lawlor had previously been 'in Paris in 1934 as a civilian to study the language'.[28] He was attached to various French units but did not attend the staff course as he was obliged by the outbreak of war to return to Ireland on 4 September. A further thirty-eight years would elapse before the first Irish officer, Comdt Michael Mullooly, finally attended the École Supérieure de Guerre Interarmée in Paris in 1977.

These tentative early steps at the accessing of diverse foreign command and staff courses settled eventually into a pattern of almost yearly attendance at Camberley or Fort Leavenworth, with diversity provided by courses in Hamburg and Paris. Pre-war attendance at Fort Leavenworth was followed by a prolonged hiatus between 1939 and 1962. This hiatus was filled by regular post-war attendance at Camberley. Arrangements were in place for participation at Camberley in 1940 and 1941. Financial approval had been granted for attendance at the course but, 'owing to the short notice received by the Officers who will undergo the 1940 Course, the British War Office agreed to waive the entrance examination in their case'.[29] This generous approach by the War Office, which seems to have overridden the earlier objections of the UK chiefs of staff, did not, however, survive the outbreak of the war, and the first two students, Lt Col P.J. Hally and Comdt J.J.G. MacCarthy, did not report to Camberley until 1946. Even then it was a concession which Col J.J. Flynn maintained was facilitated by a meeting between the Chief of Staff Gen. Dan McKenna and Maj. Gen. Freddie de Guignand, Field Marshall Bernard Montgomery's chief of staff. The meeting occurred during a visit de Guignand made to Ireland after the North African campaign with Gen. Bucknall, commander of British troops in Northern Ireland. According to Flynn, Bucknall prompted de Guignand to secure extra training resources from the British Army and:

> Amongst the facilities offered were vacancies on certain courses for Senior Officers and in particular one vacancy each year on the Staff Course at Camberley. (This one had been consistently withheld up to this time.) Quite a good will gesture!'[30]

It is not recorded whether or not de Guignand had consulted with the earlier fiercely opposed Montgomery.

During these early years, the practice was to send two officers together to Camberley, a practice which naturally benefited the individual officers but also facilitated a systematic assimilation of instruction and information for future application on return. Comprehensive course reports were submitted by the students on their return: these detailed not only the instruction provided and exercises completed, but also in-depth information on the host nation's forces, capabilities and operating procedures. In the absence of defence attachés, these were the only in-depth first-hand reports, apart from reports from short visits available to the Irish military authorities on rapid developments in technological change and their effects on tactics and strategy. As it was standard procedure for returning students to be posted as instructors to the Command and Staff School at the Military College, the individual education of the school's directing staff was continually improved. In subsequent years, it became the norm that one officer only attended at a time, a practice that was also followed when students attended courses at the non-English speaking institutions, although in these cases a shortage of language-qualified officers was a determining factor.

The earlier reluctance of the British military authorities to accept Irish officers at Camberley found an echo in a less-than-welcoming attitude to such attendance by the Department of Foreign Affairs. The department was unhappy for political reasons with the attendance of Irish military personnel on British military courses. It was a long-standing situation and, according to one official, 'There are even references which indicate that our difficulties with the Department of Defence regarding the political monitoring of that Department's direct contact with the London Embassy go back as far as 1927/28'.[31] The official clearly stated that his department 'has consistently been suspicious of the political implications of such attendances'.[32] That suspicion was exacerbated by the difficult relations between Ireland and Great Britain caused by British Army actions in Northern Ireland during the 1970s. In 1972, before proceeding with arrangements for courses and visits to UK military establishments, the Department of Defence asked Foreign Affairs 'for an indication as to whether you see any objection, in the present situation, to our going ahead with arrangements of this nature'. Defence added that 'the military authorities find these courses and visits most valuable and they would not wish to see them discontinued'.[33] A draft reply from Foreign Affairs stated that 'It seems to us that in present circumstances it would be best not to proceed for the time being at least with any arrangements of this kind'.[34] In spite of this negative response from Foreign Affairs, attendance at British military courses continued, and probably contributed to a decision by it not to authorise attendance by an official from the Irish Embassy in London at a closing-course dinner at Camberley in 1973. This decision resulted in correspondence between both departments and in an internal review of the Foreign Affairs position. This review concluded inter alia that 'The Department of Defence and the Defence Forces did not seem to appreciate fully the political implications of the attendance of Army officers at British Army Training Courses …'[35] Later invitations to the Camberley course dinner were accepted by the London Embassy and attendance at British military courses has continued.

A re-affirmation of the need and value of these courses had been provided in a 1964 board report chaired by the then commandant of the command and staff school, Col Eóghan Ó Néill. According to him, the overriding consideration was that the Defence Forces keep 'in touch with the most recent developments in military doctrine, equipment, tactics, methods and organisation'.[36] It was not just, however, a question of 'keeping in touch', but more importantly that the Defence Forces 'should profit from the experiences of other armies, without the necessity of making or enduring the difficulties they had to endure in order to acquire that experience'.[37] The board accepted that the best and most economical method was for returning graduates to be appointed as instructors in the Military College, and after three to five years there to be posted to Defence Forces Headquarters. This would ensure that:

> Our forces, if called upon to engage in active service, either in defence of country, or in an international force, are equipped with the knowledge and leadership required to perform their tasks with the lowest cost in men or material.[38]

This concern for cost effectiveness was not generally appreciated by the Department of Defence, and while the individual professional experiences of students on foreign command and staff courses was almost invariably positive, administrative arrangements often left much to be desired. In spite of the relative frequency of the courses, in many cases it proved impossible for the military authorities to agree with their Department of Defence interlocutors an acceptable, available norm for the financial arrangements applicable to these courses, in line for example with civil servants or diplomats on equivalent-length secondment. The length of the courses, and host-nation expectations that students and their spouses and families would, where applicable, participate in non-curricular and national-representative course activities, created many difficulties both financial and social. Students almost always departed without knowing the 'financial package' that would apply during their time abroad, which lead to much stress and personal financial loss that continued on their return from the course, and unwelcome and unwarranted distraction from the *raison d'être* of their time abroad: study. That this was not necessary was highlighted later by one student who reported on his return that discussions before his departure with Department of Defence officials and the director of training succeeded in agreement on 'a satisfactory arrangement'.[39] This was not a common occurrence, however, and an earlier student, Comdt J.P. Duggan, who attended the German Army command and staff course in Hamburg in 1969, described this distraction of long-distance financial haggling as being like 'a part-time amateur wrestling with a wily professional who is only interested in falls rather than fairness'.[40] While Duggan's colourful language somewhat belied the seriousness of the issue, he also states that it is 'time-consuming and an unnecessary worry and distraction for the officer concerned'.[41] His experience was unfortunately not unique and might well have been obviated if the recommendation of an earlier student, Comdt P.A. Maguire, later Brig. Gen. and CMC, had been acted upon. Maguire had attended at Fort Leavenworth in 1963 and had had, in addition to coursework, and in keeping with all other officers on the course, to maintain a high level of national representation among the international body of students. On his return, he recommended that:

> Until a more realistic attitude is adopted towards the question of allowances, family travel, entertainment, etc., no further officer should be sent to the US Army Command and General Staff School. Human nature being what it is, candidates will be seduced by the prospects of such a course, without fully appraising the financial implications of it, until it is too late.[42]

The recommendation was not acted upon, unfortunately for individual officers, as it could have led to a rationalising of an unacceptable situation, but perhaps fortunately for the Defence Forces because professional Irish officers continued to be seduced by the possibility of furthering their military knowledge and of their future usefulness to the Defence Forces and to the State.

The most important aspect of attendance at foreign command and staff courses was and is, of course, its benefit to the Defence Forces. Students on return from the courses were usually posted to the Command and Staff School, if indeed they had not been posted there before departure on the course. Their insertion or reinsertion was not always managed as efficiently as possible. Two radically different approaches were applied at different times by different College authorities. One approach, the most sensible and cost-effective, was the immediate appointment of the returnee to the DS staff. The other approach was one motivated by a misguided belief that the returnee should readjust to the realities of Defence Forces life by also performing an administrative College function. This approach, often influenced by the views of more senior instructors who may not have attended a foreign staff course, occurred infrequently but frequently enough to engender a sense of frustration in some. Occasional re-insertion difficulties notwithstanding, foreign-trained officers were vital to effective instruction in the Command and Staff School. Personal confidence, allied to up-to-date military knowledge, made it possible for them to influence the structure and content of courses and at times widen Defence Forces thinking. In its earlier application, returning officers were required to brief not only the College authorities but also the highest levels of the military hierarchy. Brig. Gen. John O'Shea, a future CMC, remembers one of his predecessors, Col Tom Feely, being particularly diligent in this matter and recalls, at least, two three-day seminars attended by the chief of staff, general staff and command OCs at which officers returned from foreign courses gave lectures in modern developments.[43]

A seamless and guaranteed outcome was not, however, assured. The major obstacles were the influential opinions of senior DS, often themselves foreign-educated, and conflicting views between principally the UK- and the USA-educated officers. It is easy to imagine how differences could arise given the disparity in size and roles of the two armies. Examples at the tactical level could, for instance, be given in defensive operations. Here the British Army favoured reverse-slope defence, much practised by Wellington, while the Americans in the 1980s favoured the concept of active defence. A concept that demanded 'little by way of depth or reserves and depends on the lateral move-ment of front line units to meet enemy main attacks'.[44] Likewise, in offensive operations, the American Army favoured mechanised and heavy divisions, formations that were limited in the British Army. Another area of debate concerned the adoption of either the British problem-solving technique, the appreciation of the situation, or the American equivalent, the estimate of the situation. This seemingly arcane debate could then be enlivened by a French-influenced officer extolling the benefits of *la méthode de raisonnement tactique*, which referenced René Descartes, the originator of all three systems. It was not in fact an arcane debate as the technique was the foundation of the ability to solve tactical and operational problems for both a forma-tion commander and his staff, the essence of the command and staff course. The ebb and flow of this internal debate often depended on the numerical dominance of UK or USA graduates on the staff of the school at any given time. While these were essentially internal and intellectually beneficial debates among staff, they inevitably at times impacted on students. Some students, not having the benefit of the experiences of their foreign-trained instructors, sometimes found it difficult to engage critically in instruction either tactical or conceptual. Some of these difficulties could have been obviated, if the Irish Defence Forces had had a considered, formulated and disseminated operational doctrine, an essential to which foreign-trained officers eventually greatly contributed. Consideration of this issue, important for all schools of the Military College, will be discussed in the following chapter on the 1990s, by which time the input of foreign graduates into military doctrine had become more apparent and dominant.

Doctrinal matters apart, the cost effectiveness of the policy on attending foreign command staff schools, as enunciated by Ó Néill in 1964, has been to date fully realised. The content and conduct of courses in all the constitu-ent schools of the Military College has been enhanced by foreign-educated command and staff graduates and indeed by their home-educated colleagues. One important feature has been the success in maintaining instruction on the command and staff course at a level above that of the brigade, albeit at times against well-meaning opposition. Pre-Emergency critics, with a back-ward longing for guerrilla warfare, were proven wrong when a two-division army was commanded and staffed on principles and techniques learned at Fort Leavenworth. Officers on overseas deployment function effectively in large formations due in no small measure to the education received on the command and staff course, where they are required to appreciate the role of formations above brigade level. Five Irish UN force commanders, one EU operational commander, two EU force commanders and numerous senior staff officers have served in such headquarters. The recent detachment of senior Defence Forces officers to the European Union military staff, the Western European Union, and to NATO Headquarters has also been facilitated by their attendance at command and staff courses. Not only was the influence of foreign-educated command-and-staff graduates instrumental in ensuring this Irish expertise for overseas missions, but eight chiefs of staff of the Defence Forces have themselves been graduates of foreign command and staff courses, amply fulfilling the view of the 1964 board that 'officers destined for the most important appointments in the Defence Forces have the opportunity of gaining the widest qualifications available'.[45]

Education and Training for Female Officers

Attendance by Irish officers at the US command and general staff course at Fort Leavenworth in 1926, four years before the establishment of the Military College, proved vital to its development. The arrival of female cadets and officers to the College in the 1980s would eventually prove to be one of the factors, along with third-level education of officers, that brought the College in line with developments in modern Ireland. Their arrival came about by the signing into law by the President of Ireland, Dr Patrick Hillery, on 6 November 1979 of the Defence (Amendment) (No. 2) Act, 1979. The act provided for the enlistment of women and the appointment of women as officers of the Defence Forces. It was largely a politically influenced decision, which provided for the law's enactment following the 1977 General Election manifesto of the Fianna Fáil Party. Following the success of Fianna Fáil at that election, a memorandum for government proposed that:

> Members of the Women's Service Corps would normally be employed in suitable existing appointments by means of attachment to other corps and units. They would, however, be non-combatant and would not be employed on duties of a security or operational nature under arms.[46]

The intention was to recruit two experienced officers and then to select a small initial group as potential officers, and that 'following a short preliminary course at the Military College, the first intake of potential officers will be sent abroad for training'.[47] Suitable candidates were not found for the two initial appointments, and while the first two intakes of potential female officers did attend courses conducted by the British Army, the concept of a separate Women's Corps did not last for long. The Military College was soon in the front line of developments that would eventually see women playing an equal role with their male colleagues in training and in operations. It would be an uneven process with many of the critical steps played out in the College.

Much deliberation took place between the General Election and the signing of the 1979 Act. The outline of the initial training requirements was agreed at a conference convened by the chief of staff, Lt Gen. Carl O'Sullivan, on 20 January 1978. It was decided:

> That a group of ten potential officers – young women of high character and Leaving Cert Education or higher – be sent to WRAC [Women's Royal Army Corps of the British Army] Officers Training College on a 5 months course early this year. On successful completion of that course they should then be commissioned as 2/Lts and after a further 2 months course in the Military College they would assume their appointments. A second group of ten potential officers do [*sic*] a similar course in Britain at the end of this year.[48]

Changes were, however, made to these decisions before the bill was enacted, and at a meeting chaired by the Minister for Defence Bobby Molloy, it was 'decided that candidates for the first 4 cadetships should hold a university degree or an equivalent qualification and should be under 25 years of age'.[49] This decision was sensible as it avoided possible complications with the existing USAC scheme and it was also intended that future intakes of male and female cadets should have identical enlistment conditions. While this did not in effect happen for the next intake of female cadets, it did not cause as much difficulty as did the implementation of a second ministerial decision that 'women (both cadets and recruits) should, as far as practicable, undergo the same courses of training as men'.[50] The minutes of the meeting record that the director of training, Col John F. Gallagher, 'had some misgivings about this but he will examine course syllabi to determine if any changes are necessary to take account of the physical qualities of women'.[51] While the minister said he was prepared to reconsider his decision, this was an issue that would continue to cause difficulties. The main difficulty facing the director of training was that the cadet course had the aim of training future officers to lead a platoon in battle whereas female officers were to be non-combatant.

Planning proceeded on the basis of the establishment of a separate Women's Service Corps (WSC), despite opposition expressed by the Tánaiste and Minister for Finance George Colley, who explained that:

> In our pre-election Manifesto we undertook to set up such a corps. I suggest however, that the motivation behind the undertaking was to give women a place in the Defence Forces other than in the Army Nursing Service, and that the establishment of a women's corps is merely an illustration of how this might be done.[52]

Colley considered the Department of Defence and military proposals not to be cost-effective and also too segregationist and protective of male appointments. While he also noted the fact that Ban Gardaí trained and carried out duties with their male counterparts, he subsequently withdrew his letter. His view was, however, to prevail, and on 29 October 1981, the Department of Finance sanctioned a decision taken at a meeting chaired by the chief of staff on 5 March 1981. The Adjutant General Maj. Gen. William Prendergast proposed that 'the nomenclature WSC had been useful long enough and that from here on would be referred to as women personnel of the P.D.F. [Permanent Defence Force]'.[53] Females would thus occupy existing appointments in the Defence Forces albeit still for some time to come on a non-combatant basis.

The first four females enlisted in the Defence Forces in March 1980. They attended a short course at the Military College and then proceeded on a British Army course for female officers at Sandhurst, receiving a total of one year's training. They were followed by a second group of four in September 1980, who completed the same training. While still members of the original WSC and restricted to non-combatant roles, no duties of a security or operational nature, and no night duties, they were still required to be trained and to be qualified for the use of small arms. One of the first group, Capt. Collette Harrison, remarked favourably on this aspect of their training, 'as women in the British Army didn't receive any weapons training at all'.[54] These eight cadets were commissioned as 2nd Lieutenants in April 1981 with the Military College given the responsibility of recommending seniority.[55] The next intake was of three cadets in November 1980. They joined the 57th cadet class, where they 'Completed a one and a half year Cadet Course which was fully integrated with male Cadet Training'.[56] The pattern for future intakes of female cadets was now set, but a handwritten question mark on the quoted annex opposite the November 1980 intake queried the full integration of members of these early intakes.

The fact that some did not have similar physical capabilities as some of their male counterparts, and were consequently not required to do all demanded of the male cadets, caused some integration difficulties. Other aspects of the training also caused disquiet among the female cadets. Lt Col Maureen O'Brien, who has commanded the 27th Infantry Battalion in Dundalk, recalled how although having completed 'platoon in attack' tests they were not credited with them in their overall results, which affected their class placing and eventual seniority. The inclusion of tactical training in the Cadet School for females was erratic, and some ad hoc courses were later completed in the Infantry School to cater for those who had not done tactical training. Nor were they all trained with light infantry weapons.[57] Training on these weapons was included for some female cadets and not for others, depending on the cadet class they joined. These inconsistencies indicated what O'Brien acknowledges was an exploratory or 'finding their way' approach by the College and by the military authorities. The conflicting requirements of non-combatant status, integrated training and potential access to all officer appointments led to the dropping of a stated aim of the cadet syllabus that 'On completion of the Course the Cadet should be competent to train and lead a Platoon'.[58] This confusion continued into other courses and Maureen O'Brien was to figure later, in the following hurdle to be faced by the College, whether or not to include female officers on the young officers course.

In November 1984, the director of training, Col Frank Kelly, addressed a lengthy memorandum to the chief of staff discussing whether or not female officers should attend the young officers course, which at that time was divided into two parts: 'Part I conducted at the Infantry School was designed to provide the tactical education and training to equip the Officer to act as Platoon Commander and Company 2ic in both the conventional and internal situation.'[59] While Part II was conducted at the School of Administration, the director pointed out that Part I was 'an operational course for junior combat leaders and is understandably physically demanding'.[60] On the understanding that female officers were still non-combatant, and presumably would not be able for the physical nature of the course, he recommended that they should not undergo the young officers course. He accepted that, given that by then most female officers had been trained on an integrated cadet course, this decision could cause a morale problem. Although he proposed that separate courses should be designed for non-combatant female officers, in fairness to Kelly he also recommended that 'the role and future employment of female personnel be examined'.[61]

The chief of staff accepted the director of training's recommendation and decided that female officers would not undergo the young officers course.[62] However, when the director further pointed out that this would mean female officers might not return to the Military College for a considerable time, he decreed that a separate standard course be devised and conducted for female officers. This decision was later rescinded and the young officers course, which was scheduled to be held in March 1986, was cancelled, and a further decision was taken to conduct two distinct yet almost concurrent young officers courses in September 1987. It is clear from such vacillation at the highest military level that the non-combatant yet integrated nature of the service of female officers was causing difficulties for those responsible for training and education. It did not prevent them, however, from drawing up two greatly varying syllabi for the male and female courses. The CMC informed the director of training that, in keeping with the policy of the chief of staff, the female course differed from the male course 'mainly in the reduction of the number of hours allotted to Tactical Operations, All Arms, and Internal Security and a corresponding increase in Command and Staff'.[63] The glaring difference occurred in tactical operations with 128 hours instruction on the male course and seventeen hours on the female course.

It was this discrepancy that prompted Lt O'Brien, then an instructor at the cadet school, to request the director of training that she be permitted to undergo the male and not the female young officers course. She pointed out that she had completed an integrated cadet course, and that she was presently instructing cadets in an integrated course. To fulfil her duties she should 'complete a Young Officers Course which would give me a detailed knowledge of platoon/company tactics, etc., as afforded by previous Young Officers Courses'.[64] She also pointed out that the 'emphasis of the female syllabus is essentially non-tactical. This would mean that my military education would no longer be as "complete" as that of the male members of my class'.[65] These compelling arguments received no support from either the CMC or from the director of training, who continued to maintain that the non-combatant status of female officers did not require them to complete a male young officers course. The adjutant general informed Lt O'Brien that she must complete the 1st female young officers course, which she did with sixteen other fellow female officers.

Since Lt O'Brien seems to have been the only female officer who formally requested permission to undergo the male course, it is not possible to assess how many others supported her stance. The stance, however, of the military authorities was clear: non-combatant status equated with non-tactical training for female officers. It seems as if little had changed in almost ten years after the first intake of female cadets. It was probably the easiest if the least progressive fallback position for an intensely traditional, conservative and paternal organisation to adopt. While separate male young officers courses would continue to be conducted over the next decade, the situation was not as clear-cut as it seemed. Female officers, NCOs and privates had been deployed to UNIFIL since 1982, on duties that, while not strictly combatant, were a long way from the non-night duties and non-security duties that had been prescribed for them. Fortunately, change was on the way. Non-combatant status for females was relinquished in 1992. The Minister for Defence John Wilson informed *The Irish Times* that for all positions in the Defence Forces 'the basis of selection in all of these areas will henceforward be suitability rather than gender'.[66] This change of policy, twelve years after the establishment of the Women's Service Corps, resulted in the conduct of fully integrated training and education for female cadets and officers.

Cooperation with the National Council for Education Awards (NCEA)

As the military authorities sought to adapt their training systems for female officers and cadets, they were also looking to have these same training systems incorporated into the wider national system of education. Their original focus was on training courses for enlisted personnel, i.e. NCOs and privates, with the intention of gaining recognition for such courses in civilian employment. This original intention led to contact with the NCEA, which under the

National Council for Education Awards Act 1979 had responsibility for granting national higher-education awards. The chief of staff, Lt Gen. Carl O'Sullivan, requested the minister for defence in 1984 to forward an application to the minister for education to have the Military College designated as an institution to which the NCEA Act (1979) applied.[67] The chief of staff saw this as a first necessary step that would eventually 'enable the PDF and the NCEA to formally commence the evaluation of all Military courses for all ranks in the PDF'. The military aim was that this evaluation should be 'for the purpose of achieving some form of national recognition'.[68] The focus was clearly on external recognition of military education provided to enlisted personnel, as the USAC scheme was giving officers a nationally recognised third-level award. It was also clearly oriented towards future employment outside of the Defence Forces as articulated in the chief of staff's proposal:

> From the individual's viewpoint such a development would have benefits in the line of professional developments and occupational mobility in that personnel who leave the PDF will have some form of educational qualification which is recognised by outside Academic Authorities.[69]

The chief of staff's initiative eventually led to the validation in 2012 by the Higher Education Training and Awards Council (HETAC), the successor of the NCEA, of Defence Forces enlisted-personnel career courses for awards under the national framework of qualifications. Before this considerable advance was achieved, attention was directed to the Military College and initially to the Cadet School.

The minister having approved the chief of staff's request, a NCEA delegation including its director, Mr Padraig MacDiarmada, visited the Military College on 26 June 1985 to assess whether the College could be designated as an institution under the act – only then could specific courses be assessed. It became apparent to the College authorities at an early stage that such a process would present some difficulties. The visitors' references to external examiners and independent monitoring of student performance prompted a military response that 'the primary function of the Military College was to train/educate cadets/officers in the skills, and to standards, determined by military needs; that this function took precedence over all other considerations'.[70] This was probably not the type of protectiveness that the NCEA delegation were familiar with. Also, the impression they gave was that, if the Military College became a designated institution, it would be through the College that the NCEA would 'exercise educational supervision over all military courses'.[71] This would obviously create difficulties for the chief of staff and the director of training. These difficulties notwithstanding, the Military College was designated as an institution to which the act applied on 8 November 1985, and sought recognition from the NCEA on 8 January 1988 so that those who successfully completed the cadet course, and who were commissioned into the Defence Forces, would be awarded a national diploma in military studies.

The NCEA responded to the College request by appointing boards of assessors in November 1989 and June 1990, who recommended that a special review group composed of three military officers and Professor Denis I.F. Lucey of UCC should be set up to consider outstanding issues. The issues were complex and led the group to acknowledge the NCEA's 'accommodating and reasoned approach in giving recognition to a Course which is academically at variance with much of its standard practice'.[72] Although the Military College was granted a certificate of approval in July 1990, the council's insistence on external examiners, restructuring of the course, regulation of examinations, library facilities and computerisation continued to cause the military authorities some anxiety. A draft briefing from the director of training to the chief of staff noted that the original intention was geared towards courses for enlisted personnel, and the requirements of the NCEA would require investment which the Department of Defence would most likely seek to find from the USAC scheme. There was the risk therefore that 'a project that set out to raise the standards of NCO education, could lower the status of officer education without in any way improving the lot of NCOs'.[73] In spite of the director's misgivings, the opinion of the special review group that 'the understanding and good will that has developed to date will go a long way in finding solutions to the outstanding obstacles without either side having to compromise its position in relation to its basic functions'[74] eventually prevailed. Cadets were awarded a National Diploma in Military Studies on completion of their cadet course following the NCEA approval on 13 July 1990. Military anxieties may have had some basis in fact, and the director of training's view that the Defence Forces should 'consider Graduate intake and link to a recognised college for Post Grad'[75] would be realised within the decade.

The Schools

As the above wider developments were being played out, the constituent schools of the College continued their educational and training activities within the structures that had been determined by the 1976 Board on Officer Education. For the schools, it was a period of relative stability as the 1979 Defence Forces reorganisation was implemented. The four brigades and ECIF continued to perform ATCP operations and to contribute troops to UNIFIL battalions. Units trained for and participated in a series of brigade exercises scheduled by the director of training. These exercises, while of relatively short duration, demanded planning and preparation and went some way towards exercising officers in the techniques of command and staff imparted at the College.

The Cadet School

Thirty cadets were commissioned in 1979, ending the intake of large cadet classes. In spite of a 1981 strength deficiency of 290 officers, cadet intake was not substantially increased. The stability mentioned above is highlighted in a briefing document provided by the director of training in 1989 for inclusion in the impending government-appointed Gleeson Commission on pay and conditions in the Defence Forces. Col Kissane noted that while courses in the Military College had continued along the same format for thirty years, they were constantly updated, the most important development being that of the introduction of third-level education. His document described the cadet course as designed:

> To train cadets for appointments to be officers in the PDF. The course lasts
> eighteen months and is divided into three six-month stages. The course qual-
> ifies students as Platoon Commanders and newly qualified officers spend
> eighteen months serving with parent units with periods of attachment to
> border units to gain experience prior to commencing third level education.[76]

Cadets were required to pass examinations to progress from one stage to the next, the chief of staff retaining the right to allow cadets who failed to repeat stages. While an overriding aim was to develop leadership, loyalty and service, the breadth of the course was extensive, and it is not difficult to understand how the NCEA staff had difficulty in fitting it into their more normal third-level patterns. The syllabus was divided into twelve blocks of instruction spread throughout the eighteen-month course. The subjects taught were 'Drill, Small Arms, Infantry Light Support Weapons, Methods of Instruction, Organisation of Training, Leadership, Tactical Operations, Corps and Service Familiarisation and Training, Related Military Subjects, Administration, Physical Training and Physical Education and Recreational Training, Academic Subjects, and School Administration'.[77] Each of the twelve blocks was further broken down into multiple subject areas providing eighteen months of intensive training, which were followed on commissioning by eighteen months of unit experience. The overall package was aimed at training and educating young officers in the basics of their military career before they embarked on their third-level academic studies. It was a successful and pragmatic response to the inherent disadvantages of an inadequate inculcation of the military ethos experienced at the early stages of the introduction of the USAC scheme. It would also prove suitable for future intakes, which included greater numbers of third-level graduates.

The Infantry School

The Infantry School continued its vocation as the busiest school in the College. The listing of courses conducted in the school during the 1980s is extensive: potential officers, FCA officers, night-vision equipment, nuclear biological and chemical instructors, sniper instructors, standard intelligence, press officers, reconnaissance commanders, assault pioneer platoon commanders. All of these courses were conducted in addition to the two main career courses, the annual young officers and standard infantry courses. This tempo of courses could only be sustained by ad hoc augmentation of the seven instructor officers of the school establishment. As was alluded to in the previous chapter, platoon commanders courses were phased out at the school with the last course, the 16th, conducted in 1981. Young officers courses recommenced with the 12th young officers course in 1980. The College authorities continued to recognise that the shortened cadet course and attendance at third-level institutions demanded an extra effort to ensure that the young officer received practical instruction in platoon and company level tactics and weapons employment. In a letter to the director of training in 1987, the CMC noted about the officers attending the young officers course 'that practical instruction in the skills and techniques of his craft should be well catered for in courses such as this'.[78] The use of the word 'craft' did not often find its way into such communications and is a recognition of the essentially workmanlike nature of platoon- and company-level tactics.

In spite of continuing ATCP commitments, the courses kept benefiting from the attachment of troops from infantry battalions during the practical phases of the course. They also, however, continued to suffer from the lack of training facilities that would have allowed for continuous tactical exercises under battle conditions. Of the 111 syllabus hours allotted to tactical training, only fifty-five were conducted outside of the school environment. A comparison can be made with a British Army platoon commanders battle course (PCBC), which was attended by many Infantry School instructors. There, an equivalent level course had two phases. Phase I comprised six weeks' training on the handling and employment of all infantry weapons, including under-battle conditions. In the following phase II, 60 per cent of the eight-week period was devoted to almost continuous 'on the ground' tactical operations again under simulated-battle conditions.[79] The Infantry School cannot be faulted for this unfavourable comparison; all Irish officers who attended the PCBC completed them successfully. The Defence Forces had not provided the necessary training facilities for them to replicate their experiences on return.

The school also conducted nine standard infantry courses during the 1980s. One of the recommendations of the study group on the redesign of the Military College referred to earlier was that the standard infantry course should be replaced by:

> A Junior Staff Course in the Infantry School for officers of all Corps. This course would have greater emphasis on staff work and less on tactics and would be of greater value as a common course for all Corps Officers than the present Standard Infantry Course. It would also be a course suitable for Women Officers.[80]

As with its overall redesign recommendations, this would also take time to be implemented. The chief of staff directed in 1984 that the standard infantry course must be completed by 'all officers of all Corps with the exception of the AMC [Army Medical Corps] and NS [Naval Service].'[81] All courses were run over a five-month period with 543 hours of instruction including a three-day field-training exercise conducted in the school. The course, apart from its intrinsic military instructional benefits, had added career importance in that Defence Forces regulations laid down that 'The Standard Course is designed to fit Officers to hold a Commandant's command and to acquire a knowledge of handling commands normally allotted to a Lieutenant-Colonel'.[82] As referred to earlier, the fact that the regulation did not state that completion of the course was a qualification for promotion, few captains would run the risk of not completing the Standard Course. The military experience of those who did, particularly students of the 49th standard infantry course, pointed to the continuing difficulties the Defence Forces had in providing robust tactical training. The fire power demonstration scheduled for the course had to be cancelled due to financial cutbacks, prompting the students to remark that it should be held, 'as many of the students had never seen HMGs [heavy machine guns] or anti armour weapons being fired'.[83] The school's response, 'that this is the type of experience which could and should be gained by officers at unit or command level prior to undertaking a Standard Infantry Course,'[84] again illustrated how the Military College continued to be the only source, albeit theoretical, of professional education for officers.

The Command and Staff School

A comparable regulatory situation pertained to the command and staff course, with the regulation describing it as being, 'designed to fit officers of all Service Corps to hold the rank of Lieutenant-Colonel and higher rank'.[85] The adjutant general detailed officers to undergo the course when they became eligible, usually by service and age. This strict procedure was somewhat ameliorated in 1982 when the branches of Defence Forces Headquarters (DFHQ), GOCs, the flag officer commanding the Naval Service (FOCNS) and the college commandant (CMC) were given some latitude in nominating students. However, this latitude caused the director of training to recommend to the chief of staff in 1989 that 'the policy whereby Command and Staff Courses and Standard Infantry Courses take precedence over overseas service & other military courses be strictly adhered to'.[86] Conflicting career demands on officers continued to cause difficulties in drawing up course nominations, in spite of a major change in Defence Forces policy concerning the command and staff course, which was adopted in 1986. Hitherto, an officer was required to undergo the command and staff course, but in November 1986 the general staff decided that 'for the future, officers of Commandant rank will be offered a "once only" opportunity to indicate whether they wish to undergo a Comd and Staff Course'.[87] This major policy change finally, but only partially, addressed the decades-long polemic as to whether or not students should be selected or detailed for the command and staff course, and whether or not they should also be required to pass an entrance examination. From 1986 onwards, all students on the course would be volunteers. This change had obvious implications for the conduct of the course and resulted in a more mature student-oriented ethos in which the student body effectively 'bought into' the course. The major factor that brought about this policy change was the prevailing limited opportunity for promotion beyond the rank of commandant. Evidence that this limited opportunity was affecting enthusiasm for spending eight or nine months in the College was found in the poor result of evaluation tests that the students were required to undergo on the first week of the course. The College authorities considered these poor results as 'evidence of an unacceptable downward trend in student preparation for Command and Staff Courses'.[88] The concern of the College was that students would arrive on the course with sufficient knowledge and background so that DS would not have to engage in remedial instruction. The CMC continued to press this point, which resulted in the policy change that required the student to apply to attend the course. The general staff did not, however, accede to his other demand that passing an entrance test should be obligatory for continuing the course.

The traditional shape and content of the course were restored after a three-year experiment in reducing the course from nine to eight months, with an extra teaching hour per day and the cancellation of the recreational half-day on Wednesdays, until then considered sacrosanct. Another short-term experiment was the attendance of two civil servants on the 43rd command and staff course. A visit from Mr J. Gallagher, assistant secretary of the Department of the Public Service to the Military College in 1984, initiated this attendance. During his visit, 'Mr Gallagher stated that it was hoped such attendance could significantly improve civil/military understanding, cooperation, and, thereby, efficiency through personal contact in an appropriate academic setting'.[89] At a subsequent meeting, Mr Seán Brosnan, assistant secretary of the Department of Defence, 'commented that at Departmental level there is constant commerce between officers of all levels'.[90] Nevertheless two officials, Mr Brian Whitney of the Department of the Public Service and Mr Gerry Girvan of the Department of Defence, attended the first two weeks of the 43rd command and staff course. While having some reservations about the specific period of the course they attended, both officials reported favourably and recommended that the experiment, with agreed modifications, should continue. It seems not to have done so.

In contrast to the short-lived experiments of cancelling the recreational half-day and the attendance of civil servants, an important, qualitative and lasting change was introduced into ATCP and United Nations operations instruction. Tactical

ATCP training had been conducted for some time at platoon and company level in the Cadet and Infantry Schools. In the Command and Staff School, it was considered at a higher level under the subject heading of internal security. On the 32nd command and staff course in 1973, ten hours were allocated to discussing post-colonial insurrection in the Philippines, Malaya and Cuba. On the 43rd course in 1985, this was increased to forty-four hours and included two ATCP exercises and a case study. A College DS captain, later Lt Col Frank Stewart produced an ATCP manual for instruction in the 1970s and early 1980s.[91] In recommending an instructional visit to border battalions for the students of the 44th command and staff course, the commandant noted that 'the majority of them have never served with a border unit'.[92] He further opined that this was a serious lack in their experience and 'a lack that, furthermore, diminishes the value of the classroom instruction given in Internal Security'.[93] By the 47th course in 1989, the subject had been renamed low-intensity conflict studies, with eighty-four hours allocated under three separate headings: counterinsurgency, internal security operations and United Nations operations. The qualitative change in this instruction was due to the influence and guidance of Lt Col, later Col, Johnny Hall, chief instructor of the Command and Staff School. With the input of Comdt Jim Goulding, a recent graduate of Camberley, Comdt Richard Heaslip and the first Officer Commanding the Army Ranger Wing, Comdt Paul Allen devised a comprehensive, relevant, up-to-date, and overdue block of instruction.

Senior Officers Courses

All of the previously discussed boards on officer education recommended training for senior officers after the command and staff course. Some went so far as to propose a separate school of higher strategic studies that would welcome students from business and administration. Most opted for senior officers courses, which 'were designed for the further education of graduates of the Command and Staff Courses and Staff Courses'.[94] The need for further professional education of senior officers became a concern of the general staff, and the Military College conducted five such courses in the 1980s, with the responsibility for their formulation and conduct given to the Command and Staff School. As this was an occasional course, and one that usually required that a command and staff course be postponed, there was at times some confusion concerning its actual purpose. In a memorandum to the chief of staff in 1987, the director of training reflected this confusion by stating that:

The aim of the Senior Officers' Course has been stated as to prepare senior officers for higher responsibilities by having them study those aspects of national and international affairs that affect security, particularly Ireland's National Security.[95]

However, he then quoted a previous chief of staff, Lt Gen. Gerard O'Sullivan, who stated in 1984 that 'a primary function of the senior officers' course was that its report should reflect a critical analysis of an officer's capabilities and firm assessment of his suitability for higher command in the PDF'.[96] The director of training reasonably, therefore, concluded that 'the course has both an educational and an assessment function'.[97] His conclusion was bolstered by the fact that boards were convened to select students for the courses. This assessment function was to cause some disquiet among officers, particularly at a period when the PDF was moving away from its traditional system of promotion on seniority towards a merit system. The disquiet led to the chairman of one of these selection boards to remark that, among his board members, DFHQ branches and GOCs, 'it was widely agreed that regardless of what system that was adopted, some officers who are NOT elected [*sic*] would feel aggrieved'.[98] The author can confirm these sensitivities as, when he was coordinator of the 6th and 7th senior officer courses, the commandant of the Command and Staff School instructed him not to compile individual student course reports.

The school's approach to the course was to appreciate the experience and seniority of the students and to facilitate them in reflecting on the input from a wide range of external lecturers. The introduction to the syllabus of the 6th senior officers course expressed this awareness of the experience of the students thus:

> Given the service and depth of experience of the student body it is unrealistic to expect that there is much that is new, concerning today's Defence Forces that the Military College can teach on this course. It is also reasonable to expect that the students of this course have much to offer in considering the future of the Defence Forces at a time which seems to pose many difficult questions as to its future role and raison d'être.[99]

The course organisers had hoped that senior members of government would contribute, but they came up against the opposition of the minister for defence. Michael J. Noonan informed the chief of staff that 'in view of the pressure on

senior personnel in the present circumstances I consider that the amount of time which officers at this level spend away from their posts should be kept to the absolute minimum'.[100] In spite of this opposition, which the chief of staff resisted, and the non-attendance of ministers, An Taoiseach Charles J. Haughey replied to an invitation from the assistant chief of staff to address the course. He 'would have liked very much to accept your kind invitation but unfortunately in present circumstances I am forced to keep my commitments to a minimum'.[101]

Despite the somewhat ad hoc and improvised nature of the courses, they were considered successful as the students during their twelve weeks at the College did have the opportunity to reflect on the wider issues affecting the changing Defence Forces.

Conclusion

The 1976 board report on officer education, which was accepted by the military authorities, confirmed a traditional view of the structure of courses at the Military College. It was, however, a structure that required adaptation to change. Female-officer and cadet training and education caused much soul-searching, and outreach to the NCEA resulted in a nationally recognised education award to the cadet course. The structure, not just of courses but of the College itself, came under some examination, which produced little result. Instruction in ATCP did, however, change. The demarcation between tactical and staff education and training for junior officers also called for development, and attendance on the command and staff course ceased to be obligatory and became voluntary. Five senior officers courses provided a valuable opportunity for a cohort of lieutenant colonels to reflect on the increasingly changing environment within which the Defence Forces would soon be required to adapt. Most of those lieutenant colonels would soon face these future challenges at the highest level of the Defence Forces hierarchy. At the end of the 1980s, the Defence Forces came under considerable outside scrutiny, probably more so than since the Emergency. Unrest over pay and conditions led the government to establish a commission, audit and review groups, and eventually a white paper on defence, all of which examined the organisation, its purpose and inevitably how the College was servicing that organisation.

9

The 1990s

An Expanded Military College

At the end of the 1980s, the Defence Forces began a quarter of a century of continuous review, retrenchment and reorganisation. From a strength of 13,500 in the late 1980s, the Defence Forces were reduced to an all-ranks strength of a little over 9,000. It was a period of intense scrutiny, driven as in other European states by a reassessment of traditional defence postures after the collapse of the USSR, but also with homegrown particularities. Unrest over pay and conditions led to the unprecedented sight of public protests by spouses of enlisted personnel outside barracks and at one stage outside the gates of Defence Forces Headquarters. This situation should not have been allowed to develop. When eventually the government did respond, its answer led to an Interdepartmental Committee, the Gleeson Commission on remuneration and conditions of service in the Defence Forces, an Efficiency Audit Group, a Price Waterhouse review, successive implementation reviews and two white papers on defence. The government also took what was perhaps the most radical step of all for many: the creation of a Representative Association for Commissioned Officers (RACO) and a Permanent Defence Force Other Ranks Representative Association (PDFORRA). All of this activity led over time to major changes in the organisation of the Defence Forces. The Defence Forces entered this period of change structured to operate with four brigades and the Eastern Command Infantry Force. The present-day structure of the Defence Forces, at the end of this quarter century of largely welcome change, comprises Defence Forces Headquarters, the Defence Forces Training Centre, the Naval Service and the Air Corps, and numbers just two brigades. Two aspects of this change are germane to the story of the Military College: the establishment of the Defence Forces Training Centre in the Curragh and the examination by the Gleeson Commission of the system of officer promotion. The commission determined that 'the selection of officers for promotion should change from 'a system based almost exclusively on seniority to a system based on merit'.[1] This was a radical change; heretofore the determining factor for officer promotion, except for officers of general rank, was the class placing which a cadet achieved on completing the cadet course.

The commission recommended inter alia that 'to be eligible for promotion, the following requirements should be met, satisfactory completion of the appropriate military Courses'.[2] Regulations had previously stated that successful completion of the standard and the command and staff courses was one of the criteria that qualified an officer for holding a certain rank. Now, with the acceptance by the government of the Gleeson proposal, an interview board would consider performance on these courses as an element of their recommendation of officers for promotion to higher ranks. Performance on career courses would or should be taken more seriously by students after the Defence Forces had instituted the new system of promotion on merit. Also, the College authorities would be required to pay greater attention to the conduct of career courses, the course placing of students on the completion of the course and the content and accuracy of course reports. While the College authorities would claim that this was always the case, a greater responsibility ensued and students would now pay greater attention their course reports.

During the 1990s, the final decade of this history of the Military College, review followed review and many of the established certainties of the Defence Forces were questioned and relinquished or modified. Also, in addition to internal reviews, the Defence Forces forged new links with international defence organisations. A senior officer was seconded in 1996 to the staff of the Irish Embassy in Brussels to serve as an observer at the Military Committee of the Western European Union (WEU). This secondment upset the Fianna Fáil spokesman on foreign affairs Ray Burke, who angrily warned, 'I am deeply concerned about the trend of this Government which is to get us more and more involved with the WEU and NATO through the Partnership for Peace'.[3] Nevertheless, further Irish officer appointments were made to Supreme Headquarters Allied Powers Europe (SHAPE) at Mons, Belgium, then to NATO Headquarters in Brussels, and on

1 December 1999, Burke's Fianna Fáil colleague David Andrews signed Ireland's agreement to join the Partnership for Peace programme. The College also saw change; yet another Board on Officer and Cadet Training, the amalgamation of the General Training Depot with the College, the establishment of a new school – the United Nations Training School Ireland (UNTSI) – and a major input by the staff of the Command and Staff School to Irish military doctrine. Each of these aspects will be covered in this chapter, in addition to an overview of the work of the now-four constituent schools of the College.

The 1992 Board on the Review of Cadet and Officer Training and Education in the Permanent Defence Forces

The Chief of Staff Lt Gen. James Parker DSM, on whose watch the initial external scrutiny of the Defence Forces began, appreciated the importance of the Gleeson Commission. He instructed the board in his 1992 Convening Order 'to carry out a comprehensive review of cadet and officer training and education in the PDF and to make recommendations on any changes necessary consequent to the Report of the Commission on Remuneration and Conditions of Service in the Defence Forces'.[4] The board, chaired by Col James J. Farrell, a future CMC and GOC Southern Command, included Lt Col John Martin, also a future GOC, and Comdt James Sreenan, a future chief of staff. It determined that its role was more than just examining existing structures. The board was also required to 'set about defining the qualities and skills required by the officer body of the future', what its members termed 'the officer for the 21st century'. To achieve this definition, the board analysed the roles assigned to the Defence Forces, the first and foremost of which they determined was to defend the State against external aggression, and other factors, including the representative associations, promotions systems and career profile, technological change and economic and sociological factors. The board members were conscious of the differences between training and education. They viewed training as 'the development of knowledge, skills and techniques for the performance of tasks' and thought that the 'aim of education should be to achieve sufficient broadening of the mind primarily for the betterment of the Defence Forces'.[5] Not surprisingly, given the complexity of the tasks facing the future officer, a simple definition was not forthcoming, but the board affirmed that:

The primary purpose of the officer is to lead and to lead in war. There is always the danger that in the peacetime quest for a rationalized cost effective organisation this fundamental role might be lost sight of. The development of leadership potential must be the basis of all officer education and training.[6]

The wide-ranging report covered areas such as the training and education of Air Corps and Naval Service cadets and officers, leadership, management and administration. The board considered the activities of the Military College under three groupings: induction training, junior and mid-career education and training and command and staff and senior-officer training. Whereas no major changes were recommended for the cadet course, the board suggested that the educational qualification for entry into the Cadet School should be raised and that 'the cadet selection process should include provision for an assessment centre at which structured assessment of applicants should be conducted'.[7] The USAC scheme should be continued and should aim to satisfy Defence Forces technical requirements. The board recommended that more attention should be paid to graduate intake to the Cadet School. Junior and mid-career courses should continue with a tactically oriented young officers course, surprisingly of only four weeks' duration, followed by a standard infantry course. The board accepted that the aim of the standard infantry course, which should be renamed as a junior command and staff course, was valid insofar as it 'is designed to double as an Infantry Company Commanders Course and an Infantry Battalion Operations Officers Course'[8]. All officers should complete the course and it 'should be a factor in selection for the Command and Staff Course and for promotion'.[9] The board recommended no major changes in the conduct of the command and staff and senior officers courses. They were cognizant of the impact that the pending system of promotion on merit would have in the future and were convinced that a senior officer's education should not cease with the command and staff course, but should continue to fit him/her for increasingly demanding senior appointments.

The board also addressed an issue raised by students then attending at the College, particularly those on the command and staff course. It was reported that 'many officers indicated perception that too much time was devoted to the conventional operations aspects of the course'.[10] The board accepted the fact that instruction on UN and ATCP operations had more credibility than conventional operations but insisted 'that conventional operations must remain the bedrock of the course'.[11] Students also expressed concerns regarding the relevance of the course for promotion and marketability outside the Defence Forces. The board could only speculate on a future system of promotion but recommended that access to the command and staff course should be through application and selection. Regarding marketability, the board raised the possibility that post-graduate recognition might be pursued with the NCEA.

This necessarily brief summary of what was a lengthy and closely analysed and argued report indicates that the board recommended few radical changes to either the existing content or structure of courses at the Military College. This could be construed as an endorsement of the College, or else it could be seen as highlighting the difficulties of foreseeing in 1992 the requirements of the twenty-first century. How the board's recommendations were implemented will be examined in the section on the schools. Two developments at the College that were not covered by the board, perhaps because they were not included in the Convening Order, will now be discussed: the amalgamation of the Military College and the General Training Depot and the establishment of the United Nations Training School Ireland (UNTSI).

Amalgamation of the Military College and the General Training Depot (GTD)

Earlier chapters have recounted a movement towards the amalgamation of these two adjoining establishments, the Military College housed in Pearse Barracks and the General Training Depot housed in McDonagh Barracks. First formally proposed by Col Eóghan ÓNéill in 1965, and then recommended in a 1981 study group, its rationale was to be found in a need for common tactical training for junior officers and NCOs, and in the pressing need of an improvement in infantry support weapons skills and training. An interim step had been taken in 1982, with the establishment by the chief of staff of an Infantry Weapons School in the GTD, but amalgamation was to prove difficult to achieve. Why this should be so, in spite of the obvious training advantages to be gained, is probably explained by reluctance on the part of proponents of both establishments to relinquish existing traditions, and also to a lack of material resources to effect required changes in living, training and messing accommodation. When amalgamation was eventually achieved, it came about because of a 'Government decision to make savings of £.25m from rationalisation in the CURRAGH CAMP'.[12] Responding to this decision in 1991, the chief of staff directed that among the measures to be taken, firm proposals should be presented for the 'Amalgamation of Pearse/McDonagh Barracks with the incorporation of the School of Admin, the Weapons School and the NCO School into the Military College'.[13] Earlier rationalisation had been achieved with the construction of a dining complex serving both Pearse and McDonagh Barracks, catering for students of the Military College, except for students on command and staff courses. This arrangement was to the dissatisfaction of some standard infantry course students who felt that 'by availing of meals in the Dining Centre the focal point for mess life for the students is removed from the College thus tarnishing that ethos which undergoing a career Course in the Military College should engender'.[14] The perhaps-understandable dissatisfaction of the students aside, the fact that the director of training considered it necessary to pursue a decision that had been taken ten years earlier shows how difficult it was to overcome tradition. But 'it was not the Quartermaster General's intention to change the policy outlined in 1980'.[15]

Several boards were required to develop the details of the amalgamation decision, with at one stage the Defence Forces School of Physical Training considered along with the School of Administration for amalgamation into the College. By October 1992, training imperatives had prevailed. The chief of staff, Lt Gen. Gerry McMahon, finally approved a provisional establishment in January 1995. He instructed that, with the agreement of the CMC and the director of training, component wings of the Infantry School be designated as the Officers Training Wing, the NCO Training Wing, and the Infantry Weapons Wing. This was more than a mere re-designation of titles. It was the eventual achievement of a synergy of effort and instruction in command, tactics, and weapon handling at the section-and-platoon level, the building block of all Defence Forces conventional, UN and ATCP operations. The incorporation of the NCO School and the Weapons School into the Infantry School ensured, over time, that infantry instruction in the Defence Forces followed the common doctrine then being developed within the Military College. Lt Gen. McMahon may have taken some satisfaction from his 1995 instruction, as he had followed the lengthy process through successive appointments as director of planning and research, CMC, quartermaster general and finally as chief of staff. One of the many reports on the amalgamation process had referred in passing to the 'provision of a UN School as a consequence of the recent announcement by the Minister'.[16] This UN school, later known as the United Nations Training School Ireland (UNTSI), had a much shorter gestation period than the expanded Infantry School.

United Nations Training School Ireland (UNTSI)

The 1992 board championed training in conventional warfare as the 'bedrock' of an officer's education. Nevertheless, it referred on some occasions to the comparatively limited instructional time devoted to UN operations. On the standard infantry course, a course of five months' duration, it noted 'that only two (2) hours are devoted to UN operations'.[17] This was so in spite of the fact that 'Officers of Capt. and comdt rank are required to serve with UN not just on UNIFIL service but as UNMOs [United Nations Military Observers] across the globe in widely differing situations'.[18] In discussing the command and staff course, the 1992 board affirmed that:

> While acknowledging that training for conventional operations forms the basis for operations in support of UN, nevertheless given the Defence Forces wide ranging involvement in UN operations worldwide it would appear that the 3% of instructional time devoted to peacekeeping is quite small.[19]

Little, it seemed, had changed in UN instruction at the College since Comdt Pat Maguire's 1974 student survey. The College did, however, provide the venue for a two-day UN seminar between 12 and 13 September 1991, just ten days before Lt Gen. Parker's Convening Order 'for the Board on the review of Cadet and Officer Training and Education. The seminar was organised in a series of sub-syndicate workshops and its aims were to 'Discuss aspects of the setting up of a UN mission and to discuss and assess Current Defence Forces training of all ranks for present and prospective UN Operations'.[20] Sub-syndicate number 3, tasked with examining all aspects of UN training in the Defence Forces, divided its task between examining specific unit and mission training and training provided to officers on career courses. The sub-syndicate was composed of eight senior officers, none of whom was on the staff of the Military College, although one of them had previously served there as an instructor. Their subsequent report was favourable towards specific unit and mission training but scathing of the instruction provided on Military College officer career courses.

The report noted, as would also be noted by the later board on cadet and officer education, that one hour of UN instruction was provided on the young officers course, two hours on the standard course, and thirty hours in the eight-month long command and staff course. The rapporteur accepted the conventional wisdom that conventional warfare must be taught on career courses. Once they have mastered them, officers 'will be able to adopt/modify such lessons to deal with whatever variations may arise, "you must know the air of the Blue Danube first before you can play any variations of the theme."'[21] It is not clear if the 'Blue' in the 'Blue Danube' was to symbolise the blue of the UN. Nevertheless, the Defence Forces could 'not go on forever relegating such important topics as ATCP or UN operations as "variations" especially since they constitute the primary tasks of the Defence Forces currently'.[22] Moreover, 'the derisory time allocated to UN Ops in our junior officer Course syllabi is indicative of our muddled thinking on this important aspect of our training'.[23] This criticism was uncomfortable for the College and it is to his credit that the CMC, Brig. Gen. John O'Shea, reproduced it verbatim in his seminar report. He also reported a recurring theme from all the sub-syndicates and workshops that the Irish Defence Forces, in spite of their considerable experience in UN operations, had contributed very little to the increasing institutional and academic repository of training for UN missions. Sub-syndicate number 3 recommended: 'That a separate UN wing/depot be established at the Military College to cater for all UN instruction.'[24] This recommendation was reflected in one of the overall seminar observations on the perceived inadequacy of the Defence Forces response to UN training, which suggested:

> The establishing of a more formal structure/establishment that could be responsible for:
> Preparation and training of personnel for all overseas duties.
> Promoting our image as peacekeepers both nationally and internationally.
> Co-ordinating all liaison and support structures.[25]

The opinions expressed at the seminar were representative of the views of the wider officer body, and while it cannot be shown that they had a direct influence on future developments, it was not long before their recommendation of the creation of 'more formal structure/establishment' bore fruit. UN training schools had already been established by the Nordic countries and by Austria, and it was following his experience of the Austrian school that the chief of staff, Lt Gen. Noel Bergin, decided that the Defence Forces required such a school. He requested the assistant chief of staff, now Brig. Gen. John O'Shea, to oversee its establishment.[26] Col James Mortell was duly nominated by the chief of staff as commandant of the school and reported to the Military College on 23 August 1993.[27]

Less than a month later, on 16 September 1993, the Minister for Defence David Andrews inaugurated the United Nations and International Studies School, a name that was later to cause some difficulties. The school was established in Pearse House adjacent to the Military College officers' mess, and tenders were sought for the extensive works required to convert what had been a large domestic dwelling into a suitable educational establishment. The intended works also included the construction of a replica UN military observers observation post. An indication that the fledgeling school was to be permanent was given by the visit of the President of Ireland Mary Robinson on 18 November 1993 and of An Taoiseach Albert Reynolds the following year on 19 May 1994. Col Mortell, the school commandant, outlined the aims of the school in his address to the president. They were ambitious in their content and scope:

The formulation and dissemination of up-to-date Peacekeeping doctrine throughout the Defence Forces.

Enhancement of current instruction and training on Peacekeeping within our Military Schools.

De-briefing key personnel of all ranks on their return from overseas service.

Liaison with other national UN Schools.

To attract domestic diplomats, Gardaí and foreign military and diplomatic students on relevant Peacekeeping International Studies Courses and Seminars.[28]

The school was formally established in Defence Forces regulations on 27 June 1994. Its first year was devoted to briefings, lectures, and courses for Defence Forces personnel, leading to its first International United Nations military observers and staff officers course. The chief of staff submitted the prospectus for this course to the minister for defence in July 1994. He received a minute from a Department of Defence official in November 1994 acknowledging his correspondence, and conveying the minister's direction that 'the school is to be referred to as the "United Nations Training School – Ireland".'[29] It is likely that political sensitivities regarding participation by the Defence Forces in the operations of organisations other than the UN were behind this direction. The chief of staff attempted to have the minister's direction changed by pointing out that the United Nations and International Studies School (UNISS) was the name of the school when he had inaugurated it and when it was visited by both the president and the Taoiseach. He pointed out that, 'the full title including "international studies" was devised to enable the staff to study the social, economic, political and cultural environments in which our troops operate abroad'.[30] He made the point that a military opinion had not been sought on the proposed change of name and that the Defence Forces were then engaged in missions other than traditional UN peacekeeping missions such as with CSCE, the European Union and UNHCR/NGOs. He also maintained that:

> The studying and monitoring of these areas are considered to be essential for the successful operations of our troops. The studies also enable the General Staff to offer advice to you as Minister on aspects of their performance including safety and forward planning.[31]

The chief of staff's arguments were of no avail, and John Daly informed him that while the minister had considered and appreciated them, he requested that, 'his decision as already conveyed in my minute dated 10/11/94 should stand'.[32] The school's title was changed to United Nations Training School Ireland (UNTSI) and the 1st international United Nations military observers and staff officers course was conducted there from 5 to 23 June 1995. The course was conducted for twenty-six students, six of whom were Irish while the remaining twenty were from the armed forces of Brunei, Egypt, Holland, Italy, Lebanon, Poland, Romania, Sweden, UK, USA and Zambia, constituting a considerable enhancement of the international reputation of the Irish Military College. In his course report, the executive officer of the school, Lt Col Oliver MacDonald, judged it as being successful in its aim of introducing 'middle ranking military officers to the theory and practice of United Nations Peacekeeping'.[33] Lt Col MacDonald noted that many other countries were conducting such courses, and that while UNTSI could conduct two such courses each year, it must keep abreast of developments. During its early years, UNTSI consolidated its instructor base and experience and developed the range of seminars, lectures and courses it offered to the Defence Forces and to foreign participants in peacekeeping operations. By the end of the decade, UNTSI had become a nationally and internationally recognised and respected institution for peacekeeping education and training. Lt Col McDonald's report had also noted that 'doctrine for UN is in a state of flux. This needs to be monitored closely by the

School. The staff must create studies to form the basis of a corpus of doctrine.'[34] It was not, however, just the staff of UNTSI who were to be concerned about doctrine. Nor was peacekeeping doctrine the only concern of the Military College. The wider question of operational doctrine was a concern for the staff of the Command and Staff School, and it is to their efforts to finally articulate an official statement of Defence Forces military doctrine that we will now turn.

The Military College Input to Irish Military Doctrine

There are many definitions of military doctrine. At its simplest it is a statement of how to conduct military operations. Irish military doctrine should derive from a political statement of defence policy, through military plans for accomplishing this defence policy, to an articulation by military planners of how military formations should implement these plans. This process should then allow teaching establishments to instruct students in the ways and means of effecting this implementation of defence planning and for formations and units to implement this doctrine in military operations. There is a tradition of cooperation, conflict and at times abdication between planners and educators on who is responsible for formulating military doctrine. In his examination of the development of American Army doctrine in the 1930s, William O. Odom noted that:

> Instead of harmonizing and modernizing the training doctrine of the Army, annual War Department training directives gave the publications of the service schools the character of training directives, thus transferring the duty of modernizing tactical doctrine from the General Staff to the schools.[35]

In discussing military doctrine in chapters 5 and 6, the two main issues referred to were disagreements between the director of plans and operations and the CMC on whether instruction at the College should be based on actual army organisation, and whether or not instruction should be given above the level of the brigade. These were important issues, touching as they do on the confidence students would have in the instruction they receive and also in its applicability to their careers. The concern shown by directors of plans and operations, such as Denis Lawlor and Thomas Gray, about the fact that there should be an agreement between College and general staff thinking seems to have diminished after the 1959 Chief of Staff's Directive on Doctrine. It did not, however, disappear and Col Donal O'Carroll recalls that while he was an instructor at the Command and Staff School in 1969, some difficulty was experienced with differing approaches between returned graduates of foreign military staff schools. This difficulty prompted a demand for the establishment of a Doctrinal Board.[36] Such a board was established at a meeting in the Military College between representatives of the director of training and the College schools. O'Carroll, who was nominated as secretary of the board, recalls that the representative from the director of training, Lt Col John Gallagher, later director of training and quartermaster general, argued that doctrine should be written by the Command and Staff School. The board, however, continued to be chaired by the director of training, or by his representative.

The Doctrinal Board's record cannot be shown to have greatly advanced doctrinal matters in the Defence Forces. This lapse was not entirely the fault of those who contributed to its workings. Military doctrine should derive from a policy that in turn should determine military planning. There was little new articulation of Irish defence policy in the years following the establishment of the board, understandably so given the predominance of ATCP operations. As the years advanced, the board's proceedings became routine and it concerned itself with matters far from military doctrine. The minutes of a meeting of 15 October 1982 are indicative of matters discussed:

> NBC training, NBC clothing, Staff manual, Marksman advanced trainer, Procurement Board, Tactical exercise and doctrine, War games exercise, Training Directive, Lessons of the 1982 Tactical Exercise, Tactical Exercises 1983, Military College Manuals, Printing Press, Weapons School, Third Level Education, Infantry Course 1983 and Procedures for nominating officers for Courses.[37]

By then the Doctrinal Board had been renamed as 'The Board for the Co-ordination of General Staff Policies and Military College Doctrine', a title that seemed to accentuate the separateness of the general staff and the Military College and to clearly ascribe doctrine as a matter for the College. The board had in fact become little more than a forum for the dissemination of matters concerning the directorate of training. On the single agenda item of 15 October referring to doctrine, 'Tactical Exercise and Doctrine', the director of training, Col Brendan Cassidy, repeated that:

The basis of all doctrine and training would be the scenarios as outlined at the last meeting of the Board involving the status of neutrality, of forced participation and of willing participation. The 1982 and 1983 exercises were based on a scenario of neutrality.[38]

Brigade exercises during this period involved a composite formation of units from all commands tasked with concentrating and opposing parachute landings. The minutes do not record any discussion on this agenda item and show that the original intention of formulating doctrine for the Defence Forces had faded from view. It was not to re-emerge for almost another decade, and when it did, in 1990, it was a result of two separate but interconnected events.

In January 1990, Col D.J. Coffey, the commandant of the Command and Staff School, requested guidance on doctrine from the CMC, and the commandant forwarded this request to the chief of staff. Then in February of the same year, the chief of staff, Lt Gen. James Parker, addressed the Conference on Security and Cooperation in Europe (CSCE). In his address, the chief of staff had defined Irish military doctrine as being, 'patently defensive, non-nuclear and embracing a Zonal Defence concept'.[39] Col Coffey in his letter to the CMC had also mentioned zonal defence, and that it was the understanding of his school, 'that the Zonal Defence concept has been accepted in principle and will be promulgated as the basic doctrinal concept for the Defence Forces'.[40] Zonal Defence was an Austrian defence posture that had been written about in *An Cosantóir* magazine by the future Chief of Staff Lt Gen, then Comdt, Colm Mangan. Austrian military doctrine aimed at making an invasion of its territory by Warsaw Pact forces so difficult as to deter any such invasion. It made much use of its geographically strong terrain and the employment of a mobile armour force as a reserve. Some felt that this could be adapted to suit Irish defence requirements, which lead to the chief of staff's inclusion of the concept in his CSCE address. Its adaption to Irish conditions was, however, unlikely for a number of reasons. Austrians were subject to national conscription and the geographic factors were completely different. Comdt Mangan's observation that 'It is now up to the people through their elected representatives to give them [the Austrian Defence Forces] the means to implement it',[41] would be equally critical for the Irish situation. Nevertheless, his article may perhaps have resurrected the debate on doctrine in and for the Defence Forces.

Col Coffey's particular concerns were with instruction in the Command and Staff School. He expressed the school's understanding of Ireland's neutrality-based defence policy and the roles allotted to the Defence Forces within that policy. He then outlined that, 'there are no universally issued and accepted doctrinal texts which form the basis of and standardise conventional operations instruction and operational procedures within the Defence Forces. There is an urgent need for such doctrinal texts.'[42] This need was in spite of the fact that the Command and Staff School had written a manual entitled *Operations Text, Part 1, Doctrine Combat Operations*, in 1987 for use in the school. Col Coffey illustrated his point by noting that existing instruction at the school included the deployment of a main battle tank (MBT) squadron with the infantry brigade. 'As well as being outdated this concept is unrealistic in that the Defence Forces has not got, nor is likely to get MBT squadrons in the short to medium term'.[43] Coffey had re-opened earlier debates on whether or not instruction should be based on actual Defence Forces organisation and equipment or on those of a modern European army. This time, the roles were reversed and it was the College that favoured the realism of actuality. This position had developed in the school over a number of years. While continuing to instruct on armoured and mechanised formations, the school had introduced an alternative enemy order of battle to the traditional one, Invasia, based on Warsaw Pact forces. The alternative was named Fantasia and was based on a British Army motorised brigade formation.[44] This was not intended to imply any invasion intentions by the British Army, but was to provide an exercise enemy order of battle which did not imply an invasion by Warsaw Pact forces, considered unlikely then and in the future

Coffey informed the CMC that the school intended to base the instruction of the 49th command and staff course in 1991 on zonal defence and requested a doctrinal directive from the chief of staff. The chairman of the Doctrinal Board and director of training, Col John O'Shea, then recommended to the chief of staff that the staff of the Command Staff School be tasked with, 'Drafting a statement for the Chief of Staff's approval which will include Defence Policy, Roles and Threat Analysis'.[45] This was a radical enhancement of the instructional responsibilities of the staff of the Command and Staff School, which was to be then followed by the convening of a special board tasked with:

Analysis of Doctrine

Restatement of Doctrine

Production of the necessary textbooks

Determine Own Forces Order of Battle (PDF and Reserves)
Determine Own Forces organisation and equipment
Determine Enemy Forces Order of Battle.[46]

The chief of staff approved the recommendation and the staff of the Command and Staff School were instructed to carry out their task in the interval between the 47th and 48th command and staff courses.[47]

The school's response to its task was a detailed and methodical formulation of a defence policy based on three elements: initiators, interests and means. This formulation downgraded the traditional primary task of the Defence Forces to defend the State against external aggression and replaced it with defence against a cross-border threat from para-military forces in the event of a universal declaration of independence (UDI) by loyalist elements in Northern Ireland. The CMC submitted this document to the director of training for the chief of staff's attention on 6 September 1990, suggesting that other staff sections might wish to comment on it. The director of training's initial response to the chief of staff was very favourable, finding inter alia 'the description of the threat current and realistic' and that 'the Defence Forces capabilities listed as those required and necessary to carry out its assigned roles are acceptable and current'.[48] He subsequently, however, revised his view and informed the chief of staff that, 'the threat analysis seems to tailor the threats to suit our capabilities'.[49] Other staff sections were as unconvinced as the director of training in his revised view. The executive officer of Operations Section rejected the downgrading of defence against a threat external to the island and considered that the Military College submission 'appeared to some extent to assume away the problem and limit the external threat to a force of 5,000 troops'.[50] He maintained that it was apparent that 'the Defence Forces Tactical Doctrine must encompass all phases of warfare and be based on a Zonal Defence policy, using conventional weapons and geared toward defeating a divisional strength enemy'.[51] For his part, the director of intelligence stated that the College estimate of a cross-border force was unrealistic and not factual and should be raised to 10,000. The director of training's resiling from his original favourable view of the College submission, and the views of the other sections of the Chief of Staff's Branch, showed a strong opposition to any attempt to downgrade the primary role of the Defence Forces as being defence against external aggression. The opposition is understandable insofar as it supported decades of tradition, and the upgrading of a cross-border threat would undoubtedly have created political difficulties. While opposition from the chief of staff's principal staff sections to the College view was emphatic, the chief of staff nevertheless proceeded with the earlier recommendation to convene a board to consider tactical doctrine.

This board, convened on 21 May 1991, was chaired by Col James J. Farrell, who later went on to chair the 1992 Board on Officer and Cadet Education. It was comprised of representatives from the Military College and the staff sections of the Chief of Staff's Branch. It was required to, 'examine and make recommendations on the tactical doctrine best suited to the Defence Forces in the context of national neutrality'.[52] The conflation of national neutrality and tactical doctrine made for a difficult task. Although the board asserted that, 'Neutrality as a national posture cannot be assumed to be a state's defence policy, nor is it a substitute for it',[53] it was required to consider tactical doctrine within the context of the State's defence policy. Tactical doctrine is the lowest doctrinal division, which an almost contemporaneous British Army document divided 'into three levels, military doctrine (highest level), operational level (theatre level) and tactical level (fighting the battle)'.[54] The board's approach to this difficulty was to re-affirm the primary role of the Defence Forces as defence against external aggression, although a 'major infringement of national sovereignty is the most remote'[55] of threats. It recommended that this defence be conducted by a modification of the zonal defence concept, which it called key area defence. Conducting such a defence implied a field army 'which on mobilisation will comprise those elements defined as required to implement a policy of Key Area Defence'.[56] The board discussed the concept of doctrine and its method of formulation, but articulated little actual doctrine other than to state that:

> Existing tactical doctrine as taught in the Military College would require little modification as Key Area Defence contains offence, defence and retrograde elements. This large corpus of tactical doctrine should be amended as appropriate and should be disseminated throughout the Defence Forces to provide the basis for instruction in all training establishments.[57]

The College should have a doctrinal cell, and 'shall be free to research, teach and instruct on formations, tactics and techniques for the continuing education of officers'.[58] As to Col Coffey's intention to base instruction on the command and staff course on zonal defence, the Board recommended that the defence of the State should be conducted using key area defence, and that:

A staff study is required to examine the practical implications of this, and to select the different types of areas involved. Force structure, Order of Battle and organisation and equipment would follow on from the selection of these areas.[59]

It is hardly surprising that this staff study was not carried out, given that the concept required a strategic headquarters, 'in a relatively remote and inaccessible location away from Key Areas and enemy avenues of approach. It should none-theless provide necessary facilities for the seat of Government on an emergency basis'.[60] Such a step would have been one too far for a state that, according to Professor Eunan O'Halpin, had adopted, 'a formal doctrine of external defence the primary subtext of which was not to enable Ireland to stand up for itself against military aggression from all comers and to police its own skies and waters, but rather to suppress militarism within the state'.[61]

But the College and, in particular, the Command and Staff School staff were not satisfied, and continued to pursue the question of doctrine; this time, however, they pursued a more nuanced approach and eschewed discussion of defence policy. Unusually, the school was granted a sabbatical between the 52nd and the 53rd command and staff courses in 1995, and in addition to the revision of the course syllabus, members of the staff undertook the drafting of the Defence Forces doctrinal manual operations TM 205. It set out to codify the ways in which the Defence Forces, a conventional combined–arms combat force, would, 'fulfil the various roles assigned by government, while providing the capacity and versatility to adapt to the new world order and its challenges in an efficient and effective manner'.[62] The authors, recent graduates of Fort Leavenworth, were aware that Ireland was moving into a new era of interna-tional involvement; Ireland had observer status at the Western European Union and would join NATO's Partnership for Peace in 1999. These developments were concrete indications of a changing Irish defence policy that need not then be included in a doctrinal manual. But the manual did recognise that:

The Defence Forces may be tasked by the Government to operate in response to national or international contingencies requiring the use of military resources. Such contingencies may involve Army, Naval and Air Corps assets, employed with national agencies, international organisations and other armed forces. In some of these activities Defence Forces personnel may be involved at all levels of operations. Accordingly, the manual addresses the strategic, operational and tactical application of military power.[63]

The prescience of the authors can be judged by the fact that in less than ten years after the adoption of the manual, an Irish officer, Lt Gen. Pat Nash DSM, would be operational commander of EUFOR in support of the United Nations mission in the Central African Republic and Chad (MINURCAT). With its operational headquarters in Paris, Defence Forces personnel would serve at this headquarters and also at both strategic and tactical levels of the mission. TM 205 was used as an instructional text in the Military College, and as the basis for brigade and other manuals. The general staff accepted the manual and the deputy chief of staff, operations, signed and declared it the Defence Forces doctrinal manual in January 2001.

The earlier doctrinal board had lapsed into a catch-all forum for discussing general training matters, a situation that caused the CMC to state that, 'The Board has changed little since it was first set up. It still has the same composition and the wide ranging agenda items are still discussed'.[64] It was reconstituted in November 1998 as the Defence Forces Doctrine and Training Committee with the assistant chief of staff as chairman, and while it still considers training matters it closely oversees and delegates most doctrinal drafting to the staff of the Military College. The Military College has now assumed a role common to many military educational establishments, that of a recognised senior actor in the development of Irish military doctrine under the direction of the general staff. To carry out this responsibility, it draws on Defence Forces operational experience both at home and abroad, on input from the doctrine of foreign armies and NATO doctrine, a consequence of Ireland's membership of NATO's Partnership for Peace programme. The doctrinal cell proposed by many boards has never emerged, but the College, in addition to its other many duties, has adequately fulfilled the cell's envisioned mission.

The Schools

Before discussing the individual schools, attention needs to be drawn to a 1995 dialogue between the CMC and the Director of Training Col William Fitzgerald on the recurring and cyclical problem of a backlog of officers eligible to undergo career courses. The dialogue is instructive insofar as while this problem had arisen in the past, on this occasion the CMC was Brigadier General Jimmy Farrell, chairman of the 1992 Board on Officer and Cadet Education. Farrell proposed reducing the numbers of students attending the command and staff course from twenty-eight to twenty-four, because of accommodation difficulties. In response, the director of training recommended a series of changes to both the command and staff and the junior command and staff courses to the chief of staff in August 1994. The rationale for the director's recommendations was twofold: firstly a backlog of eligible candidates, 139 commandants for the command and staff course and 272 captains for the junior command and staff course, and secondly the age profile of students on the courses. The average age on the command and staff course was then 41, and on the junior command and staff course it was 35. Recommended ages according to the 1992 board were 36–39 for the command and staff course and early thirties for the junior command and staff course. The changes proposed by the director for the command and staff course were an increase in numbers on the course, a reduction of its length, and an 'increase in the frequency of the courses from one per year to three courses every two years. His proposals could be achieved by conducting a portion of the syllabus through distance learning and the remainder by residential teaching'.[65] In the case of the junior command and staff course, the changes recommended were an increase in the number of courses and students and a reduction in the length of the course by four weeks. In these recommendations the director gave a hostage to fortune by remarking that, 'the present syllabus (TS.INF 22/94) is considered to be an excellent syllabus but could be reduced in length by approximately 139 hours (4 weeks)'.[66]

The CMC accepted that while the director's solution to the difficulties, 'has its own internal logic, there is every possibility that the remedy will be more injurious to the professional development of the officer body than the problem it seeks to address'.[67] He argued that 'were our students fully experienced in field operations in a conventional context or there were demonstration units readily available then the Command and Staff Course probably and the Junior Command and Staff Course certainly could well be restructured and reduced in length'.[68] The CMC was re-affirming here that PDF officers professional education would be greatly impaired without College courses. He emphatically rejected distance learning as an option and argued that the backlog should be managed by selection, and that 'the question of dealing with high age profiles should be tackled by means other than reducing professional standards'.[69] The chief of staff accepted the CMC's arguments; distance learning was not introduced, a slight increase in the frequency of junior command and staff courses was allowed and the command and staff course was not changed. A major decision was also taken in 1995 by the general staff to allow officers over the age of 45 to opt out of attending the course.[70] The officers concerned would thereby forfeit the opportunity of further promotion but could have decided that such promotion was unlikely. The increasing influence of the representative associations can be seen in a directive from the adjutant general stating that this decision, which had been reached at a general staff meeting on 20 March 1995, was, 'a matter affected by representation and will be pursued as a policy proposal through the representative process'.[71] Such issues were no longer solely a matter for dialogue between the CMC and the director of training.

The Cadet School

The methods and standards of cadet eligibility changed during the 1990s with educational standards being raised from two grade Cs in higher papers in the Leaving Certificate to three grade Cs. Physical testing of candidates, in addition to a medical examination, was introduced, and there was a gradual move towards the introduction of professional assessment tests for army applicants, as already applied for Air Corps and Naval Service applicants. As the 1992 Board on Officer and Cadet Education did not recommend any changes in the cadet syllabus, stability in instruction was maintained with the aim of providing cadets with 'the basic skills of the infantry platoon commander'.[72] The emphasis here must be, however, on the 'basic skills', as the newly commissioned second lieutenants had much to learn on reporting to their units. A notable feature of cadet training was the assimilation and integration of female cadets into all aspects of cadet training, and by the 63rd cadet class complete integration had been achieved.[73] Another change was that of the entry profile of cadets, with the percentage of graduate entrants continually increasing, leading by the end of the decade to a majority of cadets entering the cadet school with third-level qualifications. This change in entry profile called into question the USAC scheme and the overall scheme of officer education in all the constituent schools of the College. Cadets continued to benefit, however, by the award of a national diploma-level qualification titled 'Special Purpose Award', level 7, in Management, Leadership and Defence Studies. The cadet school also witnessed an innovative, highly political but also short-lived initiative, the posting of a cadet to the British Army's Royal Military Academy Sandhurst. We have seen earlier how in 1929 the British chiefs of staff were more than willing to accept Irish cadets into Sandhurst albeit as an alternative to attendance at their staff college. This offer was renewed and accepted almost seventy years later with the confirmation by the British Military attaché of the offer 'of a vacancy on the Commissioning Course at RMA Sandhurst commencing 2 May 1999 to an Officer Cadet'.[74] The cadet nominated went on to win the Overseas Sword for the best overseas cadet before returning to be commissioned at the Military College. The officer subsequently resigned his Irish commission and was commissioned into the British Army. The venture has not been repeated.

The Infantry School

The Young Officers Course

The Infantry School continued to tackle the conundrum of bridging the instructional gap for infantry officers between commissioning and the standard infantry course/junior command and staff course. The shortening of the cadet course demanded by attendance at university led to a deficit in tactical training. As has been mentioned before, active full-strength armies fill this deficit by posting newly commissioned officers to the command of a platoon-size unit. This facility was not readily available in the Defence Forces of the period. The object of the young officers course, as expressed at the beginning of the 1990s, was 'to provide the academic and tactical background to take the young officer through his years as a senior lieutenant and on to his promotion to captain'.[75] Academic background was a misnomer, as the course focused on tactical operations at platoon and company level, with just forty-four hours devoted to staff duties. Another confusion and misnomer was that of 'young officer' for a course that had taken over from the more focused platoon commanders course. In the 1960s, before USAC, the young officers course was indeed that, with mostly second lieutenants within a year or two after commissioning attending the course, but by the 1990s, the student age profile had greatly changed. Time spent on third-level education and overseas service had ineluctably raised the age level of students due to attend the course. USAC, overseas service and the pressing demands of unit commanders for junior officers, a vital element in UN and ATCP operations and unit training, resulted in a reluctance by GOCs to nominate students for the course. Previous mention has been made of the obstacles to realistic tactical and live-firing instruction on this course, caused by a lack of appropriate training facilities. This lack continued throughout the decade, not without efforts by the military authorities to alleviate it, culminating with a proposal from the director of training to the chief of staff in 1997 for the construction in Glen Imaal of a battle inoculation range modelled on a Dutch Army range.[76] This development eventually led in 2005 to the introduction of the much-needed discipline of live-firing tactical training (LFTT). This training, which in time became obligatory for every soldier in the Defence Forces, eventually went some way towards remedying the long-standing lack of realistic tactical training while handling live ammunition.

The anomaly that the young officers course was not mandatory for promotion, or for posting overseas, meant that some junior officers, notably infantry officers, did not complete the course. All cavalry and artillery officers must complete their corps young officers course. The delegation of authority to GOCs to nominate students from lists prepared by the director of training resulted in the director's view to a 'belief that instead of being mandatory there is some element of option for the attendance at courses'.[77] The decision to reschedule the 19th young officers course from 1988 to 1989 can be ascribed to this view. To overcome these difficulties, the director of training proposed the shortening of the course, that officers who had not completed a young officers course would not be detailed for overseas service, and that the course should be completed before an officer attended third-level education.[78] Only the first of these proposals was accepted, with the 20th young officers course, conducted from June to July 1991, being shortened from eleven to six weeks' duration. The course was deemed to be too short and subsequent courses were increased to eight weeks.

The nomination of students for the course also showed that the issue of female officers attending this, the most physically demanding of courses, had not yet been resolved. The director of training did not accept a recommendation from the CMC that a female officer who, through injury, had not been able to attend the female young officers course, should be allowed attend the 20th young officers course. The director held to the fact that female officers remained non-combatant and that the physical nature of the course made it inappropriate for the officer to attend.[79] Finding students for the course continued to prove difficult, causing the chief of staff in 1995 to approve a radical, 'once off "course credit" for completing an Infantry Young Officers Course for certain categories'.[80] The director of training noted that, 'this credit cleared a backlog for Young Officers who had not completed their Young Officers Course' but 'this procedure was considered an exception and it is not intended to deviate from this policy for current or future YO Courses'.[81] The director's intention notwithstanding, the young officers course continued to be problematic with a 2002 submission maintaining that, 'any changes made to YO training will have serious knock-on effects to officer training at every subsequent level'.[82] The inference here from Brig. Gen. Saunderson, GOC of the Defence Forces Training Centre, was that any attempt to modify this course could only lead to increasing the deficit in tactical and troop-leading expertise of junior officers. It must have been discouraging that seventy years after the establishment of the Military College difficulties were still being experienced in providing realistic tactical courses for the junior infantry officer.

The Standard Infantry/Junior Command and Staff Course

A recommendation of the 1992 Board on Officer and Cadet Education was that the standard infantry course should be renamed the junior command and staff course, thereby recognising the amount of syllabus time devoted to command and staff instruction. This recommendation was effected with the re-designation of the 55th standard infantry course as the 1st junior command and staff course in 1993. The course was mandatory for promotion to the rank of commandant and hence to senior-officer ranks. All students nominated for the course were issued with advance notice of pre-study requirements. They should, in theory, have reported on the course with an in-depth familiarity with all aspects of the organisation of the infantry battalion and the enemy order of battle, Fantasia. The course was also mandatory for officers from corps other than the Infantry Corps, except for the Naval Service, Air Corps and Army Medical Corps, and was considered as part of their corps standard courses. A justification for this all-corps designation was that the command and staff instruction at battalion level was, 'designed to give a knowledge of Command and Staff procedures applicable throughout the Defence Forces'.[83] This was a defensible argument given that all corps officers rising to senior ranks must be aware of the capabilities and procedures of the main manoeuvre arm of the army component of the Defence Forces.

The changing climate of merit-based officer promotion engendered some dissatisfaction with the tradition of determining a class placing for each student on completion of a course. This requirement often resulted in minimal differences in marks between students awarded high and low class placing. Students complained that it was only the placing that mattered to promotion interview boards, and not narrative reports on the students' performance on the course. The commandant of the Infantry School, Col Desmond Travers, sympathised with this view and reported that, 'students perceive their efforts and that of their colleagues solely in terms of class placing and that they consider this too to be the perception of those who peruse these reports'.[84] The students' view had been shared earlier by the adjutant general and by the chief of staff, who had requested a more equitable system.[85] The CMC, Brig. Gen. Colm Mangan, recognised that some students had difficulties but maintained that some indication of class placing should remain as, 'the over-riding considerations in student assessments must be to ensure that the interests of the Defence Forces are paramount and that the system is fair to the student'.[86] He maintained that the junior command and staff course was at an appropriate point in an officer's career for a peer-group assessment, and while not favouring a change to the system, nevertheless proposed that the first fifteen students be placed and the remainder shown as qualified or passed. The question remained difficult to resolve. In 1999, the director of training, Col S.P. Duffy, attempted to draft an amended administrative instruction, covering inter alia course administration. He noted that 'given the complex nature of the consultative process which applied to Admin Instrs, it will not be possible to have a working draft in circulation to meet the needs of the Defence Forces Annual Training Directive (DFATD) 2000.'[87] The representative associations had achieved a long reach.

Col Desmond Travers was the initiator of battlefield tours, an innovative addition to the school's activities, innovative, that is, for the Irish Military College. Recognising that military history instruction at the school required revision, he secured the services of Dr Geoffrey Sloan of the Strategic Studies Department at the Britannia Royal Naval College Dartmouth. Dr Sloan conducted a two-day module at the start of the 6th junior command and staff course comprising seminars and workshops. For the next course, Travers proposed to the chief of staff, with the approval of the CMC, that the two-day module be repeated and that students then research and make presentations on aspects of the D-Day landings in Normandy. A battlefield tour to the locations of the student presentations with Dr Sloan as a guide would then follow. Much preparatory work had been completed before this proposal with staff sections in Defence Forces Headquarters and with British and French military authorities.

Travers noted in his proposal to the chief of staff that, 'the value of Battlefield tours and Staff Rides is well documented and these are an integral part of Military History Studies in most military educational institutions around the world'.[88] Not that practices in other military institutions would be a guarantee for success in the Irish environment, but the ground had been well prepared. The proposal was accepted; finance was provided and battlefield and European tours became a continuing and 'integral' part of military history studies in the Infantry and the Command and Staff schools.

The Command and Staff School

The approaching millennium brought with it a greater awareness of the importance of the command and staff course for the careers of officers aspiring to a higher rank. As the course was 'designed to fit officers of all Service Corps to hold the rank of Lieutenant-Colonel and higher rank',[89] it obviously came within the purview of the new merit-based promotion system. For a limited number of years, automatic extra points were awarded by promotion-interview boards to candidates who had passed the course with distinction or merit. Inevitably, the new system created contradictions and some controversy. The 1986 general staff decision that officers would be offered a 'once only' opportunity to attend the course had to be reconsidered, as it was felt that officers who had 'opted out' of the command and staff course had done so under the existing seniority-based promotion system. The new merit-based system for promotion could have changed their career prospects. The officer in charge of Officers Records was therefore directed to request all GOCs that, 'Commandants who opted not to undergo the Command and Staff Course be advised that they may now re-apply to the Director of Training to undergo the Course'.[90] Other concessions also became problematic. Technical officers, and particularly officers of the Air Corps and Naval Service, had been permitted to complete, erroneously according to the Command and Staff School, a staff-element only of the course and to be credited with the entire course. Some such officers now requested that they be allowed to complete the full course, considering that an interview board would view their achievement in a lesser light than that of colleagues who had completed, often with high placing, the full course. Individual officers' awareness of the value of the course was matched by the school's awareness of its increasing importance within the changing Defence Forces, with a consequent need for qualitative improvement of the instruction provided to students.

The course syllabus was revised and restructured after the 48th command and staff course to enable, 'specific objectives which are better geared to the overall requirements of the Defence Forces and more understandable and meaningful to the students'.[91] Formal continuous assessment was introduced and students were authorised by the chief of staff to make direct contact with serving personnel and to have access to official documentation for research projects. Steps were made towards the provision of improved library services with the nomination of an officer to attend a librarian's postgraduate course. Information technology came into the College with the installation in 1989 of a Local Area Network to the Command and Staff School. Influenced, if not indeed encouraged by the advent of the merit-based promotion system, the school returned to its earlier conviction of a need for a selection system so that the command and staff course would 'be used to educate and identify the prospective candidates for higher rank'.[92] The school introduced a new element to its argument, the cost benefit of the course. It was no doubt influenced by the increasing emphasis on cost efficiency. It calculated that the cost of an officer attending the course was in the region of £20,000 and that, 'before allowing any officer to complete the course there should be a reasonable guarantee that the service will benefit from his participation'.[93]

The revival of this issue led to the setting up in 1995 of a working group to yet again consider the case for selection for the command and staff course.[94] The working group, presided over by Col Edmond Heskin, commandant of the Command and Staff School, consulted widely. It recommended the introduction of selection, but also expressed some reservations. It felt that the temporary problem of too many officers being available to attend the course at a particular time, caused by the 1970s large cadet intakes, should not be a determining factor. They also expressed themselves not to be in a position to accurately forecast the future demand of the Defence Forces for command and staff graduates. Their caution was justified as a subsequent reduction in the strength of the Defence Forces resulted in a form of natural selection whereby the school can adequately cater for those volunteering to attend the course. Nevertheless, the director of training's wish to increase numbers and to shorten the course still lingered. Numbers were increased to thirty in 1997, but an attempt to shorten the course, this time with a module-based syllabus, was strongly resisted. The then commandant of the Command and Staff School, Col Michael Mullooly, maintained that while such a system had benefits, it was not considered suitable since:

The planning, conduct and maintaining of military operations is the primary
element of the Course. The remainder of the curriculum is arranged around
this primary element so that the study programme proceeds sequentially and
progressively throughout.[95]

This primary focus on military operations led the Command and Staff School,
in a parallel process to the Infantry School's championing of live-firing tactical
training and fire-control computer simulation, to promote the need for the
provision of a battlefield simulation system in the College. Information technology had made it possible for armies to simulate military operations without the
actual deployment of troops. Irish officers had experience of such systems in
operation in the British and American armies and, following recommendations
by the CMC and the director of training, the chief of staff approved an investigation of simulation for the Defence Forces. The College had recommended
the provision of simulation principally as a means of providing realistic real-
time and accurate assessment of decisions taken by students on course exercises.
The strength of simulation is that it can build in and react to the variables of
combat thereby giving a concrete judgement on the effectiveness of the advice
of staffs and the decisions taken by commanders. The board set up to pursue
the acquisition of simulation emphasised this point when it noted that, 'Military
College Command and Staff exercises fail to accurately represent tactical movement, tactical deployment and combat attrition'.[96] Simulation would not be
restricted to the Military College as Defence Forces units and formations and
outside agencies could also benefit from it. The advantages of acquiring simulation were apparent; cost, training, maintenance and infrastructure being the only
restraining impediments. These were eventually overcome with the installation
in 2003 of a command and staff trainer in the Military College.

Widening horizons were not limited to equipment acquisition but also
extended to international recognition of the Command and Staff School. In 1998,
Col Bill Torpey, the US military attaché to Ireland, informed the director of training that the US Army had given 'approval for the Irish Command and Staff School
as an equivalent to our Course at Ft Leavenworth'.[97] This approval occurred sev-
enty-six years after the attendance of MacNeill and Costello at the United States
Army Command and General Staff School at Fort Leavenworth. The approval was
followed by the attendance of Maj. Tom Climber of the US Army on the 55th
command and staff course in 1998. Maj. Climber was the first foreign officer to

attend the command staff course, but he was not the first of an increasing number of foreign students attending the Military College.[98] International recognition extended beyond students when Comdt Pat Muldoon, a graduate and former instructor at the Command and Staff School and a graduate of Camberley, was selected, also in 1998, as a member of the DS staff of the Zambian Command and Staff College. The posting was not repeated but showed nevertheless that the Zambian experience of the Irish Military College, begun at cadet level and continued through the Infantry School, extended to an appreciation of the merits of the instruction provided by the Command and Staff School.

Internationally recognised though the instruction was, the school recognised that it must be continually improved and remain anchored to wider national standards. It was the consensus in the school as far back as 1992 that post-graduate recognition should be sought from the NCEA,[99] but the realisation of this ambition would take time. The chief of staff engaged with the director of the NCEA, Pádraig Mac Diarmada, in 1996 suggesting that a post-graduate award be made to graduates of the command and staff course.[100] This post-graduate engagement with the NCEA did not continue and the focus switched to discussions between the National University of Ireland Maynooth (NUIM), Brig. Gen. James Saunderson, GOC the Defence Forces Training Centre, and the Commandant of the Command and Staff School Col Len Mullins. These discussions resulted in students of the 59th command and staff course enrolling on a Master of Arts degree in Leadership, Management and Military Studies. The school re-positioned itself to serve the needs of the 21st century. The Defence Forces received from Dr Peter Foot of King's College London, the external examiner of the NUIM granted degree, the recognition that, 'by incorporating a University-accredited Masters programme into its Command and Staff Course, Ireland belongs to the mainstream of European and North American professional military education (PME)'.[101]

Conclusion

The 1990s were a decade of continuing and necessary disruption, which saw the Defence Forces changing to meet not just its perceived needs but, more importantly, the needs of the State. Organisations and attitudes came under stress particularly with the introduction of the representative associations and a merit-based promotion system. A 1992 Board on Officer and Cadet Education and Training reviewed the entire scope of this activity but substantially approved and re-affirmed current practice. The College changed with the wider Defence Forces. It established a United Nations Training School reflecting its long experience in peace operations. The Infantry School incorporated the NCO School and the Weapons School from the GTD, ensuring a long-expressed view that infantry tactical training should be the same for junior officers and NCOs. It also finally moved towards the introduction of live-firing tactical training, while battlefield simulation was introduced into Military College. The Infantry School introduced battlefield tours, an initiative that was followed by the Command and Staff School. All schools of the College now taught a common tactical doctrine. All schools of the College now taught a common doctrine, developed by the Command and Staff school, which extended beyond the tactical to include both operational and strategic levels. This school looked to the future with a redesigned syllabus and a move towards a university-accredited master's degree as an integral part of the command and staff course. Its continuing preference for selection for the course proved not to be necessary with the decreasing strength brought about by continuing changes in the Defence Forces. During the final decade of this narrative, an expanded Irish Military College had adapted to many changes in the wider Defence Forces, while continuing to maintain its traditional methods and instructional focus on the education and training of cadets and officers.

Conclusion

Past, Present and Future

In 1966, Michael Howard, the British historian and decorated Second World War veteran, outlined his understanding of the requirement for officer and cadet education and training. According to Howard the requirement was threefold:

> The need for character formation and character training to turn the boy into a man and the man into a leader; the need for technical training to enable him to handle the growing complexity of technological tools which will be at his disposal during his career; and, third and not least, the intellectual and moral education of the officer as a young man as a whole, the stretching of his mind.[1]

Ignoring, if possible, Howard's blinkered lack of awareness of gender equality, his understanding, more than thirty years after the establishment of the Irish Military College, is apposite. It remains apposite fifty years later and can be a suitable criterion against which to measure the effectiveness and impact of the College. With some modifications, a lesser emphasis on 'technological tools' and a greater emphasis on career-long education, the Military College has aimed to fulfil the requirement as outlined by Howard. The 1992 Board on Cadet and Officer Training and Education provided a more focused enunciation of the requirement. The board asserted that 'The primary purpose of the officer is to lead and to lead in war. The development of leadership potential must be the basis of all officer education'.[2] It has been the intention of this work to consider the Military College within the wider context of the Defence Forces, emphasising its function of supporting their allotted roles. The board assertion of 'leadership in war' more than sixty years after the establishment of the College epitomises the understanding of the Defence Forces and of the Military College of the context within which the College understood its vocation.

While the government and the civil service set about the necessary task of demobilising the army after the Civil War, military authorities set about professionalising the forces that had gained independence for the State and then assured its survival and stability. They looked outside the State as they recognised that the army's experience was insufficient or inappropriate for defending the State against armed invasion. Their initial efforts centred on the US Army but quickly led to the realisation that the US model could not be transposed to Ireland. The decision to adopt British Army organisation, weapons and training soon followed, and was in keeping with a government instruction that defence plans should visualise coordination with Britain. Military planning proceeded on the understanding that the Defence Forces would defend the State, but national economic planning proceeded on the basis that resources could or would not be made available for such a defence. Military planning included the establishment, in 1930, of the Irish Military College in Keane, later Pearse Barracks at the Curragh. In its early years, the College trained cadets at the Cadet School, senior officers at the Command and Staff School and infantry officers at the Infantry School. The inclusion of the Infantry School at the Military College was a compromise arrangement as separate schools were eventually established outside of the College for the other corps of the Defence Forces. This arrangement resulted in a deficit of specific, infantry tactical training.

The gap between the military responsibility of training for defence and the provision of resources resulted in much of the instruction at the Military College being class-bound. The low strength of most units meant that cadets and officers had little opportunity to lead troops in sustained unit or formation training. This lacuna became apparent on the outbreak of the Second World War when activity at the College was relegated almost entirely to the training of potential officers. Nevertheless, the command and staff training provided by the College since its establishment built a solid foundation, which enabled the expanded Emergency Army to train and to deploy in the field two full divisions. A second demobilisation after the Emergency, and the low strength of many units, again saw the College as the main source of education and training for officers. This period saw lengthy debates between GHQ and the College as to whether or not instruction should be based on an idealised organisation or the actual organisation of the Defence Forces. The College favoured, if not an idealised organisation, at least one that equated to a modern European organisation.

Internal security and United Nations deployment demands saw Defence Forces roles moving away from the defence of the State against external invasion. While this led to a passive acceptance of the unlikelihood of such a role, it continued to be the background and focus of much Military College instruction. Over time, however, students and College authorities alike recognised that invasion scenarios constituted a convenient and valuable framework for instruction in command and staff techniques. More emphasis was given to instruction in the two predominant Defence Forces roles of aid to the civil power and United Nations operations, leading to the establishment of a new school at the College, the United Nations Training School Ireland. The expansion of third-level education in the State prompted the provision of such education to cadets and later officers. A decision by government led to the opening of cadet and officer ranks to females and the necessary adaptation of traditional yardsticks and instruction. External examination of the Defence Forces towards the end of the period covered by this work demanded a change in the officer-promotion system from one based largely on seniority to one based on merit. This change inevitably brought a greater scrutiny of the Military College and its instruction. Concurrent with this scrutiny was recognition that the College should continue its engagement with external educational establishments and the inauguration of a master's degree element to the command and staff course and voluntary attendance on the course.

Such a brief survey does not, however, answer the question as to whether or not the Irish Military College has been successful in its endeavours. A standard yardstick for answering such a question is to consider how effectively the education and training that officers receive contribute to their performance in battle. This is often unflattering for military education and training. The British Army, upon which the Defence Forces based their organisation, equipment and training, performed inadequately during the early stages of the Second World War. Col Ian Jacob, of the British War Cabinet Secretariat, remarked that 'We have for twenty years thought little about how to win big campaigns on land; we have been immersed in our day-to-day imperial police activities'.[3] The US Army, which provided the Defence Forces with its first external instruction, also, initially, fared badly in the Second World War. General George C. Marshall acknowledged that 'some of the divisions sent to North Africa in the fall of 1942 were only partly trained and badly trained'.[4] This example cannot be satisfactorily used for the Irish Defence Forces as they have not, since the establishment of the Irish Military College, been engaged in war. It can, nevertheless, provide a partial, yet inconclusive, judgement concerning the officers who commanded and staffed the Defence Forces during the Emergency. Trained, in the main, at the Military College and at corps schools, they responded to a difficult challenge and succeeded, as Gen. McKenna reported, in ensuring that 'Two Divisions operated as complete units in the field'.[5] Combat is not, however, foreign to Defence Forces. Later, when deployed to the Congo, Irish officers planned, led and executed a successful battalion in attack, based on the education, training and procedures learned in the College. The operation order for Operation Sarsfield by the commander of the 36th Irish Battalion, Lt Col Michael Hogan, was an example straight from a Military College textbook. The aim of the operation was 'the destruction of Gendarmerie resistance in E/Ville Area'[6] and the operation order was a model of clarity and precision, and included the mission 'to be prepared to seize and hold the TUNNEL'.[7] This task fell to A Company and was carried through successfully, in spite of strong resistance and casualties.

Performance in war is not, however, sufficient or adequate for judging the worth of the Military College. The founders of the Military College were clear in their intention that it would provide education and training for cadets and officers to fulfil what they saw as the primary role of the Defence Forces, defence against external aggression. Successive governments did not reciprocate this intention and but for the early years of the Emergency, the role of defence against external aggression became less and less of a priority. The 2000 White Paper on Defence confirmed the 1993 government statement that defending the State against armed aggression was the primary role of the Defence Forces, but that this was a contingency and that 'preparations for its implementation will depend on an on-going Government Assessment of threats'.[8] This contingency role was complemented by several other roles including aid to the civil power (ATCP), peace support and humanitarian operations, fishery protection, a ministerial air transport service (MATS) and the maintenance of essential services. To enable the Defence Forces to perform these roles the government declared itself committed to maintaining:

A versatile force, which is organised, equipped and trained along conventional lines, which can adapt readily to the requirements of different situations in the defence and security environment and which can participate in the broad spectrum of military and non-military operations.[9]

This statement of government policy, while it was enunciated in 2000, is but a restatement and modernisation of the policy that saw the Defence Forces responsibility extending beyond and superceding the role to defend the State against external aggression. The yardstick, therefore, against which the College should be judged, is the quality of the education and training it gave to cadets and officers to enable them to provide the leadership and execution for this spectrum of tasks.

The Military College has more than fulfilled its responsibilities. It has educated and trained for the commissioned ranks over 2,700 young civilians and imbued them with loyalty and a lifelong commitment to the State. Since the amalgamation of the General Training Depot into the Military College, it has performed an equally important role for the NCOs of the Defence Forces. It has educated and trained officers and NCOs throughout their careers to be leaders, and has prepared and qualified them for the greater responsibilities of higher and the highest ranks. The Military College is unique among the educational institutions of the State in providing this career-long, continuous education and training. This contribution has enabled the Defence Forces to respond successfully to all the tasks required of them by the State both at home and in the multiple and multifaceted overseas operations and duties conducted by Defence Forces units and personnel. Throughout the period covered in this work, the Defence Forces have adapted and modernised their organisation, equipment, procedures, education and training. The Military College has facilitated these changes through parallel changes in instruction and doctrine.

The benefits of the activities of the Military College have accrued not just to the Defence Forces. Hundreds of commissioned officers and NCOs, educated and trained in the Military College, have retired and taken up civilian positions in Ireland and throughout the world. This development has gathered apace since the 1990s. Many of these, often highly successful, former members of the Defence Forces attribute much of their success to the education and training received in the Defence Forces and particularly in the Military College. Retired Comdt Wally Young, former media advisor to the President of Ireland, has remarked that:

Since the early 1990s many officers, having benefited from a military education, have retired early and taken up management positions in the private and
public sectors. This has led to wider society benefiting from the contribution
of a dynamic group of leaders who have taken up senior positions in a range
of sectors from the Office of the President and Taoiseach, the Semi-State and
NGO Sectors and private industry. There is wide recognition within this
group of 'early retirees' of the vital link to their present contribution and the
experience and education gained within the Defence Forces; especially in
the areas of leadership, motivation and the capacity to take on responsibility.[10]

The assertion by the Commission on Higher Education that the raising of
officer education to third-level status, in addition to their military training,
'would provide a pool of exceptionally well-trained men who could make a
valuable contribution to many aspects of the country's life', has proven to be
correct, and not just for 'well-trained men'.[11]

The College has, however, had its difficulties. Mention has been made on a
few occasions of the difficulty of providing realistic infantry training at sub-unit
and unit level. It has also been stated that this is not primarily the fault of the
Military College, as in most armies such training is provided and conducted by
the individual units and formations themselves. Nevertheless, the absorption
of the Infantry School within the Military College may have contributed to a
lessening of focus on this form of training. The Military College has also suffered from a continuous lack of capital investment. An early decision was made
that Defence Forces educational and training schools would be established at
the Curragh. This decision led to the utilisation of existing premises. Maj. Gen.
Hugo MacNeill, the first commandant of the Military College, took over Keane
Barracks from the Army School of Instruction in 1930. If he had returned to
the College in 2000, he would not have suffered from disorientation. Certainly,
some changes would be obvious to him. The former McDonagh officers mess
has become the cadets mess, the Military College library occupies the former
cadets mess, simulation facilities have been provided and a minor revamp was
made to O'Connell Hall. A dining complex has been constructed and Pearse
House had been transformed into UNTSI. Following the amalgamation of the
GTD, the College has also expanded into McDonagh Barracks. Nevertheless,
all of these changes have been ad hoc and not part of coordinated planning to
provide facilitates commensurate with the important roles and responsibilities

of the Military College. Given modern Irish educational facilities, there is still a ring of truth to Col T.L. O'Carroll's assertion in 1968 that 'It is not unreasonable to state that for a seat of learning the College even compared with a country national school in these matters is ill prepared for its task'.[12]

Lack of capital investment has been endemic to the wider Defence Forces and when made available it has been prey to many conflicting demands. Nevertheless, the Military College is of such importance to the Defence Forces – successive chiefs of staff have acknowledged this importance – that it should have been accorded greater priority. While not absolving the military authorities from their responsibilities, it is clear that the lack of influence of the College commandant, indeed the actual presence of the College commandant, when priorities were being decided has been detrimental to the College. A reason for this lack has been the almost bewildering turnover of officers holding the appointment of commandant of the Military College. Without considering the similar situation of the constituent schools of the College, there have been forty-one commandants of the Military College from 1930 to 2000. If one excludes the tenancies of Costello, O'Donoghue and O'Sullivan, who each occupied the position for five years or more, the other thirty-eight served as commandants of the Military College, on average, for less than one and a half years. Admittedly, this problem was not unique to this appointment but applies to many other senior appointments. Rapid turnover can be explained by officers reaching senior appointments at the latter stages of their careers, by the demands of overseas appointments and by the increasing demands of ATCP duties.

For the commandant of the Military College, lack of influence over capital investment was just one problem. A far greater one was that of lack of influence and direction over the activities of the College, in particular over instruction at the schools. A year and a half is insufficient time for any College commandant to influence the effective direction of study and instruction. Nor were the military authorities unaware of this grave deficiency. A similar problem existed in the Command and Staff School and the Infantry School, but not in the Cadet School. Because of the vital importance of the Cadet School for the initial education on which all other career courses depend, there was a much less frequent turnover of cadet masters. Twenty-one cadet masters were appointed during the seventy-year span of this work, giving an average of approximately three years for each appointment holder. This recognition of the need for continuity should also have been given to at least the appointment of the College commandant. Continuity of appointment was a problem not only for the College and school commandants but also for the instructional staff of the schools. It was a policy that officers who attended foreign courses served as instructors in the Military College. In the case of those officers who attended foreign staff schools, the period was normally three years. But as we have seen their numbers were limited. The rapid turnover of officer appointments throughout the Defence Forces impacted on continuity of instruction in the Military College.

Lack of structured capital investment and continuity of instructional staff should not, however, be allowed tarnish the achievements of all the commandants and instructors of the Military College. Theirs has been an unselfish commitment to the ideals of service they received in the Military College, and which they in their turn passed on to future generations of students. In 1968, Lt Gen. Seán McKeown DSM presented his view of the desired outcome of the education and training of officers, which complements that of Michael Howard. In a memorandum to the minister for defence, Lt Gen. McKeown asserted that:

> In any army – and the smaller the army the more this applies – the officer must regard his job as a vocation, to which when the need arises he is expected to subordinate and sacrifice personal affairs, interests, considerations and when necessary his life. This requires the development of an attitude of mind towards his profession which can not be obtained solely by the acquisition of Military skills and knowledge.[13]

This is the ideal towards which the Military College has striven during the first seventy years covered by this work. Through the dedication and expertise of its instructors and staff, it has ensured that officers and NCOs are equipped with the military and wider mental skills that have enabled them to lead the Defence Forces to the benefit of the State and its people. It has not been an easy task, but it is a vital task that has been continued beyond the temporal scope of this work into today's Defence Forces.

The Military College Post-2000

I decided to discuss the history of the Military College from its origins until the year 2000 for two reasons. Firstly, ending the story at the dawn of the millennium would help with achieving historical distance. Secondly, the years after 2000 have seen a period of much development at the College, which will eventually require a separate study. Nevertheless, I feel it would do a disservice to the Defence Forces, which initiated the developments, and to the College and its staff to end the story without giving a glimpse of these developments. As with all organic institutions, there was no abrupt change between the College of 1999 and 2000. The 2000 White Paper on Defence accelerated the continuing adaptation and change within the wider Defence Forces and eventually within the College. The first major change was an innovative, collaborative programme in 2003 between the Command and Staff School and the National University of Ireland Maynooth (NUIM), for the delivery of a master's degree to graduates of the command and staff course. This programme, referred to earlier in Chapter 9, was but the first of a number of changes at the College. Leadership for these changes was given by the chief of staff, Lt Gen. Jim Sreenan DSM. Lt Gen. Sreenan identified a requirement for 'leaders who have developed open and enquiring minds, whose preparation goes far beyond what might have been required for the type of operations associated with the Cold War'.[14]

All schools at the College engaged in a review of their functions and instruction, leading to a reappraisal of their roles. Following this review, the College embraced the modern concept of strategic, operational and tactical divisions of military operations. The Command and Staff School renamed its course as the senior command and staff and focused on the operational level, although 'Technically the operational level is concerned with the intermediary level between strategy and tactics'.[15] The Infantry School provides command and staff instruction for officers of all corps of the Defence Forces from company to brigade on the junior command and staff course. The school also took on a new role of assessing infantry doctrine, tactics and equipment, including the monitoring and evaluation of exercises and overseas unit training. The NCO Training Wing of the Infantry School provides career courses for all NCOs, including the standard NCO course with its demanding tactical module. This course incorporated a nationally recognised Higher Education Training Awards Council (HETAC) certificate in Military Studies. In keeping with the aspiration that junior officers and NCOs should follow the same tactical training, the NCO Training Wing also conducts the young officer course when required. Before the young officer advances to this course, they must, of course, complete the course at the Cadet School. Cadets have continued to benefit from a professional level 7 HETAC award, and for some years from a bachelor's degree. This returned, however, to the professional level 7 award when the cadet course was reduced to fifteen months. Flexibility of instructional approach is required at the Cadet School with the increasing numbers of graduate entrants and while, 'discipline will remain a sine qua non however this discipline cannot be instilled by curbing the inquisitive and inquiring mind'.[16]

Inquisitive and enquiring minds are vital for the Defence Forces with change now a constant. The 2015 White Paper on Defence replaced the 2000 White Paper on Defence. The defence of the State against external aggression is once again listed as the primary role amongst the multiple roles of the Defence Forces, even though the understanding of external aggression is greatly changed. The government now requires the Permanent Defence Forces to 'be able to undertake a full spectrum of military tasks that range from supports in peace-time (ATCP, ATCA, fishery protection, MATS), operations overseas (international peace support operations and humanitarian operations) to war-fighting (defence of the State)'.[17] The chief of staff, Vice-Admiral Mark Mellett DSM, has recently aired his vision of the type of military needed for this spectrum of military tasks. Ireland, he declared, 'needs soldiers, sailors and aircrew who can act as warriors-diplomats-scholars'.[18] The education and training of the officers and NCOS to lead these 'warriors-diplomats-scholars' continues in the Irish Military College. Today the College is composed of seven constituent schools. The Command and Staff, Infantry, Cadet, United Nations Training School Ireland, Artillery, Cavalry, Military Administration and Defence Forces Physical Education schools are all fully active with over 200 students in attendance in January 2016.

Maintaining its high standards across such a range of educational requirements will continue to be a difficult and challenging task for the Military College. Already the Defence Forces recognise that their professional military education (PME) model may no longer be fully synchronised with those of other European armies and will require investment in personnel and facilities. The 2015 White Paper on Defence signalled a government intention to evaluate a possible development of an Institute for Peace Support and Leadership. This initiative is indeed welcome and could perhaps evolve into wider investment in the Military College. It is reasonable to claim that long-term capital investment in the Military College, on the lines of the investment provided for a naval vessel, could recompense the Defence Forces and the State, as much and for as long a timeframe as does a single naval patrol vessel. The traveller on the M7 might then find that the Defence Forces Training Centre and the Military College are no longer the poor relations of their neighbour, the Curragh Racecourse, reportedly soon to be the recipient of a partly government-funded investment of €65 million.[19]

Appendix

Commandants of the Military College

Maj. Gen. H. MacNeill 1930–32
Col M.J. Costello 1932–37
Maj. Gen. H. MacNeill 1937–39
Col L. Egan 1939–40
Col S. Collins-Powell 1940–42
Col J. Gallagher 1943–45
Col C. O'Donoghue 1945–50
Col J. Lillis 1950–51
Col J. O'hUigin 1951–52
Col D. Bryan 1952–55
Col T. Feely 1955–57
Col S. McKeown 1957–59
Col J. Emphy 1960–61
Col H. O'Broin 1961–62
Col C. O'Suilleabhain 1962–68
Col E. Ó Neill 1965
Col T. O'Cearbhaill 1968–71
Col F. Mac An Leagha 1971–75
Col P. Quinlan 1975–76
Col W. O'Carroll 1976–78
Col J. Ryan 1978–80

Col E. Condon 1980–80
Col D. Byrne 1980–81
Col H. Crowley 1981–82
Col D. O'Riain 1982–83
Col C. Cox 1983–83
Col J. Waters 1983–84
Col P. Maguire 1984–86
Brig. Gen. P. Maguire 1986–87
Brig. Gen. W. McNicholas 1987–88
Col P. Grennan 1988–88
Col A.C. Brophy 1988–89
Brig. Gen. A. Brophy 1989–90
Brig. Gen. M. Dowling 1990–91
Brig. Gen. J.G. O'Shea 1991–92
Brig. Gen. G. McMahon 1992–93
Col M. O'Shea 1993–93
Brig. Gen. J.J. Farrell 1993–95
Brig. Gen. C. Mangan 1995–96
Brig. Gen. P. Redmond 1996–98
Brig. Gen. C. A. Dodd 1998–99
Col D. Travers 1990–2000

Notes

Introduction

1 MA DOD/A/6975, unsigned memorandum from Mulcahy to O'Hegarty, 19.08.1922.

2 MA 2 32651, ACS to COS, 22.12.1932.

3 François Roth, *La guerre de 70* (Paris, 1990), p.575. Author's translation.

Chapter 1

1 Sean Boyne, *Emmet Dalton* (Dublin, 2015), p.209.

2 Michael Hopkinson, *Green against Green: The Irish Civil War* (Dublin, 1988), p.136.

3 Ibid., p.137.

4 Ibid., p.136.

5 Boyne, *Dalton*, p.133.

6 Unsigned and undated memo in Mulcahy Papers, UCD Archives, P/7/B/50.

7 Ibid.

8 MA Department of Defence/A/5334, attachment to letter from McMahon to O'Hegarty, 30.07.1922.

9 Ibid.

10 Ibid.

11 MA Department of Defence/A/5334, McMahon to O'Hegarty, 30.07.1922.

12 MA Department of Defence/A/5334, O'Hegarty to Mulcahy, 01.08.1922.

13 Ibid, O'Hegarty to Mulcahy, 17.08.1922

14 Ibid.

15 Ibid., Unsigned letter from Mulcahy to O'Hegarty, 19.08.1922.

16 MA 6 Tex 61.

17 Ibid., Handwritten memo from O'Connell to Gorman, 02.02.1923.

18 Hopkinson, *Green*, p.157.

19 MA Department of Defence/A/6975, O'Hegarty to Mulcahy, 13.09.1922.

20 Ibid., Memorandum, Introduction of a defined form of Military Law [*sic*], unsigned and undated.

21 Ibid.

22 Ibid, Letter from unnamed staff officer to O'Hegarty, 27.09.1922.

23 MA Department of Defence/A/5534, Unsigned memorandum, 03.10.1922.

24 Ibid.

25 Boyne, *Dalton*, p.267.

26 *An tÓglách*, Vol. 1. No 2 (New Series), 10.03.1923, p.3.

27 MA Department of Defence/A/5534, Unsigned memorandum, 18.08.1922.

28 Ibid., Mulcahy to O'Hegarty, 11.11.1922.

29 Ibid., O'Hegarty to Mulcahy, 13.11.1922.

30 Ibid., McMahon to O'Hegarty, 17.11.1922.

31 Ibid.

32 Ibid.

33 'The Passing Year', *An tÓglach*, Vol. 1. No. 20 (New Series), 15.12.1923, p.7.

34 MA Department of Defence/A/5534, McMahon to O'Hegarty, 17.11.1922.

35 'The Passing Year', *An tÓglách*, Vol. 1. No 20 (New Series), 15.12.1923, p.7.

36 *An tÓglách*, Vol. 1. No. 4 (New Series), 07.04.1923, p.9.

37 *An tÓglách*, Vol. 1. No. 7 (New Series), 19.05.1923, p.13.

38 'The Passing Year', *An tÓglách*, Vol. 1. No. 20 (New Series), 15.12.1923, p.7.

39 Defence Order No. 28, *An tÓglách*, Vol. 1. No. 16 (New Series), 20.10.1923, p.14.

40 Ibid.

41 'The Passing Year', *An tÓglách*, Vol. 1. No. 20 (New Series), 15.12. 1923, p.9.

42 *An tÓglách*, Vol. 1. No. 19 (New Series), 01.12.1923, p.8.

43 Ibid.

44 Duggan, John P., *A History of the Irish Army* (Dublin 1991), p.130.

45 *An tÓglách*, Vol. 1. No. 19 (New Series), 01.12. 1923, p.8.

46 Ibid.

47 Ibid.

48 Ibid.

49 MA EB/23. Houlihan to Gorman, 11.02.1924.

50 Ibid, Acting Secretary to COS to the Secretary, Minister for Defence, 07.04.1924.

51 Ibid.

52 Ibid., Hogan to Sweeney, 24.04.1924.

53 Ibid.

54 Author's interview with Brig. Gen. John O'Shea (Retd), 27.01.2015.

55 Jack Fagan, *The Irish Times*, 16.12.2015.

56 MA EB/23. Hogan to Sweeney, 24.04. 1924.

57 Ibid.

58 Ibid.

59 Duggan, *Irish Army*, p.142.

60 MA EB/23. Hogan to Sweeney, 24.04. 1924.

61 Ibid., Sweeney to S. McMahon, 25.05.1924.

62 Duggan, *Irish Army*, p.132.

63 MA EB/23, Sweeney to S. McMahon, 07.05.1924.

64 Ibid.

65 Ibid.

66 MA 20/Buildings/5, Acting Military Secretary to Gorman, 07.05.1924.

67 Ibid. Minutes of Army Finance Meeting, 12.05.1922.

68 MA EB/23, Sweeney to O'Duffy, 14.05.1924.

69 Ibid Sweeney to O'Duffy, 02.09.1924.

70 Ibid.

71 Duggan, *Irish Army*, p.137.

72 MA EB/23, Minutes of a Meeting, 05.09.1924.

73 Ibid.

74 Ibid.

75 MA Arrivals Book, Military College, PC Area, 6/A/2.

76 Ibid.

77 NLI Ms 22,125, O'Connell Papers, Memo to Swiss Legation London, 04.08.1922.

Chapter 2

1 Memorandum by the Council of Defence on Irish Defence Policy, www.difp.ie Vol 2, No. 323, NAI D/Taoiseach, S4541, 22.07.1925

2 NAI D/Taoiseach, S4541, Defence Policy, 13.11.1925.

3 Ibid.

4 Ibid.

5 MA S/7, Minute from Comdt Mac Aoidigan (Future Chief of Staff Maj. Gen. Liam Egan)

6 Ibid.

7 Memorandum by the Council of Defence on Irish Defence Policy, 22.07.1925, www.difp.ie No. 323 NAI DT S4541.

8 MA S/7, Minute from Comdt Mac Aoidigan.

9 Ibid.

10 NAI D/Taoiseach, S1561, Mulcahy to the Secretary of the Provisional Government, 02.08.1922.

11 B. O'Brien, Capt., The origins and Development of the Cadet School, *An Cosantóir*,

(special commemorative issue) September 1979, p.260 and footnote number 1, p.266.

12 NAI D/Taoiseach, S1561, W.Brien to the Secretary of the Provisional Government, 25.08.1922.

13 NLI, O'Connell Papers, Ms22,125, Letter from Swiss Chargé d'Affaires to J.H. McDonnell Solicitor, 08.08.1922.

14 NAI D/FIN, 1/2923, Private Secretary to the President of the Executive Council to Brennan, 15.05.1923.

15 NAI D/Taoiseach, S587, Report to President of the Executive Council by Gen. Seán McMahon, 14.08.1923.

16 Ibid.

17 Ibid.

18 NAI D/FIN 1/2923, Gorman to the Secretary, Ministry of Finance, 12.02.1924.

19 Ibid.

20 Ibid.

21 Ibid., Secretary, Ministry of Finance to Gorman, 15.02.1924.

22 NAI, D/Taoiseach, S4559, O'Duffy to Hughes, 10.07.1925.

23 Ibid.

24 Ibid.

25 Ibid., Memorandum from Department of Defence, 01.08.1925.

26 NAI D/Taoiseach, S4559 Cabinet File, Army, Courses of Training in USA

27 Ibid.

28 Ibid, Minute from Department of Defence to the Executive Council.

29 Ibid.

30 *An tÓglách*, June 1931, p.3.

31 NAI D/Taoiseach, S4559, Extracts from minutes of the Meeting of the Executive Council, 17.08.1925.

32 NAI D/Taoiseach, S3592, Secretary of State for the Colonies to Healy, 07.02.1924.

33 NAI, A13584, T.J. Kiernan to M.E. Antrobus, Dominions Office, 27.10.1925.

34 Ibid., Antrobus to Kiernan dated 16.11.1925.

35 Ibid. Minutes of a Meeting of the Executive Council, 12.12.1925.

36 NLI 9A/3023, Defence Forces Regulations, *Tactical Drill 1926*.

37 Ibid., paragraph 261.

38 Ibid.

39 Ibid.

40 Ibid., paragraph 20.

41 I am indebted to Pat Brennan and Michael Keane for providing me with this information from the Military History Bureau and the Military Service Pensions Collections of Military Archives.

42 MA MM/34, Special Memorandum No.1, Preparation for War.

43 Memorandum by the Council of Defence on Irish Defence Policy, 22.07.1925, www.

difp.ie No. 323 NAI D/Taoiseach, S4541, para 30.

44 MA Report of the Military Mission, p.112.

45 NAI D/Taoiseach, S47028, Memo dated 11.09.1928

46 Ibid.

47 Ibid.

48 NAI DFA, 5/382-3, Kiernan to Lester, 28.09.1928.

49 Lavinia Greacen, *Chink: A Biography* (London, 1989), p.101.

50 Ibid.

51 I am indebted to Ms Lavinia Greachen for allowing me to quote from the notes of her interview with Lt Gen. M.J. Costello.

52 TNA Cab 29/329, Hankey to Batterbee, 10.02.1930.

53 Ibid, Batterbee to Hankey, 11.02.1930.

54 Desmond Fitzgerald, 'Address by the Minister for Defence', *An tÓglách*, April–June 1928, p.5.

55 Maj. Gen. Hugo MacNeill, 'The Defence Plans Division', *An tÓglách*, April–June 1928, pp.7–17.

56 Ibid.

57 Memoirs of Col James Flynn, p.283, in the possession of Brig. Gen. J. Flynn (Retd) DSM. Col Flynn's memoirs provide details on the establishment of the Military College and on its first nine years, when he was successively a student and then instructor in the Infantry and Command and Staff schools. Brig. Gen. Flynn has generously allowed me access to these papers.

58 Ibid, p.285.

59 NARA Record Group 165, Military Intelligence Division Correspondence, 1917–1941, 2633-19-5, G-2 Report No. 21584, 'The Irish Free State Army', M.A. London, 28 April 1928, Copy of extract in author's possession.

60 Ibid.

61 Ibid.

62 Flynn memoirs, p.285.

63 Ibid.

64 Ibid., p.286.

65 MA MM/34, 'Special Minute No.1, Preparation for War', 1928.

66 Ibid.

67 Duggan, *Irish Army*, p.154.

68 MA MM/37, 'Special Minute No. 5.' Summary of Proposals Submitted, p.25.

69 Ibid., pp 25–26.

70 B. O'Brien, Capt., 'The Origins and Development of the Cadet School', *An Cosantóir* (special commemorative issue) September 1979, p.264 and footnote number 25, p.266.

71 MA, MM/36, Special Minute No. 3, Territorial Establishment of the Defence Forces, p.7.

72 Duggan, *Irish Army*, p.156.

73 O'Brien, B. Capt., 'The Origins and Development of the Cadet School', *An Cosantóir* (special commerative issue) September 1979, p.260.

74 *An tÓglách*, 1 December 1923, p.8

75 MA 2/14257, unaddressed memo, dated 14.12.1927.

76 Michael C. O'Malley, *Military Aviation in Ireland 1921–45* (Dublin, 2010), p.110.

77 MA 2/8092, O'Connor to Brennan, 21.10.1926.

78 MA 2/23492, Houlihan to Secretary, Department of Defence, 15.11.1926.

79 Ibid, Houlihan to Army Finance Officer, 26.01.1927.

80 Ibid, Secretary Department of Defence to Secretary Deptartment of Finance, 18.08.1930.

81 MA 2/15041, Hogan to MacNeill, 23.02.1928.

82 Lalor, H.R. Comdt., 'Fifty Years Ago', *An Cosantóir* (special commemorative issue) September 1979, p.271.

83 Ibid., p.272.

84 MA 2/23492, MacNeill to O'Higgins, 12.08.1930.

85 NAI D/Taoiseach, S7129, MacMahon to McElligot, 15.11.1929. **Note:** Under the provisions of the 1954 Defence Act, the Department of Defence included three principal military offices, the chief of staff, the adjutant general and the quartermaster general. The Act as amended in 1998 now provides for the establishment of a military element – Defence Forces Headquarters – in the Department of Defence. The head of this element is the chief of staff. While prior to the 1954 act the position was less clearly defined, any mention of the Department of Defence in this work, unless otherwise stated, refers to its civilian component.

86 Ibid.

87 Ibid, Doolin to Boland, 10.11.1929.

88 Ibid, Memo to Doolin, 04.11.1930.

89 Ibid., Boland to Doolin, 09.12.1930.

90 Ibid, D.Dagg to Secretary Office of Public Works, 30.11.1931.

91 Ibid, McMahon to McElligot, 16.01.1932.

92 Ibid, J.J. Irwin to McElligot, 12.04.1932.

93 MA MM/37 DPD, Special Report No. 5, p.24.

94 Ibid, page 27.

95 Ibid.

96 MA 2/3518, MacNeill to Sweeney, 05.09.1929.

97 Ibid, Sweeney to MacNeill, 18.09.1929.

98 Ibid, MacNeill to Sweeney, 12.11.1929.

99 Author's conversation with Mr Liam Cosgrave, 01.10.2014.

100 Flynn memoirs, p.316.

101 Ibid.

102 Ibid, p.317.

103 MA PC Area, 6/A/2, Officers Arrival Book, Irish Military College, 1924 to 3 September 1934 (inclusive).

104 MA 2/3518, MacNeill to Sweeney, 24.05.1930.

105 MA 2/4629, MacMahon to McElligot, 30.09.1930.

106 Ibid.

107 Ibid.

108 Ibid, Sweeney to L. O'hAodha, 15.11.1932.

109 MA ACS/92, Half–yearly report from CMC to COS, IMC/156, 09.04.1932, p.14.

Chapter 3

1 NAI D/Taoiseach, S4541, Defence Policy, 13.11.1925.

2 Duggan, *Irish Army*, p.159.

3 MA MM/37 DPD Summary, p.23.

4 Directory of Cadet School Graduates, *An Cosantóir* (special commerative issue) September 1979, pp.288–89.

5 MA ACS/92, Half-yearly Report from MacNeill to Brennan, 08.04.1932, p.9.

6 Ibid, p.11.

7 MA 2/31043, Confidential Report on Cadet Class 1930–1932, Costello to Sweeney, 30.07.1932, p.4.

8 MA ACS/92, Half-yearly Report, MacNeill to Brennan, 08.04.1932, p.10.

9 MA 2/2705, 3rd Cadet Course, MacNeill to Director of Training, 08.03.1930.

10 MA ACS/92, Half-yearly Report, MacNeill to Brennan, 08.04.1932, p.11.

11 MA 2/31043, Confidential Report on Cadet Class 1930–1932, Costello to Sweeney, 30.07.1932, p.2.

12 MA 2/3492, Sweeney to MacNeill, 29.08.1930.

13 MA 2/36125, Secretary Department of Defence to Secretary of the Civil Service Commission, 17.01.1935.

14 Duggan, *Irish Army*, p.160.

15 MA 2/47989, Minute of Meeting of Council of Defence, 31.08.1936.

16 Ibid, Minute to McMahon, 02.10.1936.

17 Ibid, Department of Defence minute to M.Beary, 06.10.1936.

18 Duggan, *Irish Army*, p.166.

19 MA 2/47989, Beary to McElligot, 19.10.1936, p.4.

20 Ibid, Department of Defence minute, November 1936.

21 Ibid, D.S. Almond to McMahon, 29.12.1936.

22 Ibid.

23 Ibid, Internal Department of Defence minute, 22.01.1937.

24 Ibid., MacEntee to Aiken, 05.03.1937.

25 Ibid, Internal Department of Defence minute, 15.03.1937.

26 NAI D/Taoiseach, S46931, McEntee to Aiken, 04.09.1934.

27 MA ACS/75, Instruction from Adjutant General, undated but before 19.01.1931.

28 Ibid.

29 MA ACS/92, Half-yearly Report MacNeill to Brennan, 08.04.1932, p.7.

30 Ibid.

31 William O. Odom, *After the Trenches: The Transformation of the U.S. Army, 1918–1939* (Texas, 1999), p.113.

32 I am indebted to Dr Michael Kennedy for bringing this criticism to my attention.

33 Flynn Memoirs, p.318

34 Ibid, p.319.

35 Ibid.

36 Ibid.

37 Ibid.

38 MA ACS/92, Half-yearly Report, MacNeill to Brennan, 08.04.1932, p.8.

39 Ibid., Sweeney to Brennan, 30.04.1932, p.2.

40 MA PC Area 6/A/2, Military College Arrival Books.

41 Ibid.

42 Duggan, *Irish Army*, p.162.

43 I am indebted to Dr Michael Kennedy for bringing this comparison to my attention.

44 MA 2/5704, Covering note to Tentative Syllabus of Instruction circulated by MacNeill, undated, but 1930.

45 Ibid.

46 Ibid., Sweeney to MacNeill, 29.01.1931.

47 Odom, *After the Trenches*, p.87.

48 MA 2/5704, Sweeney to MacNeill, 29.01.1931.

49 NLI O'Connell Papers, Ms.22,120, O'Connell to Sweeney, 06.11.1929.

50 Ibid.

51 NLI O'Connell Papers, Ms.22,147, Lecture and Conference précis, March 1931.

52 NLI Ms 22, 147, p.11.

53 MA 2/5704, MacNeill to Sweeney, 26.01.1931.

54 Ibid, Minute from CMC to Chief of Staff, 27.01.1931.

55 Ibid, Minute from CMC to Chief of Staff, 07.09.1931.

56 MA ACS/92, Half-yearly Report, MacNeill to Brennan, 08.04.1932, p.4.

57 Ibid.

58 NLI O'Connell Papers, Ms. 22,120, 'Felix' to O'Connell, 19.07.1935.

59 The jocular *Mishay Lay Mass* refers to the practice of singing off letters with the Irish phrase *Is mise le meas*, meaning yours sincerely.

60 MA PC Area 6/A/2, Military College Arrival Books.

61 UCDA Col Dan Bryan Papers, P71/22, Course Syllabus.

62 UCDA Col Dan Bryan Papers, P71/24, Test paper.

63 MA 434/02, Advance notice for 7th Command and Staff Course, para 3.

64 NAI D/Taoiseach, S48433, Draft Defence Forces Regulations 1933, Military Education Officers and Cadets, p.6.

65 Ibid.

66 Ibid, Almond to McMahon, 27.06.1934.

67 Defence Forces Regulations C.S.3 1937, Military Education Officers and Cadets, p.1.

68 Ibid, p.2. **Note:** In the Defence Act 'component' refers to Army, Air Corps and Naval Service.

69 Ibid.

70 NAI D/Taoiseach, S48433, Almond to Honohan, 04.03.1937.

71 MA ACS/92, Half-yearly Report, MacNeill to Brennan, 08.04.1932, p.13

Chapter 4

1 The Military College was so designated, as compared with the Irish Military College, in DFR CS3, 31 March 1937.

2 Directory of Cadet School Graduates, *An Cosantóir*, September 1979, p.288 and MA, PC Area 6/A/2, Officers Arrivals Book, Irish Military College, 1930 to 3 September 1940 (inclusive).

3 Duggan, *Irish Army*, p.198. **Note:** Emergency was the metonymic term used to describe the Second World War in Ireland.

4 NLI J.J. O'Connell Papers, Ms.22,120, Letter from J.P. Duggan to J.J. O'Connell, 14.02.1943.

5 MA 2/44315, J.J. Irwin to Gallagher, 29.06.1939 and 10.07.1939.

6 NLI J.J. O'Connell Papers, Ms.22,120, Letter from J.P. Duggan to J.J. O'Connell, 14.02.1943.

7 Michael Kennedy and Victor Laing editors, *The Irish PDF: 1940–1949; The Chief of Staff's Reports* (Dublin 2011), p.37 and others. Much of the information on the activities of the Irish Military College during the Emergency is derived from this work, which the author greatly acknowledges.

8 Ibid, pp. 37 and 281.

9 Directory of Cadet School Graduates, *An Cosantóir*, September 1979, pp.288–89.

10 Duggan, *Irish Army*, p.344, Note 22.

11 Kennedy and Laing, *Reports*, p.37.

12 Author's conversation with Mr Liam Cosgrave, 01.10.2014.

13 MA PC Area 6/A/2, Military College Arrival Books.

14 Ibid.

15 Col T. Gallagher, 'The Making of an Officer', *The Call to Arms: A Historical Record of Ireland's Defence Services* (Dublin, 1945), p.83.

16 Ibid.

17 E.D. Doyle, 'Irishman's Diary', *The Irish Times*, 17.07.2004. I am indebted to Lt Malachai O'Gallagher NS (Retd), son of Col Gallagher, for bringing this article to my attention.

18 Kennedy and Laing, *Reports*, p.18.

19 Ibid, p.37.

20 Ibid, p.106.

21 Duggan, *Irish Army*, p.162.

22 Kennedy and Laing, *Reports*, p.107.

23 Ibid., p.194.

24 Duggan, *Irish Army*, p.214.

25 Kennedy and Laing, *Reports*, p.194.

26 Flynn Memoirs, p.479.

27 Kennedy and Laing, *Reports*, p.194.

28 Debbi and Irwin Unger, *George Marshall* (New York, 2014), p. 305.

29 Kennedy and Laing, *Reports*, p.807.

30 Ibid, p.530.

31 Ibid, p.537.

32 Ibid, p.538.

33 Ibid.

34 Ibid, p.486.

35 Duggan, *Irish Army*, p.220.

36 Ibid, p.218.

37 Kennedy and Laing, *Reports*, p.534.

38 Ibid, p.536.

39 Duggan, *Irish Army*, p.212.

40 MA CS/9/5, Donohue to McKenna, 31.01.1946, p.2.

41 Kennedy and Laing, *Reports*, p.621.

42 Ibid.

43 MA PC Area 6/A/2, Military College Arrival Books.

44 I am indebted to Comdt Terry McNulty (Retd), a member of the 24th cadet class for this information.

45 MA CS 9/5, CMC to COS, 22.12.1949.

46 Ibid.

47 Ibid.

48 MA 2/Buildings/383 Hibernian School/Military College, Memorandum from Secretary Department of Finance to Army Finance Officer, 08.12.1925.

49 MA CS/9, Lawlor to O'Donohue, 19.11.1947.

50 MA DTRG/092/04, Adjutant General's detail dated, 23.03.1948.

51 Kennedy and Laing, *Reports*, p.774.

52 MA DTRG/012/02, Instructional Circular No. 1, 1st Standard Infantry Course, p.2.

53 Ibid, Administrative Instruction, 22.07.1947, p.1.

54 MA DTRG/101/17, Syllabus of Training, Company Commanders Course, Warminster, 1946.

55 MA DTRG/012/02, Instructional Circular No. 1, 1st Standard Infantry Course, p.2.

56 Kennedy and Laing, *Reports*, p.629.

57 Ibid.

58 MA DTRG/012/02, Instructional Circular No 1, 1st Standard Infantry Course, p.3.

59 MA CS/9/1 1947 to 1952, McKenna to Traynor, 16.12.1947.

60 Duggan, *Irish Army*, p.231.

61 Kennedy and Laing, *Reports*, p.539, note 26.

62 Ibid, p.537.

63 Ibid, p.742.

64 Flynn Memoirs, p.341.

65 Ibid, p.342.

66 Kennedy and Laing, *Reports*, p.538.

67 Catriona Crowe et al editors, *Documents on Irish Foreign Policy, Volume IX* (Dublin, 2014), No. 180 NAI DFA/10/P12/6, Brennan to McCauley, p.206.

68 Ibid, No. 301 NAI DFA/Ottawa Embassy D/3, Minute from J.J. Hearne, p.359.

69 Ibid, pps. xix–xx.

70 archives.nato.int/uploads/r/null/9/9/99321/DC_025_ENG_PDP.pdf, paragraph 1, p.2.

71 Ibid, paragraph 9a, p.5.

72 archives.nato.int/uploads/r/null/7/1/7198/AC_19-D_141_ENG.pdf, paragraph 1, p.1.

73 http://archives.nato.int/uploads/r/null/1/3/135720/SGWM-541-59_ENG_PDP.pdf.

74 MA DTRG/090/01/ 12th Command and Staff Course, Syllabus of Training, pp. 20, 21.

75 Kennedy and Laing, *Reports*, p. 628.

76 MA DTRG/090/01, 12th Command and Staff Course, Admin Instructions, 09.09.1949.

77 PDF Regulations C.S.3 31 March 1937, Military Education Officers and Cadets, p.2.

78 MA DTRG/090/01, Syllabus of Training, 12th Command and Staff Course, p.2, July 1949.

79 Ibid, Letter from Comdt Éamonn de Buitléar, PSO Chief of Staff to GOCs and CMC, 01.04.1949.

80 Ibid., handwritten memorandum by Comdt Éamonn de Buitléar, dated 05.04.1949.

Chapter 5

1 Duggan, *Irish Army*, p.235.

2 MA CS/9, May '53 to Dec '54, Directive from COS to CMC 19.06.1954

3 Field Manual 100-5 Operations, glossary-3, quoted in William O. Odom, *After the Trenches* (Texas 1999), Introduction.

4 Ibid.

5 MA MM/34, Special Memorandum No. 1. Preparation for War, 1928.

6 NAI D/Taoiseach, S13620D, Memorandum from COS to Government, 30.08.1951, p.4.

7 MA CS/9, '53 to Dec '54, letter from DPO to CMC, 06.05.1953.

8 Ibid.

9 Ibid.

10 MA CS/9, May '53 to Dec '54, letter from DPO to CMC, 05.09.1953.

11 Ibid.

12 MA CS/9, May '53 to Dec '54, Memorandum from DPO to COS, Nov. 1953.

13 MA CS/9, May '53 to Dec '54, Letter from DPO to CMC, 03.08.1954.

14 MA CS/9, May '53 to Dec '54, Directive from COS to CMC, 19.06.1954.

15 MA CS/9, May '53 to Dec '54, annotated but unsigned and undated memorandum.

16 Ibid.

17 Ibid.

18 Ibid.

19 Ibid.

20 MA CS/9, May 1953 to December 1954, Covering note, 25.05.1954.

21 Ibid. Unsigned and undated document concerning Draft Establishment proposals.

22 Ibid.

23 Ibid.

24 Ibid.

25 Ibid.

26 Ibid.

27 Ibid.

28 Ibid.

29 Ibid.

30 MA CS/9, May 1953 to December 1954, Memorandum from PO Section, 25.05.1954.

31 Ibid.

32 Ibid.

33 Ibid.

34 MA CS/9, May 1953 to December 1954, Directive from COS to CMC, 19.06.1954.

35 Ibid.

36 Ibid.

37 Ibid.

38 Ibid.

39 Ibid.

40 Ibid.

41 Ibid.

42 Ibid.

43 Ibid.

44 Ibid.

45 Ibid.

46 Odom, *After the Trenches*, p.4.

47 MA CS 9/5, Lt Col McKeown to COS through CMC, 01.12.1949.

48 Ibid.

49 MA CS 9/5, Convening Order for Board of Officers signed by COS, 31.08.1951.

50 MA CS 9/5, Reply to questionnaire from Lt Col Joseph Emphy, 27.11.1951.

51 Author's interview with Col Donal O'Carroll (Retd), 23.01.2015.

52 MA CS 9/5, Reply to questionnaire from Lt Col Joseph Emphy, 27.11.1951.

53 MA CS 9/5, COS to the Minister for Defence, 06.01.1951.

54 MA ACS/360/03, April 1952, p.59.

55 Author's interview with Brig. Gen. John O'Shea (Retd), 27.01.1925.

56 MA DTRG/090/05, CMC to DTRG, 09.10.1963.

57 Lt Liam Donagh, 'Cadet School Regimental Colour', *An Cosantóir*, Special Commemorative issue, September 1979, p.259.

58 Ibid. **Note:** 'Full unit' might not be the correct term to use, as only formations e.g. a brigade were authorised to carry a regimental colour.

59 MA DTRG/085/02, CMC to COS, 03.12.1955.

60 MA DTRG/085/02, DTRG to COS, 05.04.1951.

61 MA CS 9/1, Command and Staff School 1951 to 1954, Letter from COS, 26.07.1951. **Note:** While certain courses are shown in Defence Forces regulations as qualifying an officer to hold a certain rank, this qualification is just one of a number of criteria which were outlined in DFR A 15 as being necessary before an officer could be recommended for promotion.

62 NAI D/Taoiseach, S1360D, Memorandum from COS to Government, 30.08.1951, p.7.

63 MA ACS/008/08, Syllabus of 16th Command and Staff Course (Modified) 1952–1953.

64 MA DTRG/085/02, Draft of Entrance Examination, CMC to DTRG, 30.07.1953.

65 MA DTRG/085/02 DPO to DTRG, 23.02.1954.

66 MA DTRG/085/02, Instruction from DTRG, 26.04.1954.

67 Ibid.

68 Ibid.

69 MA DTRG/105, DTRG to COS, 04.01.1956.

70 MA DTRG/105, DTRG to CMC, 14.12.1955.

71 Ibid.

72 MA DTRG/105, CMC to DTRG, 10.02.1956.

73 Ibid.

74 Ibid.

75 MA DTRG/085/02, CMC to COS, 03.12.1955, paragraph 2.

76 MA CS/9, May 1953 to December 1954, Directive from COS to CMC, 19.06.1954.

77 MA CS/9, General Correspondence from 1955, *Directive-Tactical Doctrine*, 27.04.1959, paragraph 7.

78 Author's interview with Col Michael Mullooly (Retd), 07.02.2015

Chapter 6

1 MA DTRG/082/03, Minutes of a COS Conference, 20.04.1959, p.1.

2 MA DTRG/31/15, Quoted in 'The Irish Language and the Defence Forces', Lt Col Joseph Young in Students Submissions, 7th Senior Officers Course.

3 Ibid.

4 Ibid.

5 MA DTRG/107/07, Quoted in memorandum by the Assistant Chief of Staff, February 1959.

6 MA ACS/486, DTRG to COS, 04.02.1959

7 MA ACS/486, DTRG Letter, 20.02.1959.

8 NAI D/Taoiseach, S13620D, Secret memorandum from the Minister of Defence to Government, 23.07.1958, paragraph 4.

9 Ibid., paragraph 3.

10 NAI D/Taoiseach, S13620D, Cabinet Minutes, 29.07.1958.

11 MA CS/9 from 1955, COS to CMC and others, 27.04.1959.

12 Ibid, Covering page.

13 Ibid, paragraph 2.

14 Ibid, paragraph 7.

15 Ibid, paragraph 7.

16 Ibid, paragraph 7.

17 Ibid, paragraph 9.

18 Ibid, paragraph 7.

19 MA CS/9, DPO to CMC, 29.04.1959.

20 MA COS/1050, Military College Notes 1965/66.

21 Ibid., The Selection, Training and Education of Officers, 1965, p.3.

22 Ibid., p.4.

23 Ibid.

24 Ibid., p.3.

25 Ibid., Plan for Officer Education, p.2.

26 Ibid.

27 Ibid.

28 MA CS/95 Cadets 1953 to 1961, Unsigned Memorandum, November 1959.

29 MA DTRG/10707, S.A. O'Broin to DTRG, 17.06.1960.

30 MA CS/95 Cadets 1953 to 1961, CMC to COS, 25.11.1960.

31 Duggan, *Irish Army*, p.242.

32 *An Cosantóir*, September 1979, Directory of Cadet School Graduates, pp 291–292.

33 Author's conversation with Brig. Gen. Frank Colclough.

34 Cyril M. Mattimoe, 'Cadets at Arlington', *An Cosantóir*, September 1979, p.274.

35 Ibid.

36 Dáil Éireann Parliamentary Debates, Vol. 47, No. 4, p.12.

37 NAI 2000/14/60, Mac Bradaigh Sec DOD to McCann Sec DFA, 10.08.1964.

38 NAI, 2000/14/60, letter from Acting Permanent Secretary of the President of Zambia to Irish Ambassador in London, 26.07.1964.

39 NAI, 2000/14/60, memo from Keating, Counsellor Irish Embassy, London to Sec DFA, 05.08.1964.

40 NAI, 2000/14/63, Handwritten note from K. Kaunda to S. Lemass, 16.07.1966.

41 MA CS/9/5 Cadet School, Cadet Training, unsigned and undated but Covering Note dated, 11.08.1961.

42 Ibid.

43 Ibid.

44 MA DTRG/092/19, DTRG to COS, 02.05.1966.

45 Ibid.

46 *Dáil Éireann Parliamentary Debates, Dáil Éireann*, Vol. 180, No.7, 23 March 1960, quoted by Capt. Barry O'Brien (Retd) in *Pen and Sword*, MA Thesis, UCG, 1978. Capt. O'Brien's thesis details the establishment and early development of university education for cadets and officers in the Defence Forces. I am deeply indebted to him for allowing me quote extensively from his thesis and for his generous help and cooperation.

47 MA, CS 9/5 Cadet School, Unsigned memorandum to Judge C. Ó Dalaigh, 14.02.1961.

48 Ibid.

49 Ibid.

50 Barry O'Brien, *The Pen and the Sword* (UCG, 1978), p.92.

51 Ibid., p.94.

52 Ibid., p.95.

53 Ibid., p.96.

54 Commission on Higher Education (1960-67) (Dublin, Govt. Publications, Stationery Office, 1967), p.339.

55 Barry O'Brien, *The Pen and the Sword* (UCG, 1978), p.101.

56 Ibid., p.105.

57 MA Annual Reports 1965, CMC to COS, 18.02.1965, p.4. Author's translation.

58 Ibid., Author's translation.

59 Ibid., Author's translation.

60 MA DTRG/092/21, Minutes of a Conference held at the Military College, 07.11.1968. p.3.

61 MA DTRG/082/03, Adjutant General to Officers Commanding Commands, 04.02.1959.

62 Ibid.

63 MA CS/9 from 1955, COS to CMC and others, 27.04.1959, paragraph 7.

64 *The Irish Military College – A Short History and Statement of Objectives*, undated, p.5, Copy in author's possession.

65 Ibid.

66 MA CS/9 from 1955, COS to CMC and others, 27.04.1959, paragraph 2.

67 Richard E. M. Heaslip, 'Ireland's First Engagement in United Nations Peacekeeping Operations: An Assessment', *Irish Studies in International Affairs*, Vol.17 (2006), pp 31–42.

68 MA. COS/25, Draft replies by Plans and Operations Branch to a questionnaire from the students of a command and staff course, undated and unsigned but *circa* June 1964, p.3. **Note**: The director of plans and operations, Col C.E. Shortall, informed the CMC that as some of the questions submitted by the students 'particularly those dealing with high policy, would be very difficult to formulate, and, indeed, it would be unwise to place replies to some of the questions on a permanent record such as this. Consequently, it is NOT proposed to submit any written document from this Rng. (Branch)' Ibid., 30.06. 1964. The replies, however, remained on file.

69 Ibid.

70 MA DTRG/090/05, CMC to COS, 09.10.1963.

71 MA DTRG/090/05, S. Ó Laoghaire to CMC, 02.11.1963.

72 MA DTRG/090/05 CMC to DTRG, undated but annotated 14.12.1963.

73 MA DTRG/090/05., Secretary DOD to COS, 09.01.1964.

74 MA Annual Reports 1961, CMC to COS, 28.02.1962, p.1.

75 MA Annual Reports 1966, CMC to COS, undated but 1966, p.2. Author's translation.

76 Ibid, p.3.

77 MA Annual Reports 1969, CMC to COS, 06.02.1969, p.3.

78 NAI D/Taoiseach, S15063, Progress Report DOD 1949, undated and unsigned.

79 MA Annual Reports 1966, CMC to COS, p.7. Author's translation.

80 MA Annual Reports 1968, CMC to COS, p., 06.02.1969, p.4.

Chapter 7

1 NAI D/Taoiseach, 2005 7 484, Memorandum from Rúnaí an Rialtais to An Rúnaí Príobháideach an tAire Cosanta, 24.10.1972.

2 Author's recollection of conversations with former colleagues.

3 NAI D/Taoiseach, 2005 7 484, Assessment of Possibilities of Military Intervention, paragraph 8, 14.06.1974.

4 NAI D/ Taoiseach, 2009/135/443. Memorandum for the Government, June 1978.

5 NAI D/Taoiseach, 2009/135/443, Memorandum for Government from the Minister for Defence, 23.05. 1979, p.17.

6 NAI D/Taoiseach, F. Murray to M. Kirwan, 25.05.1979, paragraph 2.

7 MA ACS/088/02, Board Report on Officer Training 1972, Introduction p.1.

8 Author's interview with Col John Norton DSM (Retd), then Secretary to the Board,

08.05.2015.

9 MA ACS/088/02, Board Report on Officer Training 1972, p.2.

10 Ibid., p.1.

11 Ibid.

12 Ibid., p.2.

13 Ibid., p.4.

14 Ibid., p.6.

15 Ibid., p.14.

16 Ibid., p.6.

17 Ibid.

18 Ibid., p.7.

19 Ibid.

20 Ibid., Part II, p.1.

21 MA ACS/436, CMC to COS, 28.11.1977.

22 MA PC4E8, Report on Officers Education and Development 1976, p.1.

23 I am indebted to Brig. Gen. Patrick Purcell (Retd) for bringing this to my attention.

24 MA PC4E8, Report on Officer Education and Development 1976, p.1.

25 Ibid., p.2.

26 Ibid., p.3.

27 Ibid.

28 Ibid., p.9.

29 Ibid., p.8.

30 Ibid., p.9.

31 Ibid., p.6.

32 Ibid., p.10.

33 Ibid.

34 Ibid.

35 Ibid., p.14.

36 Quoted in MA DTRG/12/01, Briefing by Staff Officer of DTRG to Command and Staff Course, undated but probably 1985.

37 MA ACS/088/02, Board Report on Officer Training 1972, p.2.

38 Barry O'Brien, *The Pen and the Sword* (UCG, 1978), p.114.

39 I am indebted to Brig. Gen. Patrick Purcell (Retd) for bringing this to my attention.

40 This register, which holds details of all cadets, beginning with the first cadets appointed in 1927, is held in the Cadet School. I am indebted to the cadet master, Lt Col Tom O'Callaghan, for allowing me examine and quote from it.

41 Barry O'Brien, *The Pen and the Sword* (UCG, 1978), p.115.

42 I am indebted to Brig. Gen. Paul Pakenham (Retd) for this clarification.

43 MA Annual Reports 1960s, CMC to COS, 13.04.1970, p.6. Author's translation.

44 Barry O'Brien, *The Pen and the Sword* (UCG, 1978), p.121. I am again indebted to

Barry O'Brien for his kind permission, which allows me to develop this section from his MA thesis.

45 Board to Examine the Scheme for the University Education of Officers and Cadets, quoted in Barry O'Brien, *The Pen and the Sword* (UCG, 1978), p.126.

46 MA 1970s Infantry Courses, Report 38th Standard Infantry Course 1975, p.1.

47 MA 1970s Infantry Courses, Report 1st Platoon Commanders Course 1971, p.2.

48 Ibid.

49 MA 1970s Infantry Courses, Report 4th Platoon Commanders Course 1974, p.3.

50 MA 1970s Infantry Courses, Report 16th Platoon Commander's Report 1981, p.2.

51 MA 1970s Infantry Courses, Report 16th Report, 14th Platoon Commanders Course 1978, p.4.

52 MA DTRG/089/02, DTRG to the General Staff, February 1977, paragraph 2.

53 MA DTRG/089/02 Letter from DTRG, undated and unsigned.

54 MA DTRG/089/02, File copy of Memorandum from the Deputy Adjutant General, undated and unsigned.

55 MA DTRG/088/10, Report on 4th Potential Officers Course, RSM P. Butler and Sgt J. Harris, undated, p.7.

56 Ibid.

57 Ibid., p.8.

58 Ibid., Course Commander's Comment, Comdt F. Studdert.

59 Ibid.

60 MA COS/0765, Student Survey on UN Operations, 33rd Command and Staff Cse, 1973/74.

61 MA ACS/436, Report on 31st Command and Staff Course, 02.11.1971, p1.

62 Ibid.

63 Ibid.

64 Ibid.

65 Ibid., p.2.

66 Ibid.

Chapter 8

1 NAI D/Taoiseach, 2009/135/443, Memorandum on Reorganisation of the Defence Forces, unsigned 18.02.1977.

2 Ibid.

3 NAI D/Taoiseach, 2009/135/443, Memorandum from H.J. Dowd Assistant Secretary to the Government to the Private Secretary of the Minister for Defence, 29.06.1979.

4 Ibid.

5 MA DTRG/12/01, Briefing by Staff Officer of Director of Training to Command and Staff Course, undated but probably 1985.

6 MA COS/1050, Report: The Selection, Training and Education of Officers,

18.05.1965, p.6.

7 MA COS/47, DTRG to OC Curragh Command and CMC, 06.10.1978.

8 MA ACS/407/03, Report: Structure and Organisation Military College – General Training Depot, 10.11.1981, p.1.

9 Ibid.

10 *The Irish Defence Forces Handbook 1988*, p.43.

11 TNA Cab 21/329, D.J.M. Byrne to the Secretary of the Air Ministry, 22.10.1929.

12 NLI Ms 46, 687 6, Emmet Dalton papers.

13 TNA Cab 21/329, C.O.S. 208, Report by the Chiefs of Staff Sub-Committee, 06.12.1929, paragraph 6.

14 Ibid., paragraph 13.

15 Ibid.

16 Ibid., paragraph 16.

17 TNA Cab 21/329, Draft Memorandum by Sir H.F. Batterbee, 23.11.1929.

18 Ibid.

19 Ibid.

20 TNA Cab 21/329, C.O.S. 221, Joint report by the Secretary of State for Dominion Affairs and the Chiefs of Staff Sub-Committee, 03.03.1930.

21 TNA Cab 21/329, Note of a conversation with General McMahon, Secretary to the Department of Defence, Irish Free State, Maurice Hankey, 24.10.1930.

22 NAI D/Taoiseach, S587, Report to the President of the Executive Committee by General Seán McMahon, dated 14.08.1923.

23 NAI D/FIN, S 004 010 57, Secretary DoD to Secretary DF, dated 21.12.1938.

24 NAI D/FIN, S 004 010 57, W. Doolin to Seán MaEntee Minister for Finance, dated 09.01.1939.

25 Ibid.

26 Ibid.

27 Ibid, Annotation by Minister for Finance, dated 07.01.1939.

28 MA 2/56319, Tréanlamhach to Sheehan, 16.05.1939.

29 MA 2/58163, Sec DOD to Sec DFIN, 12.06.1939.

30 Flynn papers, p.486.

31 NAI, DFA, 2009/120/2109, Swift to Whelan, 04.09.1973.

32 Ibid.

33 Ibid., Ó Cearnigh to McCann, 10.02.1972.

34 Ibid., Draft reply for Ó Cearnaigh, Feb. 1972. **Note:** It seems that such a reply was sent, as a later draft referring to this correspondence stated, 'You will note that at the time, we suggested in reply to your query, that for political reasons it would be best not to proceed then with such arrangements of this kind for 1972/73'.

35 Ibid., Lillis to Gavigan, 15.03.1974.

36 MA COS/1050, Report of a Board on Foreign Courses and Visits, 1964, paragraph 2.

37 Ibid.

38 Ibid.

39 MA DTRG/048/11, Comdt S. McCann, Course Report US Command and General Staff Course 1989–1990, p.7.

40 MCL Comdt J.P. Duggan, Report on 1969/70 General Staff Course (69), Command and Staff School, Hamburg Germany, p.17.

41 Ibid.

42 MCL Comdt P.A. Maguire, Report on US Army Command and General Staff Course, 1963/64, p.11.

43 Interview with Brig. Gen. John O'Shea (Retd), 27.01.2015.

44 MCL Comdt Brian McKevitt, Draft manuscript Report on US Army Command and Staff Course No. 36, 1980–1981, paragraph 16.

45 MA COS/1050, Report of a Board on Foreign Courses and Visits, 1964, paragraph 2.

46 NAI D/Taoiseach, 2009 135 404, Summary of a Memorandum for Government, 07.06.1979 paragraph 4.

47 NAI D/Taoiseach, 2009 135 404, Memorandum for Government from the Minister for Defence, 07.06.1979, paragraph 10.

48 MA COS/1448, Minutes of a General Staff Conference, 20.01.1978, p.2.

49 MA COS/1448, Notes of a Meeting held on 30 October 1979.

50 Ibid.

51 Ibid.

52 MA COS/1448, Colley to Molloy, 12.09.1978.

53 MA DTRG/36/04, Minutes of a Conference held at the Office of the Adjutant General, 05.03.1981, p.2.

54 Wesley Bourke, 'Here Come the Girls', *An Cosantóir*, 70:10 (2011), p.15.

55 MA DTRG/36/04, Minutes of a Conference held at the Office of the Adjutant General, 05.03.1981, p.1.

56 MA DTRG/36/04., Annex A to Trg 820/Y.

57 Author's interview with Lt Col Maureen O'Brien, 28.08.2015.

58 MA COS/2209, Cadet Syllabus 1988, p.1.

59 MA DTRG/36/04, DTRG to COS, 03.05.1984, p.2.

60 Ibid.

61 Ibid., p.3.

62 MA DTRG/36/04, DTRG to CMC, 27.03.85.

63 MA DTRG/36/04, CMC to DTRG, 02.07.1987.

64 Ibid., Letter from Lt Maureen O'Brien to Director of Training, 20.08.1987. I am very grateful to Lt Col O'Brien for sharing her experiences with me and for allowing me to quote from her letter.

65 Ibid.

66 Rowan, Michael, 2012, *Status, Role and Equality: The Experience of Women in the Irish*

Defence Forces, MA Thesis, UCG, p.34.

67 MA COS/2050, COS to Minister for Defence, April 1984.

68 Ibid.

69 Ibid.

70 MA DTRG/35/08, Report from CMC to COS, 02.07.1985, p.2.

71 Ibid.

72 MA DTRG/35/04, 1st Draft of Board Report on the NCEA's General Conditions of Approval for the Standard Cadet Course, May 1991.

73 MA DTRG/35/02, Draft briefing note from DTRG to COS, September 1990, paragraph 11.

74 MA DTRG/35/04, 1st Draft of Board Report on the NCEA's General Conditions of Approval for the Standard Cadet Course, May 1991.

75 MA DTRG/35/02, Draft briefing note from DTRG to COS, September 1990, paragraph 14.

76 MA DTRG/36/04, DTG to DP&R, 31.08.1989, p.2.

77 MA COS/2209, Syllabus of Training, Standard Cadet Course 1988/89.

78 MA DTRG/36/04, CMC to DTRG, 02.07.1987.

79 MA DTRG/053/02, Report on Platoon Commanders Battle Course, 1985.

80 MA ACS/407/03, Structure and Organisation Military College – General Training Depot, 10.11.1981, p.5.

81 MA COS/2092, DTRG to GOCs, November 1984.

82 Defence Forces Regulation C.S.3 1, Part I, paragraph 4.

83 MA DTRG/02/01, General Course Report 49th Standard Infantry Course 1987/88, undated p.2.

84 Ibid.

85 Defence Forces Regulation C.S.3 1, Part I paragraph 4.

86 MA DTRG/150/10, DTRG to COS, 14.02.1989.

87 MA DTRG/150/10 DTRG to GOCs and FOCNS and CMC, 10.11.1986.

88 MA DTRG/13/03, Report on the 44th Command and Staff Course, 27.08.1986, p.2.

89 MA DTRG/13/02, CMC to COS, 14.05.1984.

90 MA DTRG/13/02, Report of a meeting held on 02.08.1984.

91 I am indebted to Col Richard Heaslip for much of this section. Col Heaslip was the first officer commanding the Army Ranger Wing and conducted low-intensity conflict studies in the Command and Staff School during the middle to late 1980s.

92 MA DTRG/13/03, CMC to DTRG, 14.01.1986.

93 Ibid.

94 Defence Forces Regulation C.S.3 1, Part I paragraph 6a.

95 MA DTRG/141/04, DTRG to COS, 24.07.1987.

96 Ibid.

97 Ibid.

98 MA ACS/433/15, ACS to COS, October 1988.

99 MA DTRG/141/04, Syllabus 6th Senior Officers Course.

100 MA DTRG/141/04, Minister for Defence to COS, 14.08.1988.

101 MA ACS/002/03, An Taoiseach to ACS, 30.11.1988.

Chapter 9

1 *Commission on Remuneration and Conditions of Service in the Defence Forces*, paragraph 2.2.6.

2 Ibid, paragraph 2.2.9.

3 John Cooney, *Sunday Tribune*, 28.07.1996.

4 MA COS/2324, Report of the Board on the Review of Cadet and Officer Training and Education in the Permanent Defence Forces, 23.09.1992.

5 Ibid., pp 17–18.

6 Ibid., p.18.

7 Ibid., p.3.

8 Ibid., p.52.

9 Ibid., p.5.

10 Ibid., p.62.

11 Ibid., p.63.

12 MA COS/1444, COS to GOC C Comd and CMC, 19.09.1991.

13 Ibid.

14 MA DTRG/02/01, DTRG to Quartermaster General, 19.07.1990.

15 MA DTRG/02/01, Deputy Quartermaster General to DTRG, 24.07.1990.

16 MA COS/2208, Study Group Report on the Amalgamation of the Military College and the General Training Depot, 23.07.1993, p.2.

17 MA COS/2324, Report of the Board on the Review of Cadet and Officer Training and Education in the Permanent Defence Forces, 23.09.1991, p.55.

18 Ibid.

19 Ibid., p.63.

20 MA DTRG/152/09, Report by CMC on UN Seminar, 17.09.1991.

21 MA DTRG/152/09, Report from Sub-Syndicate 3, paragraph 1c (2) (b).

22 Ibid.

23 Ibid.

24 Ibid., Paragraph 1c (2) (c) ii.

25 MA DTRG/152/09, Report by CMC on UN Seminar, paragraph 5b.

26 Author's interview with Lt Gen. Bergin DSM (Retd) 02.08.2013.

27 United Nations Training School Ireland, History of Activities, Author's copy.

28 MA COS/2048, Address by Col James Mortell to Mary Robinson President of Ireland, 18.11.1993.

29 MA COS/2048, John Daly DOD to COS, 10.11.1994.

30 MA COS/2048, COS to Minister for Defence, 14.11.1994.

31 Ibid.

32 MA COS/2048, John Daly to COS, 18.11.1994.

33 MA COS/1324, Report on 1st International UNMO and Staff Officer Course, paragraph 3.

34 Ibid., paragraph 19.

35 Odom, *After the Trenches*, p.222.

36 Author's interview with Col Donal O'Carroll (Retd), 23.01.2015.

37 MA DTRG/131/08. Minutes of a meeting at the Military College, 15.10.1982.

38 MA DTRG/131/08. Minutes of a meeting at the Military College, 15.10.1982, p. 2.

39 MA COS/2405, Lt Col C.J. Crean to DOPS, annotated received 03.04.1990.

40 MA COS/2405, Commandant of the Command and Staff School to CMC, 25.01.1990.

41 Comdt Colm Mangan, 'Zonal Defence', *An Cosantóir*, Vol. 44, No. 5, 5 May 1984, pp 153–157.

42 Ibid.

43 Ibid.

44 Author's recollections and confirmation with former Command and Staff School DS.

45 MA COS/2405, DTRG to COS, 17.04.1990.

46 Ibid.

47 MA COS/2405, DTRG to CMC, 27.04.1990.

48 MA COS/2405, DTRG to COS, 28.09.1990.

49 MA COS/2405, DTRG to COS, 06.12.1990.

50 MA COS/2405, Lt Col C.J. Crean to DOPS, 03.04.1990.

51 Ibid.

52 MA COS/2405, Convening Order by the Chief of Staff, 21.05.1991.

53 MA COS/2405, Report of the Board on Tactical Doctrine, 30.10.1991, paragraph 6.

54 Dr Paul Latawski, 'The Inherent Tensions in Military Doctrine', *Sandhurst Occasional Papers No.5*, Royal Military Academy Sandhurst, 2011.

55 MA COS/2405, Report of the Board on Tactical Doctrine, 30.10.1991, paragraph 9.

56 Ibid., paragraph 34 g.

57 Ibid., paragraph 39 e.

58 Ibid., paragraph 40 d.

59 Ibid., paragraph 40 b.

60 Ibid., paragraph 25 c.

61 Eunan O'Halpin, *Defending Ireland: The Irish State and its Enemies Since 1921* (Oxford, 1999), p.350.

62 TM 205 Defence Forces Doctrinal Manual Operations, Pre-Publication Edition, February 1997.

63 Ibid.

64 MA COS/2405, CMC to DTRG, 28.10.1992.

65 MA COS/2100, Letter regarding Command and Staff Course from DTRG to COS,

10.08.1994.

66 MA COS/2100, Letter regarding Junior Command and Staff Course from DTRG to COS, 10.08.1994

67 MA COS/2100, CMC to COS, 15.02.1995.

68 Ibid.

69 Ibid.

70 MA COS/2096, TRG/803, 27.06.1995.

71 MA COS/2091, Directive from Adjutant General, 20.04.1995.

72 The Board on the Review of Cadet and Officer Training and Education in the Permanent Defence Forces 23.09.1992, paragraph 10.3.

73 Author's interview with Comdt Anita Hogan (Retd), 25.09.2015.

74 MA COS/2050, letter from DTRG to CoS, 16.06.1998.

75 MA DTRG/11/11 Young Officers Course Syllabus.

76 MA COS/2050, DTRG to COS, 18.12.1997.

77 MA DTRG/36/07, DTRG to COS, 27.09.1989.

78 Ibid.

79 MA DTRG/36/07, DTRG to CMC, 22.03.1991.

80 MA COS/2050, DTRG to GOCs, 29.04.1997.

81 Ibid.

82 2002 Submission from GOC Defence Forces Training Centre to Deputy CoS (Operations), undated, Author's copy.

83 Report of the Board on the Review of Cadet and Officer Training and Education in the Permanent Defence Forces, paragraph 4.24, 23.09.1992.

84 MA COS/2050, Commandant of the Infantry School through CMC to the COS, 17.09.1997.

85 MA COS/2091, Adjutant General to COS, 05.01.1996.

86 MA COS/2091, CMC to COS, 17.01.1996.

87 MA COS/2050, Letter from DTRG, 22.09.1999.

88 MA COS/2091, Commandant of the Infantry School through CMC to the CoS, 07.10.1997.

89 Defence Forces Regulation CS3, paragraph 6(ii).

90 MA COS/2083, Officer in Charge of Officers Records to GOCs, 15.05.1992.

91 MA DTRG/12/12, CMC to DTRG, 16.07.1991.

92 MA DTRG/12/10, Appendix 1 to Course Report 48th Command and Staff Course, paragraph 8.

93 Ibid., paragraph 3.

94 MA COS/2092

95 MA COS/2083, Commandant of the Command Staff School to CMC, 30.09.1997, paragraph 5.

96 MA COS/2094, Board Report Command and Staff Simulation, 16.07.1996, p.3.

97 MA COS/2083, Facsimile from Torpey to O'Carroll, 02.02.1998.

98 This distinction probably goes to Lt Jean Paul Le Duc, a reserve officer of the French Army. Le Duc was a mortar expert with Société Nouvelle des Etablissement Brandt. Brandt were providing mortars to the Defence Forces at this time. Le Duc attended the 22nd standard infantry course from September to December 1956, where he improved his English and gave instruction on the Brandt mortar. See NAI DFA, 341/91/2 and MA DTRG/092/10.

99 MA DTRG/12/12, Course Report 49th Command Staff Course, 28.07.1992, paragraph 12 c.

100 MA COS/2050, COS to Director of the NCEA, 05.09.1996.

101 Dr Peter Foot to the Registrar NUI Maynooth, 03.03.2003, Author's copy.

Conclusion

1 Michael Howard, Education in the Armed Forces, *Royal United Services Institute*, 15.11.1972.

2 The Board on the Review of Cadet and Officer Training and Education in the PDF, 30.09.1992, p.18.

3 Quoted in Max Hastings, *Finest Years, Churchill as Warlord 1940-45* (London,2009), p.14.

4 Unger, *George Marshall*, pp.167–168.

5 Kennedy and Laing, *The Chief of Staff's Reports*, p.194.

6 MA, Unit History 36 Irish Battalion, ONUC.

7 Ibid.

8 White Paper on Defence 2000, p.23.

9 Ibid., p.27.

10 Author's conversation with Comdt Wally Young (Retd), 17.01.16.

11 Commission on Higher Education (1960-67), (Dublin, Government Publications, Stationery Officer, 1967, p.340.

12 MA Annual Reports 1968, CMC to COS, 06.02.1969 p. 4.

13 MA, 3/35116, COS to Minister for Defence, 15.03.1968.

14 Lt Gen. Jim Sreenan, 'Change at the Military College' *An Cosantóir*,Vol. 65, No. 3, May 2005, p.7.

15 Ibid.

16 Ibid., p.8.

17 White Paper on Defence 2015, p.61. **Note:** ATCP stands for aid to the civil power, ACA for aid to the civil authority and MATS for Ministerial Air Transport Service.

18 Lorna Siggins, 'Man of the sea highlights many roles of Defence Forces in a more complex world', *The Irish Times*, 18.11.2015.

19 Brian O'Connor, 'Landmark day for Irish racing's HQ', *The Irish Times*, 29.10.2015.

Index